ACCLAIM FOR
TOGETHER ON TOP OF THE WORLD

"I read the book in just two sittings and I can't count how many times I cried. As a mountaineer, I was especially impressed with Phil's overcoming his numerous life-threatening health issues, and Susan's perseverance to push herself beyond her established boundaries . . . I was inspired by their loving marriage and mutually supporting partnership and hope that all of us readers might find that depth of happiness in our lives."

> —Aron Ralston, author of *Between a Rock and a Hard Place*

"Phil and Susan's astounding accomplishment of being the first couple to scale the Seven Summits is beautifully articulated and poignantly told."

> —Dick Bass, first person to climb the Seven Summits

"An amazing story of the triumph of love and determination."

> —Nando Parrado, author of *Miracle in the Andes: 72 Days on the Mountain and My Long Trek Home*

"Phil Ershler is a world-class climber and guide. Susan Ershler is a first-class businesswoman. But their story is not just about climbing and business. It is about two people in love who switch leads in life's hard climb. A great read—inside or outside a tent!"

> —Jim Whittaker, author of *A Life on the Edge: Memoirs of Everest and Beyond* and former CEO of Recreational Equipment, Inc. (REI)

"An uplifting account of survival and achievement in the face of great adversity. A captivating story of love and adventure set amongst the world's most challenging mountains."

> —David Breashears, expedition leader, Everest IMAX Film

TOGETHER ON TOP OF THE WORLD

TOGETHER ON TOP OF THE WORLD

The Remarkable Story of the First Couple
to Climb the Fabled Seven Summits

A SAGA OF LOVE AND COURAGE

PHIL AND SUSAN ERSHLER

with Robin Simons

GRAND CENTRAL
PUBLISHING

New York   Boston

Grateful acknowledgment is made to reprint the following: "My Choice" by Chris Hooyman. Used by permission of Nancy Hooyman.
Wedding poem by Greg Linwick. Used by permission of Greg Linwick and Lee Linwick.
Everest Route photograph by Craig John. Map design used by permission of Mike Ellerman.

Grand Central Publishing
Hachette Book Group
237 Park Avenue
New York, NY 10017
www.HachetteBookGroup.com

Printed in the United States of America

Originally published in hardcover by Hachette Book Group.

First Edition: April 2007
First Special Sales Edition: December 2009
10 9 8 7 6 5 4 3 2

Grand Central Publishing is a division of Hachette Book Group, Inc.
The Grand Central Publishing name and logo is a trademark of Hachette Book Group, Inc.

The Library of Congress has cataloged the hardcover edition as follows:

Ershler, Phil.
    Together on top of the world : the remarkable story of the first couple to climb the fabled seven summits / Phil and Susan Ershler, with Robin Simons. — 1st ed.
        p. cm.
    ISBN: 978-0-446-57905-6
    1. Mountaineering.   2. Mountaineers—United States—Biography.   3. Ershler, Phil.   4. Ershler, Susan.
5. Mountains.   6. Continents.   I. Ershler, Susan.   II. Simons, Robin.   III. Title.

GV200.E77   2007
796.522—dc22
                                                                        2006025779

ISBN 978-0-446-57091-6 (Special Sales Edition)

TO
ARTHUR AND FRANCES ERSHLER
AND
ROY AND MARY ELLERMAN

WHO TAUGHT US THAT
ANYTHING IS POSSIBLE

AND WHO SUPPORTED US
EVERY STEP OF THE WAY

ACKNOWLEDGMENTS

We did not reach mountaintops alone, nor did we complete this book alone. All along we have been surrounded by the most generous, supportive, and expert partners we ever could have wished for:

Robin Simons, who dedicated endless hours to researching and writing this book. Her ability to take years and volumes of data and tease out the truest and most important elements helped us find all the layers in this story.

James Levine and his colleagues at Levine Greenberg Literary Agency. We felt Jim's passion for this business, his knowledge of the industry, and his belief in us every step of the way.

The entire team at Grand Central Publishing. From the day we first met in New York we felt their commitment to this project and knew their support and expertise would be second to none.

Linda Hasselstrom, award-winning author, for her invaluable guidance and counsel during this entire process.

John Whetzell, CEO of Northland Communications Corporation, who introduced us and thereby set this whole story in motion.

Dan McConnell who shared our story with the world.

All of our Everest Sherpas, led by Ang Passang, and with special thanks to our Everest summit partners, Dorjee Lama and Danuru Sherpa.

George Dunn and Eric Simonson, for thirty years of partnership and support.

Jerry Lynch and Lou Whittaker, for their guidance and mentorship throughout the years.

Drs. Marty Greene, Phillip Chapman, and Steven Medwell, and the nurses and staff at Swedish Medical Center for their incredible patience and care.

The great leaders for whom Sue has worked; the incredibly talented team members who worked for her; and her many corporate clients; so many of whom are still great friends today. You gave her the opportunity to succeed in business while pursuing her dream.

All of Sue's speaker partners who have supported her in the field of professional keynote speaking. Your support and friendship have been invaluable.

All of Phil's climbing partners and clients. His vocation and avocation are one because of you.

Walt Yeager for his mentorship throughout the years. Walt promoted Sue in the corporate world and supported her throughout her entire career. It is amazing the impact a great mentor can have on helping us reach our dreams.

The wonderful community of friends and family who have wholeheartedly supported our endeavors and made our lives inestimably richer along the way.

THANK YOU TO ALL OF YOU FOR BELIEVING IN US AND OUR STORY.

Contents

PREFACE

Most stories have a single beginning and a single ending. This one has a few of each. The most obvious ending came on May 16, 2002, when Sue and I stood together on top of Mt. Everest. That day we became the first couple to climb the Seven Summits—the highest mountain on each continent—together. "You made it, baby!" I hollered in Sue's ear. Not the most romantic way to acknowledge a pivotal moment, but if you don't holler you can't be heard over the wind. If we'd been down at sea level we might have thought of some other ways to celebrate, but we had oxygen masks dangling from our faces, down suits covering every inch of skin, and 30-pound packs strapped to our backs, so that was the best we could do. But we didn't have to get personal to tell each other how we felt. We'd spent the last two months getting to the top of Everest—two months shoehorned into a 6- by 6-foot tent, sharing every meal, every ache, every thought, every fear. There wasn't much we didn't know about each other. And because mountaineering (like life) doesn't always work out the way you want, we'd done it all the year before on our first summit attempt as well. That's where those multiple beginnings come in. It's hard to know where the story really starts.

I do know that for Sue and me it had different beginnings. Sue knew the minute we climbed McKinley in 1995 that she wanted to do the Seven Summits. She was new to mountaineering then (she had three mountains under her belt) but she loves a challenge, and in the world of climbing there are few that are more famous than the Seven Summits. Ever since Dick Bass became the first to do it in 1985 hundreds of people have tried, but by 1995 only thirty had succeeded. She made noises about it but I pretty much ignored her. For one thing, I'd already done the Seven Summits and I wasn't interested in doing them again. Second, I thought the idea would pass. Third, I obviously hadn't conveyed to her the vast difference between climbing Mt. McKinley and Mt. Everest.

So that was the end of the discussion—or so I thought. But my guiding business was growing and over the next few years I had the opportunity annually to take groups of customers up many of the Seven, and once or twice a year Sue used her hard-earned vacation days to come along. So before I saw what was happening, in addition to McKinley we had knocked off El-brus in Europe and Kilimanjaro in Africa, Aconcagua in South America and Vinson in Antarctica, and even little Kosciuszko in Australia, which on any other continent would be considered a Sunday stroll. And then all that was left was Everest, Mother Goddess of the World. Surely Sue didn't expect me to take her *there*. But she did. And as time went on, and I realized how truly serious she was, I, too, began to get pulled in. I began to see that it wasn't just a matter of climbing Everest, or of finishing the Seven Summits; it was an embodiment of something we'd been working toward ever since we'd met. For seven years, in the mountains and at home, we'd been growing a partnership. We'd been learning about each other, coming to trust each other, putting ourselves in each other's hands. Everest would place the ultimate demands on that partnership—but it was also where the partnership would shine. I realized that I wanted that experience as much as she did. When I summited Everest in 1984 I became the first American to do so from the less-climbed north side, and I was sure my pleasure was unsurpassable. But now, when I thought about doing it with Sue, I knew that standing on top with her would be even better.

What I couldn't know at that time was that the partnership was about to be tested in a way I had never imagined, and that the challenge would not be on Everest, but right here at home. Nor could I know that when we did finally stand on top of Everest, the story would not be over.

Unknown to both of us, other endings were still to come.

Phil Ershler
Kirkland, Washington
May 2006

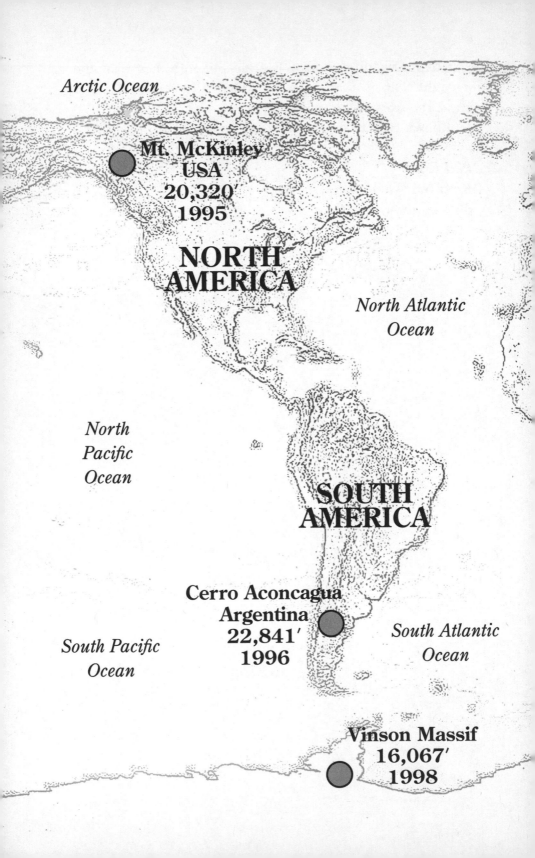

Arctic Ocean

EUROPE

**Mt. Elbrus
Russia
18,481′
1993**

ASIA

**Mt. Everest
Nepal
29,035′
2002**

AFRICA

**Mt. Kilimanjaro
Tanzania
19,339′
1992**

*Indian
Ocean*

AUSTRALIA

**Mt. Kosciuszko
7,308′
1999**

ANTARCTICA

TOGETHER ON TOP OF THE WORLD

January 2001

Susan,
Is it good to have all your dreams realized before 50? Thanks for making that happen.

Love,
Phil

February 2001

Phil,
Well, here we go. Almost time to leave for the big one. Have I told you lately you are my hero?
I love you. Can't wait to be stuck together for several months.

Love,
Sue

1

DREAMS BREAK ON EVEREST

May 2001

At 26,000 feet, the wind howls like a freight train. I lay in the pitch black, willing the tent to hold its ground, trying not to think about the fact that by 10:00 tomorrow morning either we'd be standing on top of Everest, thumbing our noses at everything that had conspired against us, or we'd be back here in this frozen, wind-beaten sardine can of a tent listening to five years' worth of hope and effort whip away. *Which way?* The wind taunted me with the question.

Earlier in the evening we'd learned that a climber from another team had not returned from the summit. Inside my sleeping bag, my hands and feet had gone numb; my desire to complete the climb had flickered. But Phil had talked me through it. "What's changed?" he asked. "We knew yesterday that people die up here. Is the mountain less safe today? Are we less capable?" I rallied. I felt eager. I couldn't wait for the alarm to go off at 9:00 p.m. so we could head up to the summit. The image I'd carried for so long—the two of us, arm in arm on top of the world—came back stronger, clearer than ever. But now, staring into the dark, feeling the cold penetrate the nylon walls, that clarity once again receded.

I heard the beep of Phil's alarm, then the whoosh of gas as he lit the tiny stove. A professional mountain climber, Phil is conditioned to get up in seconds. It would be a matter of minutes before he prodded me to do the same. But I had no desire to get out of my bag. With two layers under my down suit, a hat on my head, gloves on my hands, and two pairs of socks on my feet, I was actually warm, and the churning that had roiled my stomach for much of the last two months had vehemently returned. We had already delayed our summit attempt by a day because of the weather. Shouldn't we wait one more day? But that was impossible. It was May 21, the end of the season. After tomorrow, Sherpas would start dismantling the ropes that fix the route to the summit, and below us the already shifting Icefall would become impassable. Phil crawled out of the tent and a jet of cold air came through the tiny opening. Between the wind gusts I heard him talking with another climber and then, above their voices, a different sound, hypnotic and haunting. It took a moment to realize what it was: Ang Passang, leader of our climbing Sherpas, chanting. Ang Passang was praying for our safety! It must be even worse than I thought! *Stop! Relax, Sue,* a calmer voice told me. *Ang Passang is a devout Buddhist. He probably prays every morning. You just heard him today because he's right outside your tent.* I closed my eyes and let his voice wash over me, and for one brief moment I was able to drift—fearless—in his steady, musical prayer. Then reluctantly I pulled my boot liners out of my sleeping bag where I kept them so they wouldn't freeze.

The world above 8,000 meters—26,000 feet—is no place for the human body. Even if you wear an oxygen mask your brain gets too little oxygen, so your thinking is slow, your movements are labored, your circulation is impaired. The simplest tasks—just zipping your jacket or lacing your boot liner—take twice as long as normal. It was ninety minutes before I'd managed all the zippers and Velcro, forced down a little coffee and a cookie, and jammed my warm feet into my outer boots, which were cold as ice. When I emerged from the tent it was into a swirl of stinging snow. All around, under the muted glow of headlamps, our three climbing partners and five Sherpas were hunched against the wind, strapping on harnesses and crampons and checking each other's equipment. I did the same and then, one by one, we fell into line and began the slow march toward the rope that would guide us to the summit.

The South Col of Everest, where climbers pitch Camp 4, is a flat expanse of ice and rock 3,000 feet below the summit. I'd thought the flatness would make the crossing easy, but within moments I realized I was mistaken. The surface was a corrugated sea of frozen shallow waves that I had to straddle with my crampons. It was riven every few yards by narrow, snow-covered crevasses. I couldn't lift my eyes from the ground lest I step into one by accident. My muscles were sore from the day before, my pack felt heavier, my headlamp cord froze where it snaked against my neck. And no matter how I adjusted it, my ascender, swinging from my safety harness, hit my knee with every step. To take my mind off my misery, I experimented with different rhythms: *step . . . breathe . . . step . . . breathe . . . breathe . . .* I yearned for the moment when the hypnosis of climbing would take over.

We had been going for twenty minutes when I heard a commotion behind me. I turned just in time to see Charlie Peck righting himself after a stumble. Charlie and John Waechter were the two friends we'd invited to join us for the expedition. Charlie had been Phil's client on Mt. McKinley in the 1980s and had since become a friend. He was a natural choice for a partner because he's one of the few people you can imagine spending two and a half months with clinging to the side of a mountain. But Charlie had been having a hard time the last few weeks. He'd gotten the "Khumbu crud," a deep high-altitude cough that's almost impossible to shake and that makes climbing even harder. He'd been through more pain than the rest of us just to get to the Col. Phil came up behind him and in the merged light of their headlamps, I saw them talking. Phil said something, Charlie shook his head, Phil clapped Charlie on the back. Then Charlie turned around. *Wait!* I thought. *Charlie's going back! If he's going, I should too!*

Stop it! I told myself sharply. *Don't go there. Focus.* But even as I argued with myself, Phil's light began edging forward. Rhythmically, it shrank the ground between us until I was standing in its circle of light. Phil took my gloved hand in his and gave it three quick squeezes: *I . . . love . . . you.* Then, carried forward by his nimbus, I bent my head, resumed my breathing, and continued moving.

Phil can do that for me. He is my husband, my mentor . . . my hero.

I was thirty-five—already "old"—when I met him; I'd given up on getting married. But within hours of meeting him I knew that I was wrong. I was a high-heeled, high-powered sales executive and he was a fleece-and-jeans mountain guide; we couldn't have been more different if we tried. But he was the most compassionate and genuine man I'd ever met. From the get-go I was as lustful as a teenager. Pretty quickly, though, the lust grew into deep, deep love, unlike anything I'd ever known. By that time he'd taught me to love the mountains the way he did, and I'd begun using every vacation to join him on his climbs. So it seemed only natural that before too long we would attempt what no couple had done before, to climb the Seven Summits, the highest mountain on every continent, together.

What we couldn't know was how close we would come to not making it. Not because of danger on the mountains, or because we lacked the skill or teamwork to pull it off, but because life had something else in store for us. In 1999, seven years after we met, three years after we married, six months after we made the sixth of our Seven Summits, while we were training for our millennium climb of Everest, Phil was hospitalized with cancer. On the day we met I couldn't have imagined the degree to which I would allow my lifelong independence to soften into intimacy; the degree to which I would open up and take him in, make his life my life, his breath my breath. Nor could I imagine the depth of terror and pain I would feel when our life together was threatened. But Phil is as much a mountain as he is a climber: rock solid, undeterrable. And if there is one quality we share, it is the absolute refusal to let someone or something tell us no. We knew Phil might not survive. We knew he might never climb again. We still know the eventual outcome is uncertain. But we weren't going to let cancer tell us no without giving it everything we had. So cancer thwarted us in '99, but we took our five pounds of luck and six pounds of determination and made it here in 2001. Take that, cancer! Life is short, but for the moment it's ours, and we're living our dreams.

• • •

How do you explain to someone why you want to climb Mt. Everest? When I summited from the north in 1984 it was because I wanted to get my ticket punched; I wanted to validate what I'd been doing for the last fifteen years of my life. When I got back, my business partner, Eric Simonson, said, "Most of us *think* we can climb Everest, but now you *know*." I guess that was a lot of it. I wanted to know.

Seventeen years later a lot of that was still operating. I was fifty years old, I'd survived cancer, I still wanted to know. But so far, this trip wasn't showing me what I wanted to see. I wasn't talking about it to the others, but things that had been relatively easy when I did this south-side route back in 1983— sleeping at altitude, scaling the steep ice of the Lhotse Face— were giving me trouble. And for all my admonitions—*Dig deep, Phil, pull on your reserves*—I knew the well wasn't very deep.

Fortunately, the hyper-safety-conscious side of me had anticipated this situation. I was practical enough to know that having just survived colon cancer I wasn't in top-notch condition, and for that reason I'd asked Greg Wilson, a longtime friend and climbing buddy, to join us as another guide. Greg and I were on Everest together in '84 and he'd summited himself in '91. Throughout this climb he'd been a strong, reliable partner. Now, as we headed out of camp, I let Greg take the lead. John accompanied him up front, followed by Sue and our Sherpa, Dorjee Lama. Behind them were Charlie, Ang Passang, and our other Sherpas, Phu Tashi, Dawa Zangbu, and Passang Yila. Underfoot, the snow was soft; traction was easy. From the spacing of the lights I could see that everyone was moving steadily. I was walking in a slow rest-step myself, gradually getting my rhythm, wondering whether the weather would clear as we got to higher elevation, when suddenly I felt my left foot stick in the snow. I pulled hard and the boot came up without its crampon. *Darn!* I'd noticed the crampon was loose when I'd put it on and hadn't taken the time to adjust it. A stupid rookie mistake. I called myself a few names, retrieved the crampon, and put it back on.

We were almost at the fixed rope when I saw Charlie's light fumble. I pulled up beside him.

"Lost my water bottle," he shouted over the wind. He motioned in the direction the bottle had gone, off the side of the mountain.

"I'll give you one of mine," I yelled back.

He shook his head. "I'm outta here."

"You sure? We can slow up." Sometimes, if I can get someone to push just a little harder, the going gets better.

But he shook his head again. I knew he was thinking about his family. Charlie had been having a harder time than usual because of his cough, and I think he was feeling a little less aggressive than the rest of us because of his wife and two young children. Now he looked like he was in no mood for a discussion. So I clapped him on the back and he turned around. Ang Passang went with him.

I pushed myself to catch up to Sue. Sue had really impressed me on this climb. She'd been strong and steady right through the toughest sections, and never complained even when I knew she felt like garbage. That's the way she's always been about climbing. I thought about our decision to come here, on a path that led through six other summits as well as cancer. If climbing Everest in the 1980s was my way of validating my own life choices, climbing it now with Sue was a way of validating everything that she and I had built together.

At the rope, the snow gave way to slick, hard ice and the pitch rose to about 30 degrees. I clipped in and began to climb. The steps were high but easy to find, and after thirty hours of lying in the tent it felt good to be moving upward. Five steps up, I kicked into the ice, felt the crampon grab, then felt my foot give way beneath me. The crampon had come off again. I pulled off my glove. The cold cut like a razor. It took five tries to tighten the single screw because I could leave the glove off for only thirty seconds at a time. It annoyed me that I'd made such a careless mistake. The crampon itself was no biggie: I'd fixed it; it wouldn't be any more trouble. But at 26,000 feet, it's the simple mistakes that kill you. My good friend Marty Hoey's climbing harness opened while we were on Everest in '82. Closing it, she probably didn't loop the belt back through the buckle. Then she leaned back to get out of someone's way, and a second later she was gone.

With the crampon on, I continued up the slope. Charlie had been right to turn around. He knew he wasn't firing on all cylinders and that the only safe thing was to go back down. What I didn't appreciate, although I'd seen the evidence, was that I wasn't firing on all cylinders either.

Our route was taking us up the triangle face, the exposed pyramid of ice and rock that culminates in the summit. Higher than everything around, the triangle is scoured relentlessly by wind and snow. Above my oxygen mask, my face felt sand-blasted.

We'd been climbing for about an hour when I realized that my eyelashes and eyebrows were covered in ice. I brushed them off but minutes later the ice formed again. That was odd. In a decade of climbing in the Himalayas I'd never experienced that before. I exhaled deeply, hoping my breath would somehow warm the air above my mask, but minutes later the ice re-formed. What was going on? The ice was merely an annoyance but it unnerved me. It was one more *issue,* and as a guide, I don't want to be the one with issues. It was one more reminder that I was letting myself and my teammates down.

I was also feeling growing concern about the weather. What had begun, back on the col, as wind-driven snow had deteriorated into a full-blown storm. The temperature had dropped significantly and the snow was now so thick I could barely see. I knew we were on the broad, featureless face of the triangle and that steep bands of rock occasionally punctuated the surface, but I knew these things by feel rather than sight. Occasionally, the ground beneath me would harden and I'd find myself feeling for a toehold in the rock; then I'd have to transfer my body weight to my arms and pull myself up on the rope. Ten or twenty steps later the angle would lessen and the snow would return. I was grateful for these occasions; they were the only landmarks that gave me any sense of progress. Occasionally I'd stop and scan the route ahead, hoping for some sign that we were closing in on the Balcony, the narrow ledge where we would rest, get fresh oxygen, and assess the situation. But looking for a visual clue was useless. All I saw was a snowy haze, as if I were looking at the world through wax paper.

Over the next half hour the visibility worsened—to the point where it was hard to get my footing. Half the time I'd kick my crampon into a step only to have it slip back out when I transferred my weight. Each step up meant a half step back. If I was having this much trouble, how was the rest of the team managing? Our Sherpas had stashed a fresh bottle of oxygen for each of us at the Balcony, enough to get us to the summit and back to the Balcony, where we'd trade back to our half-full bottles on the way down. But if it took longer than expected to reach the top of the Balcony, we would run out of gas. We were also racing time. Late-afternoon storms make it imperative to get off the summit by early afternoon, so regardless of where we were, as it got close to 1:00 we would have to think about heading down. I looked up for the umpteenth time to check the progress of the team. Their lights were faint pinpricks in the blizzard: Sue and Dawa Zangbu about 100 feet above me; John, Greg, Passang Yila, and Phu Tashi another 100 feet ahead of them. I had begun to fall behind.

With a pang of shame I turned up my oxygen. Seventeen years ago I'd made it to 2,000 vertical feet from the top before putting on a mask, and then descended the mountain without it; now here I was upping my gas. But for some reason I didn't feel the head-clearing that should have come with increased oxygen. I turned it up a little more; still no appreciable difference. What was going on? I kicked upward, figuring I'd swap out the bottle at the Balcony. But as I continued to climb, my exhaustion was accompanied by another feeling that I now realized I'd been resisting for several hours: a growing sense of dread.

Five years before, in 1996, twelve climbers had died on Everest in one of the worst disasters in the mountain's history. Caught in a storm just below the summit, Rob Hall, an Australian guide with a well-earned reputation for safety; Scott Fischer, an American guide with years of Everest experience; and ten of their co-leaders and clients perished. Several others barely survived. There hasn't been a climber on Everest since who hasn't been accompanied by their ghosts, and there's probably not a guide in the world who hasn't dissected that disaster again and again, desperate to steal some shred of learning from the tragedy. We had paid tribute to those climbers at the stone shrines at the foot of the mountain and, although we hadn't talked about it, I'm sure they were in all of our minds for much of the climb. But now their ghosts were making themselves more insistent. We were at the same altitude, in the same location, they had been when they died. We had the same level of experience they had, the same concerns for safety, the same professional and personal ambitions. We had the same amount of time and the same amount of oxygen. But we also had one thing they didn't have. They had clear weather going up, and only abstract worries that a storm might develop. We already had the storm.

• • •

We were barely an hour outside of camp when I realized I couldn't feel my toes. I wiggled them but it was like trying to wiggle disconnected blocks of wood. I began to worry about frostbite.

The steps we were climbing had been made by someone with legs much longer than mine. When Phil kicks steps he makes them short so anyone can use them, but these steps were like benches. I had to pull myself up with my ascender just to get from one to the next. After each one I had to lean over my ice axe and take two or three long breaths before I felt ready to move on. With each step, Greg's and John's lights got farther ahead. But I knew Phil's light was behind me. On fixed ropes he always climbs behind me so he can hold the rope taut and offer help. How many times had he taken extra weight from my pack, talked me through something, or made me laugh when I thought I couldn't take it any longer?

Now, to keep myself going, I chanted mantras that I'd written in my journal:

You have the ability; now believe, believe, believe.
Olympic athletes perform through the pain.
Nothing lasts forever, even this pain.

When those stopped working I goaded myself by reciting the names of other climbers who had reached the summit.

About three hours in, we stopped for a snack. The cold high-calorie gel felt good on my raw throat, but I had little desire to swallow it. I had read that I might burn as many as 10,000 calories on summit day and I knew I needed to eat, but it had been days since I'd had any appetite whatsoever. Less than five minutes later we were chilled to the core and it was time to move again.

The stop made climbing harder. My quads and knees ached from the constant lifting and my biceps burned from the effort of pulling myself up. The 17-pound oxygen bottle dug into the top of my back. *It isn't worth it,* I told myself, and the words echoed with each breath. But I couldn't turn around. I had seen us standing on the summit a thousand times. That vision had sustained me through two years of training, had propelled me this far up the mountain. There was no way I was turning around now.

A voice in my head began a litany of complaints: *My throat is burning, my joints are aching, my hands are freezing . . .* Another voice countered every outburst with another mantra: *The pain is temporary, you have all the right training, you can do this . . . you can do this . . .* I tried to hold that last thought, to superimpose it on each step, but instead, what filtered up from the back of my mind with all the intensity of a hallucination was the infuriating awareness that if only I hadn't been so eager to achieve this ridiculous objective, I could have been home at this very moment, in front of the fire watching 60 *Minutes* on TV.

We'd been climbing for five hours when a cluster of lights appeared above me. I felt a clutch of dismay: Something must have happened to the team ahead of ours—a rope mix-up, or a rescue that would require Phil and Greg's assistance. All this preparation and our ascent would be derailed! I craned my head as far as the oxygen tank would allow to see what was going on. Slowly the lights thinned to a horizontal line, as if a pearl necklace had been laid out on a table. It wasn't a problem: We had reached the Balcony. This was the landmark I'd been waiting for since we left the South Col, the last major resting place before the top. For one absolutely blissful second every pain, every lick of cold, vanished. We were only 1,400 feet from the summit, more than halfway to our dream.

• • •

The Balcony is a 15-foot shelf at the top of the triangle face. Step too far without turning and you'll find yourself skating down the Kangchung face to the glacier 10,000 feet below. I was not excited about moving around the Balcony in a white-out; especially since the wind seemed strong enough to blow us off the ledge. I unclipped from the rope just long enough to slip in between Greg and Sue, sat down on my pack, and pulled my oxygen bottle out to trade it for a new one. But when I went to disconnect the regulator, I could barely see it. I bent my head so my light would shine directly on it, but the connection was a blur. I looked over at Greg and Sue who seemed to be switching their own bottles without a problem. *This is stupid, Phil! You should be able to do this in your sleep!* But no matter how much I squinted or chastised myself, I couldn't bring the darn thing into focus.

"Hey, Dorjee," I hollered, "give me a hand with this, will you?" I couldn't believe I was asking him for help; usually I was the one doing this for others. But if Dorjee thought there was anything odd about my request, he was polite enough not to say so.

With the new bottle on, I settled onto the ledge. Looking out away from the mountain I could see what I hadn't seen earlier: lightning flashing in the distance. Each strike lit up the sky as if a silent explosion had erupted just over the horizon. The strikes were not close enough to be a danger, but they magnified the uneasiness that had now thoroughly permeated the night. I pulled a candy bar out of my suit but couldn't bring myself to tear it open. I felt heavy, not from the altitude or the exertion but from the decision that had, without my choice or participation, already made itself in my mind.

One of the ironies of climbing is that reaching the summit is often anticlimactic. It's not that you're not thrilled to be there; it's just that for some time already you've known it was a fait accompli. You've passed that point when it dawns on you that since you've gotten this far and can still feel your fingers and toes and still have gas in your tank, there's no way you're not going to make it. At that point you start thinking about how to get down. As I sat there on the Balcony looking into the snow, my calculations were going in the other direction. I'd turned up my oxygen, my face was frozen, I couldn't see well enough to disconnect my own regulator . . . It looked like a duck, it quacked like a duck; I had to call it what it was.

I glanced over at Greg, who looked like he was having his own misgivings. "What do you think?"

He didn't answer. I knew he was wrestling with the same question I was, the question mountain guides all over the world ask themselves: In the face of uncertainty is it safe to go on? There's rarely an easy answer. Much as we tell ourselves and our clients that we're going to Everest, or K2, or McKinley for the experience, the truth is we're going there because we want to summit. Customers have taken weeks (or, in the case of Everest, months) away from work and home; they've spent thousands, or tens of thousands, of dollars. Getting them to 27,000 feet is a great experience—but it's not the summit. But at the same time, we can't jeopardize anybody's safety. So over and over again we struggle with the same equation, totaling our strengths and weaknesses, the consequences of overshooting and the probability that that will happen, until we arrive at a measure of acceptable risk. "It might be better up top," I said.

He nodded.

"It's still early, you and John are strong, you can turn around if it gets worse. I think you should keep going."

Even with the poor visibility I could see his surprise. "What about you and Sue?"

I shook my head. For a split second I felt the sadness well up, and then the mechanics of the situation took over. "I can't see a bloody thing," I said. "I gotta go down."

"We'll turn too."

I waved that away. "Go for another half hour and make a decision then."

He chewed on that for a moment, then nodded.

For just a moment I considered sending Sue with him. I trusted him implicitly, knew that his decisions would be the same as mine. But I couldn't ask him to take two climbers in that kind of weather.

So Greg leaned over and yelled to John, Passang Yila, and Phu Tashi that they would go for another half hour, and I turned to Susan. If I had any inkling of how disappointed she would be later, the part of me that knew we had to get down didn't pay attention. I simply said, "I can't take you up in this. We have to go down. Can you live with that?" And she nodded yes.

• • •

My immediate reaction was relief. We're out of here! We've made it this far; we haven't died; we're together; that's all that matters. I leaned in to hear Phil and Greg's conversation and the plans for going down. To my surprise I heard Greg say something about going for another half hour.

"Phil . . ." I grabbed his arm. "Shouldn't we go for half an hour?"

But he shook his head.

So John, Greg, and their Sherpas continued up into the whiteout and Phil, Dorjee, Dawa Zangbu, and I turned to go down. Going down was easier than coming up. It was a whole different movement on my body, dropping each foot into the step, letting gravity do most of the work. It was still dark though, and the wind cut through my gloves so that my hands stung with cold. Dawa Zangbu insisted that I swap my gloves for his, and my frozen fingers immediately sucked up the warmth left from his hands.

We'd been dropping for about two hours when the sun began to rise over the lip of the distant mountains. The air was still thick with snow but at least now there was a little light. I could see Phil's teal-green back bobbing down the slope ahead of me. With the uneven footing, he looked like he was drunk, bobbing from one foothold to the next. But as I followed his trail, stepping where he stepped, I realized that it wasn't the footholds that caused him to bob; he was tripping. Every few steps, his foot would slide out from under him and he'd have to scramble to get his balance. I'd never seen Phil trip before; usually he walked with such precision. I thought something must be bothering him and that shortly it would pass. But ten minutes later he turned around and waited for me to catch up.

"Sue," he said, "can you look in my eyes? They're real bad and I can't figure out what's wrong."

I got up close. Before I could even look in his eyes, I saw a giant icicle, longer and wider than my middle finger, hanging off the bottom of his mask. "Well, for one thing, you've got this icicle," I said, reaching up and breaking it off. I'd been poking my own mask religiously every fifteen minutes to prevent it from icing up. The exhale hole through which your breath is expelled ices over if you don't clear it repeatedly with your finger.

Immediately he took two huge gasping breaths.

Phil had forgotten to clear the exhale hole! All this time he'd been getting too little air. I looked up into his eyes. Instead of their normal brown they were a purplish color. The skin beneath was white as paper, and his eyebrows and lashes were covered in frost. I felt my own face, but it was clear.

"My goodness, Phil, you're frozen, and your eyes are purple!"

With the hole blocked, his exhaled air must have been migrating up through the crack between his face and his mask, freezing as it hit the air and blowing frozen vapor across his eyes. His eyes, lashes, and eyebrows had frozen.

Even with the purple I could see the flash of recognition in his eyes. "Jason," I said, and he nodded.

Jason Edwards, a guiding friend of Phil's whose team had passed ours going down, had come back from Everest a few years before saying that "nipped corneas" had temporarily blinded him and forced him to turn around. Other stories of frozen eyes traveled through the climbing community from time to time, but we'd never paid them much attention.

Phil must have sensed my alarm because he put his hand on my arm. "It's no big deal," he said. "It only lasted a couple of days. I'll call him when we get down."

His tone was as calm as his words and reassured me. Maybe it was wishful thinking, but I needed to believe that Phil was unconcerned. He gave me a hug, then we started back down the mountain.

The light rose as we descended, but it didn't help Phil's vision. If anything, the tripping was getting worse. His walk took on a dogged determination that told me he was in a big hurry to get down. I would have given anything to rest—between the cold and the jolting, my knees felt like they would shatter—but I didn't say so. Finally, when I simply couldn't help it, I stopped for a moment to catch my breath. It was full daylight now and although the air was still thick with snow, the Khumbu valley was visible in a glaciated panorama before us. Opposite, the sharp, ridged face of Pumori was catching the morning light, and immediately below, where the triangle face opened into the flat cradle of the South Col, were the blue and green humps of our tents. "Look, Phil! The tents!" I shouted. He turned and looked in the general direction I was pointing, then continued down the route. It sent a shiver through me to realize that he couldn't see them.

• • •

I hated telling Sue we had to turn around. It's never easy to pull the plug—even on Rainier—but beyond summiting, our job was to stay alive. I haven't yet seen a mountain that was worth getting killed for. I was relieved when Sue didn't protest.

Hard as it had been going up, going down was harder. I couldn't see the steps below me and could only guess where to put my feet; with no depth perception, I couldn't tell how far to let my body drop. I held on tightly to the fixed rope, thankful each time I stumbled that it stopped me from going very far. I was furious with myself for letting this happen. The exhale hole! How could I have been so stupid? The fact that it had been fifteen years since I'd climbed with oxygen was no excuse. But at the same time I felt a tremendous sense of relief. It was the *mask* that had caused my problems! If it hadn't been for the cancer, I would have looked at my equipment, found the ice, cleared the hole—this never would have happened. But the cancer had shaken my confidence, had made me assume that *I* was ailing. What a total relief to find it wasn't entirely me!

It didn't even occur to me to worry about my vision. I trusted my eyes would clear, as Jason's did, in several days. But when I couldn't see the tents at the South Col, I felt a rush of alarm: What if I couldn't see tomorrow? We had two days of steep descent ahead of us, including a day crossing ladders in the Icefall. Without my eyes, I'd be a danger to myself and a liability to the team. But I forced the thought away. Right now my only job was to get us back to camp.

I felt a little sheepish telling Charlie that I'd forgotten to poke my exhale hole; every rookie knows to do that. But he put his arm around my shoulder in a way that said, "I'm just glad you're alive, buddy!" and then we all crawled into our tents to get out of the cold.

The first thing I did was get on the radio to Greg. To my pleasure, they'd made it as far as the Hillary Step, a 60-foot vertical face just below the summit. The weather had cleared considerably and they were waiting their turn at the rope along with the members of another team. When I knew they were okay, I called around to lower camps looking for Jason. I found him at Camp 2, and he assured me that his eyes had, in fact, gone back to normal after a couple of days. After that there was nothing to do but lie in the tent, stay in touch with Greg, and wait.

• • •

Around noon the radio crackled to life. Greg's voice came through the static loud and clear. "We made it!" Phil let out a whoop and yelled to Charlie and the Sherpas. "Now don't stay up there! Get your butts down," he said to Greg, and we all had a good celebratory holler. Then we snuggled down into our sleeping bags to await their return. Phil closed his eyes; I stared up at the blue nylon of the tent and felt the first stirrings of disappointment. They had made it and we hadn't.

In all my climbs with Phil there was only one other time I'd not made the summit. We'd been on Rainier two days after an avalanche swept the upper mountain. Phil and his partner, George, decided that the slopes above were not yet stable, and at 2,000 feet from the summit they turned us around. Even with that external cause, I felt the sharp sting of disappointment. Now, I chastised myself for feeling that same angry regret. I had no right to be disappointed: If it weren't for Phil, I'd never have been here at all. And given my own difficulty climbing I might not have made the summit anyway. But that didn't soften the sense of failure. I'd had this goal and for whatever reason, I had blown it.

Suddenly I sat up in my sleeping bag. "Phil! Let's go back tomorrow! We're at Camp 4, we've got all our stuff, let's just go tomorrow."

Phil raised his eyelids and looked at me with those weird purple eyes and shook his head.

"Why not? Why can't we give it another shot?"

His expression showed uncommon impatience. "Because even if I *could* go, which I can't, we need to get off of here. We're one of the last teams. The monsoons are coming. The ladders are breaking in the Icefall. The permit's only good till the first of June. It's over."

"But—"

"It's over."

I stared at him and slowly the reality seeped in. It really was over. Everest, the Seven Summits, were history. I riled up inside, furious at the injustice of it, at the mountain for doing this to us, at myself for somehow not preventing it. I didn't get mad at Phil; I didn't blame him for what had happened, but I was outraged that it had. I should have expected it. Phil had told me all along that the odds were not in our favor—less than one in ten—but I thought we were the ones who would make it: We had the best guides, we'd made every other sum- mit. And now *bam*, gone, Just like that.

I sulked. Phil slept. Then I came up with a new plan. If we couldn't go up tomorrow, we would come back next year. It would be even better than this year. We'd be stronger, I'd know what to expect, our chance of success would be greater. I an- nounced this eagerly to Phil, expecting him to leap at the sug- gestion. Instead he rolled his eyes and turned away.

I began to cry. Suddenly it was all too much: the months of climbing, the lack of sleep, the poor food, the bad stomach, the aching throat, the utter exhaustion . . . and now I'd just missed the biggest goal of my life.

Phil said nothing. Usually when I cry he holds me, soothes me, but this time he just looked away.

For the next seven or eight hours we dozed fitfully. At about 6:00 p.m. I was awakened by one of the Sherpas shouting. Passang Yila and Phu Tashi had just walked into camp. We ran outside and hugged them, and Phu Tashi pointed up the mountain. Following his finger, on the lower portion of the triangle, we could see two red suits bobbing downward in a slow but steady progression. I grabbed the still camera, Phil (who claimed he could see well enough to at least point the camera in the right direction) grabbed the video, and we walked out toward the far end of the col to wave to them and wait. Once again I burst into tears, but this was different. Despite my disappointment, I felt so proud of them, and so relieved. In the half hour that we watched and waited, as the colored dots took on the recognizable shapes of John and Greg, my own bad feelings disappeared. Maybe it was from being up so high, from having put out so much effort, from having lived so intimately and intensely together for two and a half months; suddenly I was ecstatic—as elated for John and Greg as I would have been if Phil and I had summited too.

At 7:10 p.m. the two of them walked into camp and directly into our arms. John gave Phil a big old bear hug right around the camera. We gave them each a hot drink and got them settled in for the night, then Phil and I crawled back into the tent for our last night at the South Col. The next morning we would start our descent toward base camp.

. . .

I was happy for Greg and John. They'd worked really hard in difficult conditions, and I was proud of them. On every expedition you revel in the glory of the folks who make it because they're on your team; in a way, part of you was up there too.

That's what got me about Sue. She was acting as if making

the summit was all this trip was about. Sure, our turnaround was disappointing—but what about everything else? We'd had a great climb, two of our team had summited, no one had gotten hurt, we'd been really smooth together . . . in a million ways the trip had been a success. And she was stuck on having not made it to the top.

It was crazy to think about going back, even without my eye problem. The weather was too bad, it was too late in the season, the Sherpas wouldn't do it, we'd been at altitude too long . . . For a hundred reasons we couldn't go back, but she wouldn't let it go. After the first couple of times, she'd stopped saying it—she knew I didn't want to hear it—but even with my eyes closed I could feel her determination, her unwillingness to accept that we were done.

For the first time in the nine years we'd been climbing together, I felt uncomfortable in our tent. We'd probably spent as many nights in a tent as some couples spend in their living rooms, and it had always been pretty blissful. It was more comfortable to be with Sue than to be alone. She was my best friend, my partner, my wife all wrapped up in one. But now, for the first time, the tent felt too small.

I was relieved when daylight came and I could finally go outside. Even through the snow I could see that my eyes were better. The "wax paper" had thinned to a kind of filmy cellophane, and I could make out the sharp edges of the tents and the discolorations in the snow where it crossed the narrow crevasses.

By 9:00 a.m. we'd packed up the tents and gear and begun the descent toward base camp. John and Greg moved well despite their workout the day before; I went more slowly since I couldn't yet trust my eyes. We made it down without incident. Our two days at base camp felt like a return to civilization: real meals instead of tuna and crackers, music blaring from the radio in the cook tent, the congenial sharing of news among the five or six remaining teams from all over the world that were now packing up to go home. We were one of the last teams to leave, and it was odd to see the vibrant multicolored city of tents virtually abandoned.

In his home village of Pangboche, two days' walk out, Ang Passang threw us a party. The village had no electricity, so the Sherpas cooked dinner on a woodstove and we ate by the light of a lantern. The booze flowed, we put Motown on the boom box, and we danced and drank till we dropped into our sleeping bags right there on the floor. At that moment there was no difference between us, whether we were American or Nepali, whether we'd summited or almost made it. To a person we were drunk with pride, friendship, exhaustion, and exhilaration. And we were all ready to go home.

We were in the hotel in Kathmandu when Sue used the word "failure." We were packing up, putting all the climbing gear in duffels for taking on the airplane, and the minute I heard the word, I lost it. "We just put a complicated Everest expedition together, and for all intents and purposes it came off flawlessly, and you're calling it a failure? This trip was not a failure!"

"I didn't say the trip was a failure. I said *I* was a failure, because I didn't do what I set out to do."

"Well, all I heard was the word 'failure,' and I can tell you this trip was no failure. You know, just because you stand on top of Everest doesn't make it a success. If you all end up hating each other, if you behaved like a bunch of jerks, if you cheated some of the Sherpas . . . then, sure, you stood on top of Everest, but was that a success? Not in my book. We had a couple of guys summit. We all looked after each other. We had a pretty good walk for the two of us. We tried to be good citizens. The Sherpas loved us. I screwed up, but nobody on that mountain hated the fact that we were there. I'm pretty darn proud of that. This trip was not a failure." I zipped up the duffel, threw it onto the bed, and walked out of the room.

On the airplane, we joked around with our teammates and acted like everything was normal, but underneath I was still boiling. There are plenty of climbing expeditions where summiting is the only measure of success, and I have no respect for them. That wasn't what I'd wanted to give to Sue. Thirty-six hours after landing I got on a plane to Ecuador with a group of clients, and for the first time since we'd met, I was genuinely happy to be away.

• • •

I had one day after Phil left before I had to go back to work. I rambled around the house—which seemed ridiculously large and also comfortingly familiar—doing laundry, reading the mail. It had been three months since I'd been alone, since my smallest movement had gone unobserved, and while part of me reveled in the privacy the larger part felt lost and terribly lonely. It was as if all the disappointments of my life, everything I had ever wanted but failed to accomplish, were wrapped up in that one broken dream. I missed the intensity of the climb, I missed the closeness of the team. I missed the overarching sense of purpose. And more than anything, I missed Phil.

I hadn't meant to imply that the trip was a failure! I'd said *I* was a failure because I hadn't achieved my objective. But that wasn't what he'd heard. I relived the fight a hundred times, replaying the scene in the hotel room again and again as if somehow I could change the outcome. But no matter how many times I did it, the reality was the same: Phil had heard the word "failure" and he was gone. I listed the ways the trip *wasn't* a failure: the fact that we'd gone at all, the fact that we'd gotten as far as we did, the fact that we'd done so well together. And when I thought back to the climb to the Balcony I added to the list the fact that Phil *had* turned us around. I was so exhausted I might not have made the summit anyway, but I might have pushed myself too far and courted trouble. Phil had said at one point that he should have let me go with Greg and John, and now I told him yet again, in absentia, that I never would have gone. Summiting without him would have had little meaning. To me, *that* would have been a failure.

Phil returned from Ecuador and left again, this time for Russia, and I spent the weeks working twelve-hour days. It killed me to sit at a desk all day after three months of climbing, but being home, waiting for Phil, wondering if we'd be going back, was even harder. In between sales calls I'd find myself back in the Icefall, feeling the ground shudder underneath me, or back in the tent at the South Col, watching Phil close those weird purple eyes and turn away. I'd have to quickly dial the next number, or immerse myself in the contract in front of me, to ground myself in the security of work.

One evening I was driving home, Mt. Rainier off to my right, pink and majestic in the waning light, when I realized that I had wounded him. Of course. Why hadn't I seen that sooner? *He* felt like a failure! He felt responsible for our not reaching the summit, and when I'd used that word I'd poured a pound of salt in his already aching wound. *Oh, Sue, how could you have done that?* I wanted to pull him back to me across the miles, hold him close, and apologize, apologize, apologize . . . But all I could do was wait, and hope that time, and absence, and distance from the climb itself would repair the rift that had opened between us.

May 7, 1951
Telegram from Frances Ershler, Norfolk, VA:

Commander Ershler
Son Born 9 lb 7 oz
Wow
Mother and Son Fine

May 8, 1951
Telegram from Commander Arthur ("Mike") Ershler, USS Franklin
Delano Roosevelt:

Hope you and man mountain both feeling fine

Love, Mike

2

HIT BY AN AVALANCHE

November 13, 1967

"Okay, you guys, get in the cars."

Ten of us on the Newport High School wrestling team stood in a ragged semicircle outside the gym. We'd never had preseason conditioning before—but then we'd never had a coach like Mr. Sipe before, either. He was an Olympic-caliber wrestler who had competed in the Pan American Games; his forearms were bigger than my biceps. He'd told us a week before the official season started that the conditioning was "elective"—and we all understood that it was an elective we would be wise to choose.

"I'm going to run you up to Newport Hills and you're going to run back."

Five of us squeezed into each car, one driven by Sipe, the other by the assistant coach. Two miles from school they let us out. A young boy holding a bicycle stared at us from his front yard.

Sipe looked us over for a moment. "Don't take the whole afternoon."

Like a school of fish, we turned and took off, and a moment later Sipe and the assistant coach cruised past us, heading back to school.

I hated running. I especially hated running when I was nauseated, which I had been since early afternoon. The bouts had been coming more frequently since summer. They'd started when Greg Linwick, my best friend, and I were on our fishing trips in the Cascades, about an hour from our suburban Seattle homes. Half a dozen times on those excursions, I'd had to yell to Greg, "You go ahead, I gotta take a piss," and then dash off the trail to heave. I hadn't made much of it, but now the bouts were coming once a week or so, and often included cramping as well as nausea.

Back at school, Mr. Sipe was waiting for us in the gym. He stood with his arms crossed, feet slightly apart, looking as if he'd been poured from concrete. We stood in front of him, wiping our faces and panting. I realized the cramps and nausea had disappeared while I was running. He looked us over, and I sensed he was making a mental note of each person's condition. "Well," he said, "none of you guys got lost. That's a start."

Despite Darren Sipe's gruffness, he was exactly the coach I wanted. I had lettered the year before as the school's 106-pounder, but I hadn't felt that my performance was particularly noteworthy, and I'd been looking forward to junior year when I hoped to become a better, and better-respected, wrestler. Now Mr. Sipe, who had come close to the Olympics himself, was offering to train us as if *we* were future Olympians. I was ready to learn anything he could teach me. Unfortunately, it wasn't at all clear that my stomach was going to cooperate.

After a couple of weeks of preseason conditioning, official practice began. Now we did nothing but wrestle. No weights, no calisthenics, just 100 percent wrestling. I had been eating less and less—skipping breakfast ("Sorry, Mom, got to catch the bus"), eating half a sandwich at lunch, and pushing the food around on my plate at dinner so it looked like activity had taken place. But even so, my stomach was acting up a lot. Two or three times a week I'd throw up or have gut-splitting cramps. I was starting to feel like I was spending half my time with my arms clamped across my middle. Mom noticed, of course. She was a great cook and normally I was happy to eat her cooking. But now, when she asked me what was wrong, I couldn't tell her. If I told her she would insist on taking me to the doctor, and then the problem would become real.

All through October I kept up my little deception, hoping the problem would go away. But by early November I was worn out from the duplicity and the chronic pain. Finally I gave in and told my mother.

The family doctor was no help. First, he told us it was constipation. When laxatives didn't help, he said it was in my head. So my mother took me to a gastroenterologist—the same one she had seen several years before when she had digestive problems of her own. Dr. Beech Barrett asked me a lot of questions and did a short exam, then scheduled me for an endoscopy, a procedure that would enable him to look directly into my stomach.

On the day of the procedure I sat on the exam table in one of those flimsy paper gowns and watched as a nurse handed him a tube. It was about an eighth of an inch in diameter and about four feet long with what looked like a matchbox-size bulge at the end. Dr. Barrett held the fat end near my mouth and told me to swallow. The next thing I knew he was snaking it down my throat. Instantly I gagged.

"Good boy, just keep swallowing."

I fought the urge to vomit.

"Just a little more."

When it was over my entire body was shaking. My esophagus felt as if I had swallowed a quiver full of arrows.

I was getting dressed when I heard the doctor talking to my mother in the hall, neither of them realizing, I think, that the door was slightly open. ". . . hard to know for sure," he was saying ". . . a good chance of Hodgkin's disease . . . yes, a form of cancer . . . surgery, yes . . ." His voice dropped a few notches. "Well, if it's Hodgkin's, he'll have about six months . . ."

When I met my mother in the waiting room her face was tight and her skin was unnaturally white. Walking out to the car I waited for her to tell me, but she merely gave me a tight little smile. Finally, when we were a few blocks from his office, I couldn't bear it any longer. "What did he say?"

"Nothing, really. He doesn't know." She looked steadily out at the rush-hour traffic.

"Are you sure?"

"Yes."

"Then why do you look so upset?"

She glanced at me for a second, then turned back to the road.

I knew I would get no more out of her. I knew she would go home and talk to my dad and that together they would decide how to tell me, so I spent the car ride thinking about what I had heard. Maybe it was a teenager's sense of invulnerability, maybe it was an intuitive knowledge of my own body, maybe it was just a stubborn refusal to accept what I didn't want to believe. Or maybe I'd just heard it wrong. But with unwavering certainty, I knew that I did not have cancer. If, in fact, I needed surgery, they would find out when they did it that something else was causing my problems.

That evening I waited for my parents to tell me, but they didn't. They told me only that I would be having an operation to pinpoint the cause of my problems. I wanted to confront them and make them tell me the truth, but I didn't. I knew they were protecting me, wanting not to alarm me until the surgery confirmed the diagnosis, but I resented their silence. I was scared enough already; having them hold out on me only made it worse.

I told no one, not even Greg. Greg had been my best friend since seventh grade. He was the one I'd learned to ski with, to wrestle with; we did almost everything together. But I had no intention of telling him the diagnosis. As long as I didn't talk about it, it wasn't real.

My surgery was scheduled for winter break. As much as I dreaded going into the hospital and getting cut, I couldn't wait to get the problem fixed. Mostly, I tried to fast-forward in my mind to January when school would start again and things would be back to normal. At home we rarely talked about it—that was probably *my* wish as much as my parents'. I could feel them keeping a watchful eye on me. Mom made bland foods that I could tolerate, and they never complained when I was too sick to do anything but lie on the couch and watch TV, but they refused to let my illness disrupt the life of our family. I still went to school and pitched in around the house, and we still sat down to dinner and discussed our days as if nothing were out of the ordinary. It was exactly how it had been when my mom's digestive problems led to surgery on her esophagus. We all knew she was uncomfortable—and often in pain—but she never complained, and life went on as normal. It was as if by deliberately continuing our routine we were sending a message to our illnesses that we were not a family who could be easily threatened. They would have to accommodate themselves to us because we weren't going to bend ourselves to them.

When school closed for Christmas vacation I checked into a room at Overlake Hospital. The week before, we'd gone to meet the surgeon. He'd explained that he would be doing exploratory surgery, which would enable the doctors to make a more accurate diagnosis, and that he might have to remove a portion of my stomach. He and Mom had assured me that if he did, I would get along fine without it, and Mom reminded me how much better she felt after a portion of her esophagus was replaced. But the idea that I might wake up with part of my stomach gone was too horrifying to contemplate. The night before the surgery I lay in the hospital bed, unnerved by the bright lights outside the door and the footsteps and voices going back and forth. Each time I drifted off, I was awakened by a nurse moving in and out of the room. I couldn't shut off my fear.

The next morning Mom and Dad walked beside the gurney as they wheeled me to the operating room. I loved them, I was glad they were there, I didn't want the attendant to wheel me away, but I was extremely mad at them for putting me through this. I knew it wasn't their fault, but I needed someone to blame.

I kept closing my eyes, trying to go back to where I had been, but every time I did a woman poked at me with her voice, pulling me into the room. When I was able to keep my eyes open, I was wheeled through corridors, miserable with pain. Then my mother was there, leaning over, putting her face close to mine.

"You look better already!"

I never spoke disrespectfully to my parents, but I felt so wretched. "Just get the heck out of here," I growled and turned away.

For the next twenty-four hours I felt completely destroyed— but alert enough that I couldn't sleep it off. My parents came in and out, and my roommate, who looked like he'd stepped out of a comic book ad for a body-building course, tried to engage me in conversation, but I was too miserable to let them talk me out of my discomfort. At one point my roommate suggested that I ask the nurse for more pain medication, but I shook my head. I thought I should be able to handle a little pain.

On my third day in the hospital, Greg and our friend Mike Green came to visit. I had finally confided to them that I was having surgery, although I still hadn't mentioned Dr. Barrett's diagnosis. I was happy to see them and was glad for the distraction, but I was also embarrassed. I hated feeling like an invalid, and having them see me that way made me feel it all the more. They pulled up chairs and Mike launched into a story about a party he'd been to the night before. Mike had a wicked sense of humor, and within minutes Greg and I were cracking up. But every time I laughed I felt like my insides were ripping open.

"Quit making me laugh," I yelled, but Mike was on a roll. "Quit it!" The pain was making me angry.

But even when he tried to stop, everything that came out of his mouth was funny. When the two of them finally left I lay in my bed, holding my stomach and groaning.

"I'd ask for pain meds if I were you," said my roommate.

I shook my head.

He lifted the tube that attached him to his IV. "Don't be an idiot. That's what they're for."

It hadn't occurred to me that Charles Atlas over there might be on pain meds himself.

A short time later the nurse came in to see how we were doing. "I think my friend over there could use a little pain medication," my roommate said.

This time I didn't protest.

Before I left the hospital, Dr. Barrett confirmed what I'd known all along: I didn't have cancer. What I had was Crohn's disease, a chronic, autoimmune disorder of the digestive tract. In Crohn's, he explained, the immune system goes on overdrive and attacks the healthy bacteria in the stomach and intestines, causing chronic inflammation. Eventually the inflammation blocks or damages the organs, at which point the diseased portions must be removed. That's what had happened to me. The surgeon had removed a sizable chunk of my stomach.

"I don't think you'll miss it, though," Dr. Barrett said rather cheerily. "You're going to feel a lot better without it."

I just hoped he was right.

For the next several days my parents tried to talk to me about the disease. They explained that it was chronic, that my symptoms would return from time to time, that I would live with and manage Crohn's for the rest of my life. But they said it would not interfere with the quality of my life. Schoolwork, skiing, wrestling, hiking—all would continue as they had before. I listened to them with half an ear. I was too glad to have the surgery over, too focused on getting out of the hospital and back to school, to really grasp what they were saying.

The minute the doctors said I could start wrestling, I taped a bandage over my incision and headed to practice. I knew I was weak and didn't expect to perform as well as usual, but we still had several weeks of the season left, enough time to regain some strength and form.

"You're back," Mr. Sipe said as I walked across the gym and into the wrestling room. I'd told him I would miss the vacation practices because I was having surgery, although I hadn't told him what kind. Now I wondered if he even remembered what I'd said. He looked at me as if he thought I'd been playing hooky.

He paired us up and we went to work practicing takedowns. My opponent was a sophomore who was my weight but several inches taller. I had a full year on him in terms of skills and practice and when I'd wrestled him in the fall he'd been no match for me, but now he took me down every time. I assured myself that in a week or so I'd be back to normal.

After the takedowns we went to work on the mat. Within a minute, the sophomore wrapped his arm across my abdomen and pulled, and the sear in my stomach was so great that I was sure the incision had ripped open. I hunched to the bathroom, lifted my T-shirt, and peeled back the bandage. The incision was still closed, but the pain had barely subsided.

The next morning I fished an Ace bandage out of the bathroom drawer and wrapped it around my abdomen as tightly as I could, thinking that would offer more protection. But the result was no better. After a few holds the bandage rolled up into a narrow wrap across my upper abdomen, and when I twisted sharply to the side I gagged with pain. I made it through two more practices before I acknowledged that I had to stop.

Telling Mr. Sipe was even harder than admitting it to myself. I had never really explained to him what had happened to me during vacation, and even now I felt ashamed to tell him that I couldn't cut it. I dressed slowly, dawdling until everyone else had left the gym. Then I stood dumbly at the door of his office.

"Yeah?" he said. Even off the mat he was strictly business.

I mumbled something about "surgery" and "recovery" and "not being ready."

When I finished he looked at me for a long time with his narrow, determined eyes. "Yup," he said finally, "it's hard to keep guys on a losing team." Then he shrugged as if there were nothing left to say and turned back to his desk.

I knew he didn't understand; I hadn't told him about my stomach. But that didn't stop me from being angry. I slunk out of the gym, muttering obscenities under my breath, furious that he had labeled me a quitter, and feeling, even though I knew the truth, that I deserved it.

As if the loss of wrestling were not enough, my father had also nixed my dream of working on the ski patrol. Since sophomore year Mike and I had planned on trying out for ski patrol when we were juniors; we'd even taken a first aid class that fall in preparation. But once my stomach problem surfaced Dad had said, "Not this year." I knew he was right, but I was pissed and disappointed. The only thing that stopped me from going into a total tailspin was the fact that my health was getting better. For the first time in months, whole weeks passed with no symptoms. Doctors had put me on the steroid prednisone, which was helping control the inflammation. I was careful about what I ate (small portions, bland foods), and for weeks at a time I could almost forget that I had a "chronic condition."

This, in itself, was cause for celebration. And then in March a new pleasure inserted itself into my life.

The previous summer, during our fishing trips in the Cascades, Greg and I had decided that we needed to learn a bit of mountaineering: So many places would open up to us if we had those skills. We decided that the following summer we would take a mountaineering class. But that spring the climbing class literally came to us. Bellevue Community College began using classroom space at our high school, and one of the courses they offered was basic mountaineering. We applied, and on the first evening of spring semester we found ourselves sitting in one of Newport's portable classrooms, surrounded by a dozen other would-be mountaineers, most of whom were at least a decade older than we were. At the front of the room was a middle-aged man in a tweed blazer who looked more like a Boeing engineer than a mountain climber. Greg and I looked at each other, our enthusiasm dimming. But before we could say anything, the man began taking items out of a duffel bag and placing them on a table: a handful of carabiners, a piton, thick leather boots followed by a pair of crampons, a pack, and finally an ice axe. My eagerness returned.

John Pollack *was* a Boeing engineer, but he was also a long-experienced Northwest mountaineer, and there was barely a peak in the Cascades that he hadn't climbed. Over the next few months, he taught us everything we needed to know to understand that we loved climbing. On Mt. Erie north of Seattle he taught us belaying, tying into the rope and anchoring one person while the other climbs. On Mt. Pilchuck he taught us how to crampon and kick steps in snow and how to use an ice axe to arrest a fall. On the glaciers of Mt. St. Helens (my first "big" summit) he taught us techniques of crevasse rescue and glacier travel.

After the surgery and the disappointments of ski patrol and wrestling, I loved being out and using my body. I loved practicing the techniques and buying the gear, and even got a job as a soda jerk so I could make enough money to afford it. Once school was out for the summer, Greg, Mike (who had learned to climb from his father), and I went climbing together. We had access to Mike's parents' Rambler or my dad's Plymouth, so the Cascades were ours, and now, just as Greg and I had hoped, we could go anyplace we looked. At the end of the day we'd get back in the car, and before we had even hit the highway we'd be planning our next climb. Perhaps I would have loved anything at that time that got me out and using my body, but climbing felt *good*. It gave me strength and pleasure and companionship, it gave me confidence in my body, and it made me feel good about myself.

When fall came and school began, we continued to go up to the mountains on weekends. When we finally hung up our harnesses it was only because Mike and I were accepted onto a local ski patrol and wrestling season had begun. But wrestling didn't have quite the hold over me that it had before. I was already looking forward to the following spring when we could get back into the mountains.

Healthwise, my senior year was a period of adjustment. I was learning the pattern of my disease: periods of remission followed by flare-ups when the symptoms would return. My older sister, Margaret, who was away at college, sent me a book about Crohn's, which I read, but mostly I learned by living with it. I learned that eating several small meals during the day worked better than eating three big ones, and that some foods sat right while others didn't. It slowly dawned on me how much of my stomach they'd taken out—close to half—and I began to think of myself as a "grazer." Once a month or so I'd have that familiar feeling of food not wanting to go down and I'd find myself clutching my stomach, waiting for a cramp to pass. Sometimes it would last for an afternoon, sometimes longer; when it faded I'd be left to wonder how soon it would come again. The unexpected pleasure, though, was that staying active—skiing, climbing—seemed to have a healing effect on my body. My parents had been right: My favorite activities were not side-lined by the disease; they were providing my salvation.

Greg and Mike had a small idea of what I was going through. They knew I had Crohn's and could see, at times, that I was suffering, but I didn't talk about it and they were tactful enough not to ask. I talked about it with no one. I didn't want people to see me as the guy with Crohn's. I was slowly coming to understand what it meant to live with a chronic disease, but that was not a matter I cared to share with those around me.

In September 1969 I went away to Whitman College in eastern Washington—far enough away that I felt independent, but close enough that I could easily see my family—and the following summer Greg, Mike, and I got up to the mountains as much as we could. Then, the winter of my sophomore year, I got a crazy idea. What if I could work in the summer as a guide on Mt. Rainier? I'd never climbed Rainier and didn't know the first thing about guiding, but I knew how to climb and I knew first aid: Why couldn't I learn to be a guide? So I wrote a letter to Lou Whittaker, co-owner of Rainier Mountaineering, the guide service on the mountain, and a few weeks later I got a form letter back inviting me to an information session at his partner Jerry Lynch's law office in Tacoma.

How did one interview to be a mountain guide? On the drive to Tacoma I rehearsed answers to questions I thought they might ask. By the time I arrived I must have lost two pounds in nervous sweat. I opened the door, prepared to introduce myself to the receptionist, but the front desk was empty. Instead, a man who looked to be six-and-a-half-feet tall and 200 pounds was sprawled on a couch in a corner in a posture that commanded complete ownership of the room. I knew instantly that it was Lou. Lou Whittaker was a legend in mountaineering. He and his twin brother, Jim, had been guiding on Rainier since before I was born, well before Jim became the first American to summit Everest in 1963. Lou himself had earned the nickname

"Rainier Lou" because he had dedicated his life to guiding and rescue on the mountain. Now, standing in front of him, I felt dwarfed. I was five feet six, 120 pounds. Although he was seated on the couch, his head was level with mine. I fished around for something to say, but was completely unnerved by the fact that he was looking me up and down as if I were a steer at market. Before I could even string two thoughts together, he made a dismissive snort. "Huh," he said, "you'll never make a guide."

I stared at him dumbfounded, too shocked even to withdraw the hand I'd already offered. Then my wits returned. *You big, dumb . . . ,* I thought. *We'll see!*

A month later I drove to the end of the road on the south side of Mt. Rainier where Paradise Lodge serves as the starting point for RMI climbs. There, under the watchful eyes of Lou, Jerry, and one or two other guides, eleven hopefuls and I demonstrated ice axe arrests, belaying, knots, cramponing, and other techniques. It was hard to feel confident knowing I was being judged, but I had two extra incentives to do well. First, we were on the snow slopes just above the parking lot and any mistake would land me 30 feet below on asphalt. Second, I was hell-bent on proving Lou wrong.

At the end of the final day of tryouts he offered me a job.

A month later I drove back to Mt. Rainier—this time as an assistant guide. I was not nervous about the fact that I had never climbed it—I had climbed other glaciated peaks, albeit not as high—but I did have a case of new job jitters. Just in case Lou was still looking to justify his first impression, I didn't want to give him ammunition. Fortunately, my first assignment seemed easy enough. Six guides would be leading twenty-four customers on the 4½-mile hike to Camp Muir, the Rainier base camp at 10,000 feet. My job was to bring up the rear. All I had to do was follow.

We set out from Paradise under a cold gray sky. There had

been massive snowfall that winter and any trail that might have been there was buried under 12 feet of snow. But even from the back of the line I could see that the way was well-marked by the colored parkas and footprints of the climbers ahead. As we hiked, the temperature dropped, and cold, hard pellets of snow began to fall. Our parkas began to rime with ice. When we reached the first rest stop there was little talking, just the deep huffing of twenty-four people trying to catch their breath. After the break, the group naturally divided into faster and slower hikers and by the final break at 9,000 feet, the group at the back had been reduced to two men, two women, and me. Separated from the rest, we now formed our own little regiment, and I felt a swell of protective pride. *My clients!*

As the snow picked up and visibility grew worse, the walking got harder. The steps kicked into the snow by the other climbers filled in before we reached them, so I moved to the front in order to break trail. But even from that vantage point I could see no sign of the footprints. *Darn,* I thought, feeling a swell of panic, *without those footprints, I don't know how to get to Muir!* I picked up the pace, hoping to catch up enough to find occasional traces of footprints, but when I looked back a few minutes later, the customers were way behind. *"Hurry up!"* I wanted to yell, but I could feel their exhaustion. So instead I hollered, "Almost there, folks," having no idea if it was true. I didn't even know if we were going in the right direction.

When we did arrive, it was not by trail or sight, but by sound. I heard voices in the fog ahead and immediately felt ridiculous for having doubted. Dusan Jagersky, our lead guide, emerged from the gray. His chest and shoulders were twice the width of mine; his hands were like paws. He leaned in toward me, shook my hand with a viselike grip, and said in his thick Czech accent, "Ah, little boy, you make it." I bridled, feeling chastised and belittled, but then I saw that he was smiling. He had meant the words not as a rebuke, but as a welcome. He was praising me. I had delivered my first clients.

I was standing in the bunkhouse a few moments later when two "cabin girls" came in, handing out bowls and spoons for dinner. They were about my age, deeply tanned, and apparently as comfortable in the thin air at 10,000 feet as most people are at sea level. One smiled and joked with the climbers; the other, who was wearing red reflective sunglasses even though the sun was nowhere to be seen, thrust a bowl and spoon at me and barked, "Use these for the seminar and return them at the end. Clean." *Whew,* I thought, *and I thought Whittaker was intimidating! I won't be having much to do with that woman!*

Fortunately, I didn't have to. The next three days were filled with the demands of teaching. We broke into small groups on the Cowlitz Glacier and taught the clients the basics of climbing. The clients were considerably older than I was, but to my surprise, they were completely attentive. They had no idea that I was a total novice! Two older men actually asked if they could be on my rope team for the summit, and both times I'd almost blurted, "You don't want to be on *my* team, Jack! I've never done this before either!" But the fact that they had asked, and the satisfaction I could see in my clients as they improved their skills, filled me with enormous pleasure. At the same time, I couldn't shake my worry: What if on summit day they couldn't tie knots? What if they couldn't ice axe arrest and they fell? The anxiety I'd felt on the way to Muir returned, doubled.

At midnight on our fourth day we gathered in the dark outside the bunkhouse, roping up for our climb to the summit. The customers stamped their feet and drew their hoods tight as the wind whipped bits of pumice into our faces. I was at the head of a three-man team, and as we set off across the Cowlitz Glacier, my customers moved steadily, cramponing well and watching the rope just as we had taught them. About two hours in we reached Gibraltar Ledge, a series of narrow shoulders, each 3 to 4 feet wide, that sloped away from the mountain before dropping steeply to the Nisqually Glacier below. My pulse quickened. The Ledge was famously precarious, an unstable mixture of rock and snow, and dangerously exposed to rockfall. How would the clients handle it? Were they steady enough on their crampons? Could they handle this much exposure? Yesterday I'd worried that *my* inadequacy might endanger them, but now I remembered a half-joke that Joe Horiskey, one of the senior guides, had told me during training. "Remember, Ersh: Number one, the clients are trying to kill themselves; number two, they're trying to kill each other; number three, they're trying to kill you." I'd laughed when he said it, but suddenly it didn't seem so funny. If one of my clients fell, he would probably take the rest of us with him.

I stepped gingerly onto the beginning of the Ledge, keeping to the mountain side of the trail while listening for rockfalls from above. Fortunately, this early in the morning ice was still cementing the rock together. When I was 30 feet out, the rope went taut then loose again, a sign that the man behind me had begun the traverse. I looked back and watched him as he worked his way across, head down, absorbed in his own steps. Irrationally, I felt that as long as I watched him, I could assure our mutual safety. But I also had to keep moving. If I didn't keep the rope between us taut, I'd have no chance of stopping him if he fell. For the next hour we moved at a snail's pace from one ledge to the next. When the last of us stepped off the final pitch, my entire body sagged with relief.

For the next hour we threaded our way up the Nisqually Chute, an area that required nothing but good cramponing and steady uphill effort, and then picked our way across the crevasses of the Nisqually Glacier. At 8:00 a.m., under a gray sky that was indistinguishable from the surrounding mountain, we stepped up onto the summit. I turned around to shake the hands of my team. It was hard to know who felt prouder, they or I.

I was coiling up the rope that had held my team together when Dusan came up to me and, with a grip so fierce I thought my bones would break, began to pump my hand. "Well, little boy," he said in his thick accent, "you make the summit."

I felt I had arrived.

For the rest of that summer I barely left Rainier. When I wasn't guiding I was down at Paradise, hanging out with the guides at the Lodge or the Visitor Center, or in the small room I shared with another guide named Larry Nielson. One night I was walking back to my room after dinner when a black sedan drove up beside me. The cabin girl with the red glasses, who I had since learned was named Marty Hoey, leaned out the driver's window.

"Hey, want to get some pie?"

Blackberry pie à la mode was a specialty of the Gateway Inn, twenty miles down the road, and since there wasn't much to do at Paradise at night, we ate it often. But I couldn't imagine why Marty was asking me. We'd spoken barely twenty words to each other since our "introduction" and most of those had been pretty gruff. She looked me square in the eye, practically daring me to say no, so I got in.

The Gateway was a rustic log-cabin-style resort, and the restaurant always had a big fire roaring in the hearth. Marty shook out her hair, which was long and dark, and pushed aside her menu. "So." She leaned forward on the table. "Tell me about yourself."

Jeez, I thought, *she's forward.* "What do you want to know?"

"Whatever you want to tell me."

So I told her about going to Whitman, about my family in Seattle, about how I got into guiding, and every time I stopped she nodded and waited for me to continue. I would have felt like I was getting the third degree except that her interest seemed so genuine. When I couldn't think of anything else to say I asked about her.

"I'm an English major at the University of Washington. I love to climb. This is my third summer working up here."

"Have you thought about being a guide?"

"Yeah, I'd like to guide. But I don't want to lead."

"You don't have to lead at first."

"I don't ever want to lead."

"Why not?" That didn't make a lot of sense.

"I don't want that responsibility."

"Huh. That's pretty honest." It was so honest I was surprised she'd said it.

"Yeah, well, honesty's an important trait to live by."

I felt almost rebuked.

"Honesty, nobility and . . . I'm not sure about the third. What do you think?"

What I thought was that I should have had the courage to say no back in the parking lot. "I don't know, Marty. It's your question. You tell me."

"Just try to name another."

I looked around the mostly empty restaurant. I didn't know! "Integrity?"

She smiled—probably the first time she'd smiled in my presence. "I like that. Honesty, nobility, integrity. I think that's it."

I felt like I'd passed some kind of test. I hadn't had a lot of one-on-one conversations with women in my life, but I sure didn't think they went like this.

An hour and a half later I was lying in bed when there was a light knock at the door. I opened it and there was Marty. Her roommate was "occupied," she said, and she needed a place to sleep. "Well, Larry's 'occupied' too, so you can use his bed," I said, and she climbed up to the top bunk and I got back into mine. I was just drifting off to sleep when she crawled in beside me.

For the rest of that summer, and intermittently for several years after, Marty and I were lovers. I'm sure if she hadn't taken the initiative it never would have happened. I was twenty years old and had avoided relationships, but she challenged me—emotionally, physically, intellectually—and little by little she chiseled away at my self-protection. Still, I was only willing to go so far. When she asked about the scar on my stomach, or why I sometimes had trouble eating, I ducked the questions. She said I was putting limits on our closeness by limiting what she knew—and she was right. But even though I'd come to care about her deeply, I just couldn't tell her more.

Everything about that summer was heady: the climbing, Marty, the community of guides—even my health, which was significantly better than when I was at college. But right on top of the list was guiding. I had gone to Rainier because I wanted to climb, but over the course of the summer I found that guiding gave me equal satisfaction. I was going up five or six days a week, but no matter how many climbs I did, each one felt new. There were new customers, new guiding partners, new weather and route conditions—and I loved the challenge of bringing all those disparate elements together to create a successful climb. I loved establishing a rapport with my clients, loved helping them push through their fears, loved watching them develop the confidence that would enable them to stand on top. The customers were all ages and came from all walks of life—from carpenters to professionals to corporate CEOs—and we were thrown together in situations where the consequences of a wrong judgment were steep. It was a crash course in communication, empathy, and group dynamics, and it made for intense trial-by-fire learning. For a guy in his early twenties it was a great way to grow up.

Back at college, I missed the adrenaline rush of climbing. I missed the intense interaction with the guides and customers, and the highs that came from knowing I'd made a difference in a few people's lives. I also missed the better behavior of my stomach. I'd had the sense that being active and in the mountains had had a restorative effect on my body, and now that I was sedentary, I could see that I'd been right. Within weeks of getting back to school my flare-ups intensified, and the background level of discomfort rose. By October I knew I'd be spending all my summers on Rainier.

One morning I was awakened by an unusually violent roiling in my stomach. I did a running shuffle to the bathroom and the minute I sat down, my insides poured loose in a gassy flood. I wasn't surprised. For the last several days I'd been dragging myself around, more tired than usual, and I'd pretty much been expecting the rest of the symptoms. But when I stood up to flush the toilet, I recoiled. My diarrhea was red with blood.

I knew I should go to the doctor. I'd had diarrhea before, but never anything like this. But I was not about to make myself go. I'd read enough about Crohn's to know the trajectory of the disease—one surgery often leading to another and another until you're carved up like a turkey, trussed with stitches, tubes, and colostomy bags—and I was not going there. So I dressed, took as many books as I could carry, and headed out of my apartment. I lived half a mile from campus, just a fifteen-minute walk, but I was so weak and my stomach was so knotted that it was hard to move my legs. *Suck it up,* I said to myself. *Get to class. Do what you do in the mountains.* So I began to "rest step" the way we taught our customers on Rainier, straightening and resting my back leg for a moment before transferring my weight, taking two full breaths with every step. It took me forty minutes to reach the classroom.

Over the next few weeks the flare-up passed; whatever it was healed itself enough that I returned to the state of fluctuating discomfort that had become the norm. In the wake of the attack I realized that, for all its ups and downs, my life had taken on a kind of regularity. The flare-ups came and went, I waited them out, then returned to whatever I was doing. I had developed a new definition of "normal." Normal for me would never be nachos and pizza several nights a week, washed down with several pints of beer. It would never be seeing the doctor only once a year for flu. It would never be taking good days for granted or believing that time was free for the wasting. It *would* be enduring bouts, several times a month, when my gut acted up. But the bouts would pass and then I would return to whatever I was doing. This is it, I realized; this is what it takes to live with this disease: resilience, determination, and a persistent belief in the future. I needed to become a master of all three.

A few weeks later, I was home for spring break and went for a routine medical checkup. I had heard that Dr. Barrett had retired and that his replacement was a doctor named Marty Greene, and I wasn't entirely happy about losing the doctor who had treated me for three years. I grew even warier when Dr. Greene entered the exam room. He couldn't have been more than ten years older than I was. How could he know enough to treat me as well as Dr. Barrett had? I was swallowing my concern when he held out his hand and said, "I know you, Phil. You may not remember, but you were the guide on my rope when I climbed Mt. Rainier."

I did a double take. He'd been my customer? I looked at him more closely and, in truth, I didn't remember, but inside I felt myself relax. *He's climbed.* I thought. *He knows what I do. He'll get that this can't limit my lifestyle.*

Dr. Greene asked about my flare-ups and I told him about the bloody diarrhea. He nodded but didn't seem alarmed. When he was finished examining me he said, "You know, we should probably get you into the hospital, get you fully checked out."

I took the "probably" to mean I had a choice, and shook my head. The flare-up had passed. If something more serious happened I would know it when it did. Until then, I would continue doing what I was doing. Crohn's would be taking me to the hospital at some point in the future, that was pretty much assured. But I had no interest in going any sooner than I had to.

After college I continued working summers on Rainier. As it had the first summer, my stomach tended to behave better on the mountain than off. I had fewer symptoms, and when it did act up, the symptoms were less severe. For some reason my third summer was the only exception. Many times that summer I lay in my bag at Muir, sick to my stomach, unable to sleep. I'd try to hold it until morning and then, during the bustle of getting everybody ready, I'd flick off my headlamp and run behind the bunkhouse to vomit. Each time it happened I'd think, *That's it; I'm done.* I walked off that mountain half a dozen times in my mind. But then we'd start climbing and I'd gradually feel better. The sun would come up and one of the clients would say, "Isn't that the most incredible thing you ever saw?" and I would think, *All right, maybe I'm not finished after all.*

Each winter I picked up work with a small manufacturer of climbing gear or in a health club as a trainer. I would have preferred to continue guiding, but there was no guiding industry in those days, no companies taking customers around the world year-round. There were only a few outfits like RMI that took customers up local mountains in the summer. I had just come back from my own climb of a Mexican volcano when I got an inspiration: In South America the seasons were reversed. When it was winter here, the big Andean volcanoes were ripe for climbing. If I could guide customers on Rainier, why couldn't I guide them in the Andes too? Speculatively, I put the word out to my Rainier customers that I would be leading a Mexican climb and, remarkably, people started signing up. So bit by bit I put together a little business leading South American climbs. I was just starting to think it might be possible to actually make a living guiding when the chance of a lifetime came sailing into my lap.

It was 1979, my ninth season on Rainier, and the other guides and I had just finished outfitting the customers with rental gear when a guide named Chris Kerrebrock grabbed Eric Simonson, George Dunn, Marty Hoey, and me and motioned us all outside. Chris was relatively new on Rainier; he'd only been guiding with us for a couple of summers, but he was strong, technically proficient, and highly motivated. We joked that when Chris led one of our longer programs, the customers had better watch out because he was always trying to take them on harder routes. Now, when we were out of earshot of anybody else, he said, "Hey, what do you guys think about going to the north face of Everest? I have a friend who works in the State Department who thinks he can get me a permit."

We all looked at him like he was crazy. Chris was one of those people who can do anything. He was a grad student at Columbia, and it was easy to imagine him having a prominent career in government or at a university and setting climbing records in his spare time. But even so, it was impossible to get a permit to climb the north side. For one thing, the north side of Everest was in China, it was the middle of the Cold War, and no Americans were getting in. For a second, the north side had been climbed exactly four times—twice by a Chinese team, once by a Japanese, and most recently by the famous Italian climber Reinhold Messner. If the Chinese were going to grant any American a permit, it would be a high-profile climber like Jim Whittaker. It wasn't going to be Chris Kerrebrock and a bunch of twenty-something, overambitious Rainier guides.

"Yeah, sure, Chris," we all said. "Just let us know." And that was the last any of us thought about it, at least seriously.

But it wasn't long before Chris did it. Although his State Department contact never came through, his father, who was a professor at MIT, did an academic exchange in China, and when his Chinese hosts asked if there was anything they could do for him while he was in their country, he responded by asking for an audience with the head of the Chinese Mountaineering Association. In 1980 he came home with a permit. Chris was good to go in the spring of '82.

Wow! It took a little while for the news to sink in. *We could actually go and do it.* Chris, Marty, George, Eric, me . . . ordinary American kids, total Himalayan neophytes . . . we were actually going to climb Everest's north side! After that, we gathered every night in the Lodge, or at the Ranch in Ashford where we lived when we weren't on the mountain, and talked through the logistics. Chris, who was an accomplished trumpeter and played with pit orchestras in New York, would take out his trumpet and punctuate our conversations. Almost immediately we realized we needed a leader: someone with a lot more experience than we had, and who could raise the hundreds of thousands of dollars it would take to get us to the top of the world and back. There was no argument there: The leader should be Lou. Lou, once he got over his own surprise, agreed, and then, for the next two years, everything took a backseat to Everest. What had begun as Chris's pie-in-the-sky dream became the main reason for any of us to eat, sleep, or breathe.

Early in our planning we added Jim Wickwire to the team. Jim was a Seattle lawyer and, unlike most of us, had bona fide Himalayan experience. In 1978 he and his partner, Lou Reichert, had become the first Americans to summit K2, the world's second highest mountain. Jim had gained added fame when he survived a near-fatal bivouac on the way down. Having climbed on McKinley with him a few years before, I could attest to the fact that he was both fearless and driven, and we all felt his strength, attitude, and endurance would be an asset to the team. In the spring of 1981, a year before we were due to leave, Chris and Jim decided to climb Mt. McKinley together. They wanted to get to know each other, and to do it on terrain that was similar to what we would face on Everest. True to their temperaments, they picked a previously unclimbed route up the Wickersham Wall and along the heavily crevassed Peters Glacier. We urged them to be careful. Glacier travel is particularly dangerous for two people because if one falls into a crevasse, there isn't enough manpower to guarantee a rescue, and their route was so remote that only a ski plane commissioned to fly overhead would be able to spot them in case of trouble. But we knew Chris and we knew Jim. We had the utmost confidence in their abilities, and we anticipated the bonding that was sure to take place and that would strengthen our Everest team.

Two weeks after they left, I was home getting ready to have dinner with my parents when I got a phone call from Lou. Chris and Jim had fallen into a crevasse. Jim had broken his shoulder; Chris was dead.

I sat with the receiver in my hand long after Lou had hung up. *Chris was dead.* People die on mountains—I knew that. Dusan had died climbing the Fairweathers, and another climber I knew, Al Givler, had died with him. But I hadn't seen either man in years, so their deaths had been remote. They hadn't had anything to do with *me*. But Chris . . .

Jim came back from Alaska, gaunt from ten days of glacier survival, in obvious physical and emotional pain. No one talked to him about what had happened. Without learning any of the details we knew it had been an accident and that he had done everything humanly possible to rescue Chris. If at some point he wanted to tell us, we would be ready to listen. At the next team meeting we discussed whether or not to continue with the climb. Jim was reluctant. The accident had made him rethink his commitment to his family; Everest now felt like too big a risk. But the rest of us had no reservations. We knew we had to go. We had to go because it was Everest's north side, because we'd probably never get the chance again, because we needed to honor Chris's dream. And we had to go because of who Chris was, and who we felt ourselves to be. Chris was a man of amazing talents and he had used them to go out and *live.* He had believed in Everest when we all "knew" it was impossible, and out of nothing he had built this opportunity. That was the model for us to follow. The lesson from his death was not a lesson about dying; it was a lesson about living. We would be smart, we would do our homework, we wouldn't take unnecessary risks. But we would go—because for us, going was a way to *live*.

Jim and Lou had numerous discussions and in the end, Jim decided that he, too, would go. Although we didn't talk about it, I suspect his reasons were similar to the rest of ours. More than any of us, he had a bone to pick with death, and a reason to assert and celebrate life.

For me the decision had added resonance. For ten years now I'd used climbing to keep the Crohn's under control. I could think of no better way to prove myself against the disease, or to validate my life, than by climbing the world's tallest mountain.

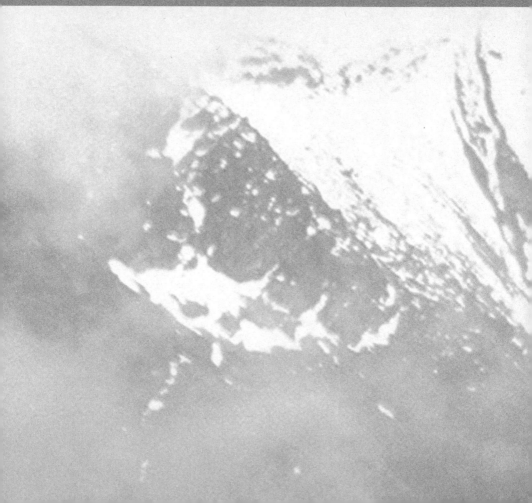

8/23/84

Dear Mom & Dad,
Base Camp at 16,800', not a cloud in the sky & the North Face of
Everest staring down on the whole scene. It's been lots of years
getting here and I want you to know that I couldn't have come close
without your love & consistent support. If I make anything of myself
the credit is yours.
   I love you both—

                                                    Phil

3

FIRST AMERICAN TO SUMMIT EVEREST'S NORTH WALL

March 10, 1982

N*ihao! Nihao!"*

The crowd swarmed around us, first cautious, then eager, calling out in Mandarin and grabbing for the Polaroid pictures that Lou was snapping and handing out. It was the same scene we'd caused earlier that day and twice the day before as our train made its way 900 miles across central China from Beijing to Chengdu. We had anticipated our own excitement at seeing China, but I don't think any of us had realized that our team of sixteen Western climbers would be equally fascinating to the Chinese. From Chengdu we flew to Lhasa where three days of sightseeing gave us our first chance to acclimatize to altitude. At 12,500 feet, Lhasa is the highest and most isolated city in the world. With its dun-colored buildings, it looked like a city carved from sand. Tall gold spires rose from a dozen temples, and saffron-robed monks paraded the streets in slow deliberate steps. Towering over the city was the Potala, the thousand-room monastery that had been home to generations of Dalai Lamas. Behind, as if we could have forgotten why we had come, the steep, rock-strewn slopes of the Himalayas disappeared into mist.

In Lhasa we boarded buses and a military transport truck and began the drive toward base camp. Outside, the ground steepened and vegetation grew more sparse; inside, we wound bandanas around our faces to protect ourselves from the rising dust. At night we lay deep in our sleeping bags in old military barracks as the temperature dropped below freezing. I was not concerned about the elevation of Everest; I had been high up before in Alaska and South America and knew that I tolerated altitude well. What I didn't know was how well I would cope living above 17,000 feet for eight to ten weeks straight. Above that altitude the body begins to deteriorate from oxygen deprivation, and even the strongest climbers have headaches, nausea, insomnia, dizziness, and loss of appetite. At the summit of Everest there is one-third as much oxygen available as at sea level; if we attempted a direct ascent we would die. Instead, we would go up and down and up again, each ascent a little higher, giving our bodies a chance to build the red blood cells necessary to carry the available oxygen throughout our bodies. We could not avoid the lower-grade maladies associated with high-altitude climbing, but we hoped to at least avoid the life-threatening hazards of cerebral and pulmonary edema, fluid buildup in the brain or lungs.

On the fifth day the truck dropped us off on a moraine of rocky scree. We were at 16,900 feet—base camp—the "storeroom" for our equipment and one of two sites to which we would retreat for recuperation after days of working the route, ferrying loads, and acclimatizing at higher elevations. From base camp forty yaks carried our gear to the foot of the Central Rongbuk Glacier, a long, narrow tongue of ice that swept down from the upper mountain. The big, squat-bodied animals followed each other like lemmings, their great horned heads low to the ground, their bells jangling. When we reached the glacier and the yaks could go no farther, we became human yaks, and for the next ten days we ferried load after load of tents, climbing gear, fuel, food, stoves, oxygen tanks, clothing, and personal effects—over a ton of gear in all—to the site that was gradually taking shape as Advanced Base Camp, or ABC. Here, for the first time, we got an unobstructed view of what we had come to climb. The entire north face of Everest rose 9,000 feet above us, a massive pyramid of snow, ice, and rock, trisected by two vertical white stripes, the Great and Super Couloirs. Our route would take us up the left-hand stripe, the Great Couloir, a broad gully filled with snow and ice that made a fairly direct route to the summit. Somewhere in that strip of white we would establish Camp 5 and if necessary Camp 6, our final jumping-off point for the summit. Looking up at the pyramid from ABC I suspect we all took an inventory of our own abilities and ambitions and, if we were really honest, even our fears. Although we didn't speak of it aloud, I'm sure that each of us thought about Chris and the fact that he had been denied his own dream.

It was the tail end of March when we finally finished setting up ABC. We sat on boxes of supplies in the dining tent and made our plans for scaling the mountain. The work would be done by rotating teams. One team would lead the way, finding a route to the next campsite, putting in bamboo "wands" or fixed rope to mark the route, and carving flat platforms into the slope for pitching tents. A second team would follow, carrying supplies, while a third rested at ABC or base camp. After a few days the jobs would rotate. We had little to go on to plan our route and campsites—only photographs taken from afar and our own observations from lower down—so each day we looked up the mountain and pinpointed the route we planned to ascend. But in the end, it would be up to each day's leaders to pick their way through the snow, ice, and rock as best they could. Once we had established our high camps, Lou, as the team leader, would designate two to four of us to make the first summit bid. If that group failed, a second and then a third would try. Although the season was short—the monsoons would start by early June—the weather looked good and we were optimistic that all of us would have a good shot at the summit.

The climb from ABC to the next camp, Camp 3, was relatively straightforward—a "walk" up broad snowfields from which we could look out to the west ridge of Everest, which forms the border between Tibet and Nepal. Just over that ridge lay the south-side base camp from which Sir Edmund Hillary and Tenzing Norgay had first summited in 1953. We were slogging up, moving steadily, roped 30 feet apart, each in our own little world, when suddenly something whistled above our heads. We knew that sound. A rock had hurled off a peak called Changtse just to our left, and our route was directly in its path. We waited a few moments for the adrenaline to subside and then began to walk again, each of us now nervously scanning the peak beside us for signs that it might happen again. Ten minutes later the whistle sounded. "Rock!" someone shouted and we hit the snow, pulling our packs over our heads. Did we need to find a different route farther from Changtse? But there was no other route; this really was the best line. So we continued upward, ears pricked for the slightest sound of rockfall, ready to drop at a moment's notice. Twice more the whistle sounded, and twice more we dropped, scanning the snow to see where the rocks had hit. When we finally saw them they were each several hundred feet from the trail. We were just far enough from Changtse that no rock would ever reach us. From then on, we took great pleasure in every whistle and yelled, "Incoming!" each time, like soldiers warning of arriving mortar fire.

Above Camp 3 the terrain became more difficult. Winter delivers little precipitation to Everest, and fierce winds scour away the snow. As a result, the upper slopes, which rise at 40 to 45 degrees, are glazed with hard ice. It was hard to dig our crampons into the surface, and climbing became a kind of dance as the crampons failed to penetrate and our feet skated along the surface. There was no way we could climb without a fixed rope to facilitate our movement up and down and to protect us in case we slipped. But our spirits and teamwork were good, and on April 9 I wrote home to my parents, "The route looks fine. Should summit about May first. I just don't see any way we won't make it."

Jim Wickwire and I had been partners for several days when we crawled into our tent at Camp 3. It was about 8:00 at night and we were lying in our sleeping bags waiting for snow to melt on the little stove, when he said, "Phil?" There was a question in his voice as if he were asking himself whether he should speak. "I've been wanting to tell you about Chris."

I felt my stomach tighten. I had been burning with questions about Chris's death—questions I would never ask of Jim and that I had made a restless peace with leaving unanswered. Now part of me was terrified to hear what he would say. Whatever images I had constructed to make Chris's death easier to live with would only be vitiated by hearing the truth.

"Go ahead," I said. My own voice sounded rusty.

So Jim began to tell me the story. They had been climbing on the Peters Glacier on their way to the Wickersham Wall. Chris had been out front carrying a heavy pack with a loaded sled behind him, and Wick had been roped behind with his own 60-pound load. And then . . . Jim's voice trailed off. "Are you sure you want to hear this?"

"I don't think that's the question, Jim. The question is, do you want to tell it?"

"I want you to know exactly what happened."

So I turned off the stove—perhaps so we wouldn't have to look into each other's eyes—and Jim told me in detail about the accident. He had been watching the sled when Chris broke through into a hidden crevasse. Only the sudden jerk of the rope had made him look up in time to see Chris disappear, and before he'd had time to react, the sled and he had both slammed into the crevasse on top of Chris, their combined weight acting like a pile driver forcing Chris down, wedging him between the 18-inch walls. Jim, his shoulder broken in the fall, managed to climb up to the surface, where he then tried everything he could think of to get Chris out. But with the ice walls hard as rock and having only inadequate tools, he was unable to free him. Finally, as darkness descended, even Chris acknowledged that there was nothing to do. He dictated messages to his family and counseled Jim to signal a bush pilot for a rescue because it would be too dangerous to walk off alone. Then he said goodbye. For the next five and a half hours, Jim lay on the surface listening as Chris sang to himself, slowly succumbing to hypothermia. By 2:00 a.m. Jim could no longer hear him.

When Jim finished we lay in silence, the darkness pressing down from above. I knew Jim was harboring guilt about the accident, but none of us thought for a minute that he had any culpability. We knew in our hearts that he had tried everything humanly possible to get Chris out.

"It wasn't your fault, Wick. There isn't one of us who thinks you could have done anything differently."

Jim turned away and his sleeping bag rustled. He was silent for a long time. A Park Service report had already exonerated him, acknowledging that he had done everything possible. But all the logic in the world wasn't going to erase the sense of responsibility he carried.

Underneath us the mountain rumbled. I thought perhaps Jim had fallen asleep, but then his voice came again. "He asked me to do him a favor . . . to take his trumpet mouthpiece up and leave it on the summit."

I smiled. An image of Chris at the Ranch in Ashford, wailing out a jazzy version of "Amazing Grace," came into my mind. "That's great," I said. "It belongs there."

"I told him I didn't know if it would be me, but I'd be sure it got there."

It pleased me to think of Chris's mouthpiece in Jim's pocket. In a small way it was like having him with us again. I was pleased for Jim that he had this way of giving back to Chris what Chris had given to us. And I had no doubt that Jim would get there to deliver it.

When we'd been on the mountain for six weeks and established the route as far as Camp 5, Lou announced the summit team. To no one's surprise it was Wickwire, Larry Nielson, Dave Mahre, and Marty. Wickwire, Nielson, and Mahre were strong climbers and a good team, and there wasn't one of us who didn't want to see Marty become the first American woman to summit Everest. Dan Boyd, a good friend and fellow Rainier guide, and I were assigned to fix the route above Camp 5. The summit team would come up behind, site Camp 6, and attempt the summit the following day.

By May 15 we had pushed the ropes partway to Camp 6, which we had hoped to site at around 26,500 feet, 2,500 feet shy of the summit. It had been slow work on hard ice, and the time we could stay up high ran out before we were through. So we started down, and the summit team headed up, planning to finish the job themselves. At about 26,000 feet I ran into Dave and Larry, and then a few minutes later Wick. We chatted for a few minutes and then continued on our separate ways. A short time later I felt the fixed rope tug below me and Marty's red bibs emerged from behind a bulge in the ice. She was breathing hard, working on that rest-step we all knew so well. When our paths crossed, we sat down on the ice to talk. It had been eleven years since we had first met at Paradise, and in those intervening years we had remained close. During the first few years we had gotten together and broken up numerous times, pulled together yet unable to commit. But over the following years our relationship had matured into a close and intimate friendship. We were among each other's biggest and most trusted supporters. Earlier on the trip we had teamed and tented together a bit, but it had been over a week since we'd spent any time together. Now we sat and looked out at the vast flank of ice and rock, which, except for an abrupt ice cliff a few hundred feet below, extended as far as we could see. Overhead the sky was so starkly blue it was almost black. We talked about the expedition, about how we each were doing, and I teased her about all the publicity she would get when she got back home.

"You know, you should be going up, not me," she said. "You've done so much work for this trip."

"Bull crap."

She looked at me closely for a minute. With her dark sunglasses I couldn't see her eyes, but I recognized the intensity of her gaze. Finally she said, "You and I still have a lot of things we need to talk about."

"Yeah," I said. It was the familiar theme, that lingering sense of *what if?* Unfinished business, opportunities not yet extinguished.

We stood up and gave each other a hug. The little blue earrings she always wore felt cold against my cheek. Then she moved up toward the summit and I moved down to rest at Advanced Base Camp.

At ABC I slept the sleep of the dead. It was pure luxury to sleep in a flat camp where the tent wasn't pitched at an angle and I didn't slide into my tent mate or the wall several times a night. There were seven or eight of us at ABC, and the next day we were sitting around reading or repairing equipment when the radio in Lou's tent squawked. I couldn't make out Lou's words but a few seconds later he came out of his tent and in a voice that filled me with dread called us together. We gathered around in a loose circle, already running scenarios in our minds.

"That was Wick," he said. "Marty came out of her harness. She's gone."

For a moment we all stood there, stunned. Then wordlessly we roped up and went to look for her. The route she had fallen would have taken her in a straight line down the north face into a bergschrund at the bottom of the slope, a gap where a glacier had begun pulling away from the side of the mountain. It was an enormous area; there was little chance we would find her and no chance we'd find her alive, but we went. I walked mechanically. With one part of my mind I contemplated the task of searching: where she might have landed given the contours of the face above, how we should array ourselves in order to have the best chance of spotting her. I was thankful that her red bibs would make her easy to see. With another part I repeated the words, "Marty's dead, Marty's dead," as if saying them over and over would eventually imbue them with meaning. The feeling that welled up was not grief, but anger. *Darn it, Marty, for doing whatever you did up there that made this happen!*

At the edge of the bergschrund we unroped and fanned out. I walked across the pitched ice toward the rocky flank of the mountain where a yawning gap marked the spot where the glacier had split away. From there I could look up and see the entire north face rising 9,000 feet above me, its sharp edges carving like glass into the dark sky. Just yesterday I'd sat up there with Marty; tomorrow she was supposed to be on top. Suddenly the enormity of what had happened hit me. Marty was *gone.* We would be here tonight and tomorrow and the next day; we would go home to our families and friends; we would gather together and tell stories about this climb—and she would not. She would not be at Rainier next summer. She would never tease or hint again at what might have been between us. She was gone. And despite all of our searching and talking and hoping and wishing, there was nothing I or anyone else could do to change that.

Alone, in the shadow of the mountain, I dropped down on my knees and wept.

Larry, Jim, and Dave came down from the mountain the next day. By that time we'd each called off and restarted the expedition ten times in our minds. But all together we decided that we had to continue; Marty would have been mad at us if we didn't. So Lou designated George Dunn, Eric Simonson, and Larry Nielson to go back up. I chose to stay at ABC. I had lost my desire to climb. Two days later, the three of them attempted the summit. Eric got hit by a rock that injured his knee and was forced to turn back. George accompanied him down. Larry pushed on, only to turn around, frostbitten, at 27,500 feet. A few days later, George, Wickwire, and Dave Mahre made a second attempt, but bad weather at 24,000 feet forced them to turn around. The first American Everest north face expedition was over.

Before we left we had a ceremony for Marty at base camp. Lou carved a memorial and we set it up under the lofty pyramid of the north face. I took a small degree of pleasure in the fact that Marty now had the biggest tombstone in the world.

We all dreaded going home. We dreaded dealing with the media, which had been primed to celebrate Marty's climb. We dreaded seeing Marty's mother, who had lost her only remaining child. And most of all, I think, we dreaded our own feelings. It was one thing to deal with Marty's loss on the mountain where there were a million things that needed doing or deciding, moving or packing, in preparation for our departure. It was another to walk back into our normal lives where she had been a radiant, vibrant presence. Already several of us had begun to dream about Marty, to see her coming in the door, only to wake up and find her gone.

I'd thought that Chris's death had taught me about loss, but Marty's death was completely different. For all the devastation I'd felt when Chris had died, there had been a detachment to it. It had happened far away, and he hadn't been the long-term fixture in my life that Marty was. With Marty, it was hard not to feel that a part of me had vanished too. Where did it go? Where did *she* go? Where were her half of all the memories and feelings and conversations we had shared? Could my half even exist without her energy to keep them alive? Physicists tell us that energy can neither be created nor destroyed. I had to believe that a little bit of Marty's energy had come to settle in each of us who had loved her.

Marty died in May; ten months later I was back on Everest. We had been back in the States for less than a month when Frank Wells and Dick Bass asked me to join their expedition to the south side of Everest in the spring of 1983. Frank and Dick were successful businessmen who were hoping to be the first people to climb the Seven Summits. Wells was president of Warner Bros., and Bass was a Texas oilman who also owned the Snowbird Ski Resort in Utah, and they had provided the pivotal final funding for our Everest expedition in exchange for being able to use our trip as a trial run for their own. Now they had a permit to climb the south side in spring 1983. I said yes in an instant. Despite my deflation at the end of the '82 trip, I knew even then that I would be back. Chris's and Marty's deaths had saddened me but they did not frighten me. I did not expect to die in the mountains. On the contrary, I expected to *live*: to use my body and mind to the fullest, to wake up and go to sleep amid unfathomable beauty, to live intimately and intensely with other people—in short, to be fully *human.* An expedition, I had discovered, was an opportunity to live life to its fullest. And that, every bit as much as the lure of the summit, was what drew me back. It would keep drawing me back, I knew, for a long time.

The Wells/Bass trip was very successful. No one got hurt, the teamwork was strong, and ten guys made it to the top, including Larry Nielson, who became the first American to summit without oxygen. I, too, tried to summit without gas but had to turn back 2,500 feet from the top. I was pretty certain that had I used oxygen I would have made it, but I had made my choice and was pleased with my ability to stick with it. However, I left Everest more determined than ever to stand on top, so when Lou told me he had a permit to do the north side again the following August, it took me half a second to say yes.

George Dunn, who had been on the '82 climb, was also on the team. He and Eric Simonson and I had guided together for years on Rainier, and after returning from Asia in '82 we had decided that the time was right to pool our resources and create a business, which we called International Mountain Guides. Now George and I split our attention between getting IMG off the ground and preparing for Everest. We worked with Lou to raise the money, fill out the team, plan the menus, order the food, gather the equipment, and make the hundreds of logistical arrangements required to get nine American climbers and three support staff across China and Tibet and onto the mountain. When I wasn't planning or guiding, I was in the gym training, or going on conditioning hikes in the Cascades, or climbing up to Camp Muir in the winter and skiing down. I wanted that summit, bad.

In the Himalayas you pick your dangers. Climbing pre-monsoon in the spring as we had on our first trip, the mountain is glazed with hard ice. By fall, the monsoon has blanketed the ice with several feet of snow—easier for climbing, but prone to avalanches. This time we went back in the fall, and from the start we were behind schedule. A fierce storm battered the mountain, immobilizing us at ABC. It wasn't until ten days later that we were finally able to site our next camp, at 23,000 feet, where the weather was little better. High winds slammed against the tents, and swift dark clouds obscured the top of the mountain. Each day our sense of urgency grew. The bad weather was a reminder that winter was approaching and if we didn't get the summit by early October we would go home empty-handed.

Finally, on September 18 we were able to dig out a site for Camp 5, and six days later we had a meeting in Lou's tent to plan our summit attempt. I felt little suspense about who would be on the team. From our earliest meetings in Seattle I'd understood that Wickwire, a super strong climber named John Roskelley, George, and I would make up the first team. Wickwire and Roskelley were naturals since they both had significant Himalayan experience, and Lou had practically promised the slots to George and me after our '82 expedition. Now we sat in a tight circle as Lou made his announcement. The first team would be made up of Wickwire, Roskelley, and Lou's son, Peter. The second would be George, a Rainier guide named John Smolich, and me. I looked over at George, who looked as surprised as I was. Had we misunderstood?

"Lou," I said, "I thought George and I were supposed to be on the team."

"I'm sorry, Phil," Lou replied. "You've both been performing well. You've worked hard. I want you on the second team."

Frustrated, I turned to Wickwire. "Wick, you were in those planning meetings. You remember when you and Lou and George and I talked about the team."

Wickwire looked at me, then looked away. "Not to the best of my recollection."

George and I stared at each other in disbelief. Wick was a good friend, but somehow his recollections and ours were miles apart. I knew if I opened my mouth again I would say something I regretted. Instead, I stood up and walked out of the tent.

For the next three days we hung around base camp, resting for the final push. George and I tented together. We were both furious at Lou, but at the same time we desperately wanted the expedition to succeed. The part of me inclined to sulk and mentally resign fought against the desire to put at least some of our members on top. I had to acknowledge that Lou had a point: We had four strong, experienced high-altitude climbers and it made sense to split us into two teams rather than put all our eggs in one basket. I could even see that, while being first had a certain aura, there was an advantage to going second and having another team put in the route. What I couldn't get past, though, was that George and I had not been consulted. That the decision had been handed to us as a fait accompli pissed me off more than being denied the first shot.

George and I talked about it during the day, and at night the issue permeated my sleep. I couldn't let go of my anger. We worked for Lou on Rainier, but he didn't own the Everest expedition! But the more that George and I talked, the more I began to focus on what really counted. Going first wasn't what mattered; being consulted wasn't what mattered. What mattered was that somebody get to stand on top. And given weather, illness, and the other uncertainties of climbing, regardless of who went first, George and I had as good a chance of doing that as anybody. One night I was propped up on one elbow in my bag, munching M&M's to compensate for the small meals I ate during the day, when George rolled over and looked at me.

"You eating again?"

"George, you know I eat all the time."

He lay there for a few moments watching me. "Think we're going to get a shot?"

"You know what I think? I think Smolich, you, and I are a really strong team, and I think we're going to go regardless. If Wick, Roskelley, and Peter *don't* summit, we're going, and if they *do* summit we're going. Somebody's going to get to the top of this thing, and there's nothing to say it's not going to be us."

George slid a hand out of his bag and I filled it with M&M's.

"I think this expedition's a long way from over, George. We just need to take care of ourselves and be a little patient."

On September 28 Wick, Roskelley, and Peter began their bid. From Camp 5 at 25,000 feet they climbed up and across the north face, hoping to site Camp 6 in the Great Couloir. In two days of trying they never got more than 100 yards from their tents. The wind was too fierce, and on October 5 they were forced to come down. Now it was our turn. The next day, George, John, and I left ABC. The weather was good, we were feeling strong, the climb to Camp 4 went smoothly. Overnight, however, the wind picked up. Stepping out of the tents in the morning we had to be careful not to get blown off balance. We made it to Camp 5 by listening for gusts, getting down on our hands and knees and digging our ice axes into the snow, and then starting up again when the gust passed. If the angle had been steeper, or the slope icier, it would have been harrowing, but as it was, there was something almost comic in the image of us dropping repeatedly to all fours. It reminded me of the climb in front of Changtse, where we dropped to our knees to avoid the rocks that never came. That night Lou called on the radio to say that an Australian team that had just returned from the summit had left a tent in the Great Couloir just above 26,500 feet. Since that was where we were hoping to site Camp 6, it made sense to use it. That would be one less thing we would have to carry across the north face.

The following morning we loaded up stoves, fuel, food, oxygen bottles, regulators, a shovel, pickets, rope, ice screws, and personal gear and began climbing into the wind toward the Couloir. It was a long day with lots of breaking trail. George, who was a powerhouse of a climber, did most of the work himself. I followed, and John, who seemed to be having more difficulty than usual, brought up the rear. Late in the afternoon we reached the Couloir just below 26,000 feet and began looking upward for the tent. At 26,000 we still had not seen it. At 26,500 we stopped. It was 7:00, the daylight was gone, and after ten hours carrying 40- to 50-pound packs, we were exhausted. There was no way we could go on.

"Bivouac?" said George.

I looked at him as if to say, "Are you out of your mind?" He knew the dangers of spending the night outside, unprotected, at 26,500 feet. He knew that Wickwire's bivouac had practically cost him his life, and that most people who bivouacked above 8,000 meters came back seriously messed up. We'd always joked that bivouac was a French word for "mistake." "George," I said, "here's another idea. Let's put on our headlamps and get the heck out of here. We can make it back to the Col." It would be a difficult descent; there were no wands or fixed rope in place; we'd have to retrace our steps in the dark, but with headlamps I thought we could manage.

But George shook his head.

Man, I thought, *George is tough, but if he wants to bivouac here he's either a lot tougher—or a lot crazier—than I thought.* With no tent the chance of getting through the night without serious frostbite or hypothermia was slim; by morning we might be too compromised to get back down. And even if we did get down, that would be the end of the climb. We'd probably be so debilitated from the exposure and dehydration that we'd have blown our chance to summit. And what if one of us had a really serious problem during the night—say, pulmonary or cerebral edema, life-threatening conditions in which blood flows into the lungs or brain and immediate evacuation is critical. If that happened, the other two would be powerless to get him down. George might want to bivouac, but I had no interest in sitting like a duck on the side of a hill waiting for the elements to pluck us off.

I looked over at John, but he just coughed strenuously and spat in the snow. I pulled out the radio and called down to base camp. "Hey, Lou, there couldn't be any mistake about that tent, could there?"

"You haven't found it yet?"

"No! And if it's another four or five hundred feet farther up, we're going to have to come down. We just don't have the strength to go up there."

There was static on the radio, then John Roskelley's voice came on. "Ershler, you're a good enough mountaineer to know you can't come down in the dark. You've got bivouac gear. Dig out a platform, huddle together, and bivouac."

George answered before I could. "All right," he said, "I think we better start digging in."

I clicked off the radio. I couldn't argue with both of them.

And the fact that Smolich hadn't even weighed in wasn't a good sign.

A few yards farther on there were two slight depressions in the slope, one about a foot higher than the other. They offered a bit of a head start at knocking out ledges to lie down on. We grabbed our ice axes and the one shovel, secured the packs, and began hacking away at the snow and ice. I silently gave thanks that at least we weren't here in the spring when we would have been chipping away at pure ice. Each time I straightened up to rest, I found myself looking straight up the Couloir to the base of the Yellow Band, a section of ocher-colored rock that was the toughest technical piece before the summit. The summit was tantalizingly close—and a million miles away.

We had been digging for perhaps ten minutes when John had another fit of coughing. Afterward, I saw red drops in the snow at his feet. I looked over at George and from the expression on his face I could see that he had noticed them too. Suddenly John's uncharacteristic fatigue and violent coughing looked like more than just exhaustion and a raw throat. Along with the pink phlegm they were warning signs of pulmonary edema. If that were the case he would need to get down fast. George and I looked at each other. John had not complained about tightness in his chest or shortness of breath, two other signs of edema. Which was it: edema or a bad altitude-induced cough? We went back to digging but both of us kept our eye on John, watching for the sign at which we would decide that, regardless of the danger, we would have to get him down.

After thirty minutes of chopping we'd managed to widen the two depressions into little flat ledges. George and John pulled their sleeping bags up around their hips and sat down on the upper one; I did the same on the lower. When I looked down past my feet, the mountain fell away in a broad, steep plane for several hundred feet and then dropped off precipitously. I could just about see where we'd sited ABC in 1982, 6,000 feet below. A bit farther I could make out the silver end of the Rongbuk Glacier, where we'd made base camp that year. This was the same spot from which Marty had fallen.

For the next hour we talked quietly, wiggling our fingers and toes to prevent frostbite, nibbling at whatever snack food we had in our pockets, taking stock of each other's condition. John coughed some more but seemed to have no other signs of edema. It was too windy and we were too tired to light the stove, which meant we had only the little bit of water left in our individual bottles—way less than the several liters we would normally drink to stave off dehydration. We knew we would doze fitfully at best, and agreed that each time we woke up we would check on the others, occasionally waking each other so we could assess each other's condition. Then we each retreated into our own world.

For the next eight hours we slept and woke, slept and woke. Between the bouts of sleep I'd look up and see the stars through the blowing spindrift and think, *man, Ershler, it's October 8th. What in the world are you doing spending a night outside at 26,500 feet on the north face of Mt. Everest?* When morning finally came, we pulled our legs out of our sleeping bags and with frozen fingers began to lace our boots and put on our crampons. Half my brain screamed, *Hurry!* while the other half warned, *Take it slow. You can't afford to let your sleeping bag slide away, can't afford to drop your ice axe . . .* When I watched myself, I thought I was doing okay. At the same time, I knew that my oxygen-depleted brain was impaired, and that even thinking I was okay was an illusion.

"Either of you have any water?"

I looked over at George, who was crouched over his pack, one arm pressed against his stomach, his face tight. I wondered if he was having stomach pain from dehydration. John and I both shook our heads.

"I'm having trouble keeping anything down. I need to get some water."

George never complained. The urgency in his voice kicked

us into higher gear. We cached two oxygen bottles, some fuel, and the shovel for the other team when they came up to make high camp later and then started down. It was far less treacherous in daylight, just a matter of being careful, of not letting our exhaustion make us screw up. After four and a half hours we reached the spot where the north ridge turns up in a short rise to the North Col. At the top of the rise stood Steve Marts, the cinematographer who was filming our expedition for a documentary, his camera on his shoulder. Throughout the trip I'd given Steve a hard time for constantly sticking the camera in our faces at inopportune moments, and now I thought, *man, Steve, I can barely walk; don't ask me a question and expect me to link two sentences together.* But I managed to mumble something about how George and John are the guys you want with you in that kind of situation. About ten minutes later the two of them arrived. George gave a similar response, but when Steve asked Smolich how it had been, John only stuttered, "T-terrible." That stutter, coming from such a powerful climber, chilled me. For him the expedition was over.

After some food and water at the Col, we continued down to ABC. For real recovery, we needed to go to base camp, but we didn't have time. So instead George and I tented together at ABC, sleeping, eating, and drinking as much as we could. Lou had ordered the yaks in to base camp on October 22 to load us up for the walk out, which meant we had thirteen days left. Now, as if we were chessmen on a board, I moved us up and down the mountain in my mind, seeking all the ways that George and I might get a shot at the summit.

The following night I was awakened by the sound of moaning. When I looked over, George was clutching his stomach, obviously in terrible pain. He said he'd been vomiting. Cramps and vomiting were symptoms I knew something about so I gave him codeine, which often worked for me, but he couldn't keep it down. So I did what I do for myself: I went to the mess tent and started a couple of stoves to make him hot water bottles. For the next hour he lay with the bottles against his stomach, but the pain grew worse and he continued to vomit. Finally I realized we needed help. I woke up Carolyn Gunn, our camp manager, who was actually a vet. Jokingly, she growled, "You guys are just like the dogs I treat," but she came with me to our tent, diagnosed George as seriously dehydrated, and started him on an IV and oxygen. The next morning two team members helped him down to base camp where he could be treated by Ed Hixson, our team doctor. John, who was feeling better but still coughing, also headed down. Regardless of what happened above, we would not be going to the summit as a team.

The next day Roskelley, Wick, and Peter came down. They had gone up as we were coming down, but they had been turned back just beyond Camp 5 by the weather. The mood at ABC was somber. Up above, the climb had been stymied; below, we waited for news of George's and John's conditions. Three attempts at establishing high camp had been unsuccessful, the weather was worsening, our window of opportunity was closing, and one by one, we were losing climbers who could support a summit team. Assuming the Team 1 climbers were still healthy after so many days up high, there were really only four of us—Wickwire, Roskelley, Peter, and I—who still had the strength and ambition to give it another try.

Wickwire approached me and told me that he and Roskelley wanted to go again and that this time they wanted me to be the third member of the team. They were planning to say as much to Lou.

"Don't," I said. "If I'm going to be able to work with Lou going forward, this is a decision he has to make and I don't want you influencing it."

That night we gathered again in Lou's tent, the tension so thick you could taste it.

Lou looked at his hands as he spoke. "Wickwire's still strong.

Roskelley's strong. That leaves the third slot for either Peter or Phil."

Even in my powerful desire to go back up I didn't envy him his position.

"Phil really paid his dues up there. I think I need to give the slot to him."

Yes!

Now it was up to me.

On October 16 we began our final summit push. To avoid the wind at Camp 5, we set in a new route, crossing the north face lower down and climbing in the shelter of the Great Couloir to 25,000 feet. Peter, showing tremendous teamwork and grit despite his disappointment, worked hard at putting in the route and digging the platform for our tent. On the 18th, Wickwire, Roskelley, and I climbed to the site of our earlier bivouac and established Camp 6, carving a tiny platform and pitching our tent in the lee of a rock. To our dismay, one of the two oxygen bottles we had left there was gone. In my depleted post-bivouac state, I must have been careless and not anchored it securely. As a result we now had only one bottle of oxygen between us. Roskelley had always said he didn't want oxygen, Wickwire had always said he did; I had said I would do whatever was necessary for us to succeed. So, effectively, that left the oxygen to Wick. I was okay with that. The year before, going without oxygen had kept me from the summit and there was a chance that would happen again, but I was feeling good—stronger than I'd felt in '83—and there was an equal chance that it wouldn't. I was also pleased with my work on this trip. No matter how it turned out, nobody could discount my performance. Even without a summit, I felt that I'd had a good expedition.

On the morning of the 19th we got an early start. This was the latest Everest had ever been climbed and it was as dark and cold as it had been the night of our bivouac. I led, with Wickwire roped 50 feet behind and Roskelley another 50 behind him. As the sun rose, the sky and mountain brightened to a milky white. We moved slowly, two pressure breaths to every step. The snow was crusty and uneven from the unrelenting wind, and the route sloped upward at a steady 45 degrees between dark outcrops of rock. But I felt as good as I'd ever felt high up, and remarkably well rested given that I'd just spent the night at 26,600 feet without oxygen. A few hundred feet above I could see the Yellow Band and felt a surge of excitement. Once we were past the Band, the climbing would get easier. If the weather held—if my lungs held—this would be my time.

Just below the Yellow Band I stopped to rest. Behind me Wickwire was moving slowly, looking fatigued. Behind him, Roskelley was standing still, slumped over his ice axe. I waited as Wick made his way painstakingly up to me, then together we watched Roskelley struggle upward. I had noticed earlier that John seemed weak, had even thought with some alarm that his steps seemed unsteady. Now as he labored to close the hundred or so feet between us, he seemed so uncoordinated that I wondered if he would be able to make it. A few years earlier on Everest he had suffered from high-altitude cerebral edema, and he seemed to be displaying the symptoms again. If that were the case, we would have to turn around and get him down.

John staggered up to us, icicles hanging off his beard. His breath came in short gasps. "I'm having trouble. I can't stay awake."

Wick got out the radio and called down to Lou. "I think we better get John down."

"What's going on?"

John took the radio. "I'm just kind of passing out up here."

"Okay, that's the end of the climb. We did our best."

We turned around and started retracing our steps, and with every step I felt the juice seep out of me. To have gotten so close . . .

Back at the tent we crawled into our sleeping bags and lay

in silence with our thoughts. I was drifting off to sleep when John announced he was feeling better. Wick and I looked at him without moving.

"I took some codeine this morning because my feet hurt from an old frostbite injury. But it's worn off. I'm okay. Let's give it another try."

"You're crazy," I said. "There's no way we can spend another night at 26,600 feet and then climb to the summit without oxygen. It didn't work last year and it ain't gonna work now. We just need to get off this darn mountain and get home." I felt so strongly about it, and so ornery in my disappointment, that I almost left and started down alone.

"Look," John said, "you're doing fine. It's not going to be a problem for you to stay one more night. Then we'll just get up and climb this thing in the morning." He made it sound as if he were talking about a walk to the store.

I'd always said how important it is to choose your partners wisely, to surround yourself with people who won't let you quit. Now this was the second time that Roskelley had had a better sense of my best interest.

"All right, Roskelley," I said. "We'll give it a go."

That evening we had a long discussion about the oxygen. Roskelley, in spite of the day's events, was still determined to go without it, but Wickwire was now convinced that having two climbers without oxygen was unsafe. We would lack the brainpower to handle an emergency, and the team as a whole would stand a better chance if only one oxygen-less climber ascended. Therefore, the only solution was for the stronger climber to take the oxygen while the weaker one remained at camp. He knew I was stronger at that point and volunteered to be the one to stay. It was hard to accept his offer; he wanted that summit as much as I did. But he was adamant, essentially decreeing that the only way we would get the summit at all would be to follow his plan. So I agreed.

The next morning John and I set out, leaving Wick deep in

his bag with his journal. I led out with about 50 feet of rope between us. As we walked, I worried about how we would do above. Would John be okay without gas? I'd never been above 27,000 feet; would I be okay with it? At the Yellow Band the terrain became more difficult than we had expected. We switched leads and John did a herculean job leading up the steep rock and ice. Halfway up we reached a fixed rope the Australian team had left behind and were able to use that as a hand line. Above the Band we rested, and then switched leads again.

This was my first time using oxygen and all through the Yellow Band I had been fighting the gear. The mask was uncomfortable and had been causing my goggles to fog. But now, on the snowfield above the band, I managed to get the mask into a better position and the effects of the oxygen kicked in. My whole body began to warm and my lungs and muscles suddenly felt switched on. I climbed steadily, kicking steps through new snow in a good rhythm now, until I reached a rocky area just below the Gray Band. There I stopped and waited for John. As I coiled him in I could see that he was really cold. His beard was frozen, his teeth were almost chattering, and he was starting to shiver. "My hands and feet are gone," he said. "The heat's draining out of me."

I knew what he was talking about. The year before when I'd attempted Everest without oxygen I'd had to turn around at 27,000 feet because I could literally feel the inside of my body getting cold. Now he and I were effectively in different worlds. John Roskelley was an infinitely stronger climber than I was, but without oxygen his body was unable to generate heat or fight its fatigue. I looked up. Beyond the Gray Band the terrain might get easier. "Can you go a little farther?"

He shook his head, barely. "I think I should turn around."

The night before John had stopped me from going down; now, if at all possible, I wanted to do the same for him. Less altruistically, I wanted him to stay because we were a team. Wherever we went, we went together.

As if he could read my thoughts he said, "You should keep going, Phil. You can make it."

"Let's go a little farther and then see."

He nodded, so I led up another couple of rope lengths, 75 or 100 vertical feet, and found a spot where we could sit. We nibbled on mints and Fig Newtons. His body convulsed in its effort to stay warm.

"I can't go for another three hours and still make it back down."

I looked at him sitting in the snow a little more than a thousand feet from the top of the world. Despite my disappointment, I felt enormous respect for him. He was one of the best climbers in the world, daring, principled, independent sometimes to the point of obstinacy, but he knew when to risk and when not to. "Okay," I said, "we're going down."

"What's this 'we' crap? I don't need you to get down." I started to argue but he interrupted me. "Neither one of us is going to be able to live with himself or each other if you go down now and we both know you could have made it."

I looked away. I knew he was right, and that he was protecting himself as much as me. He didn't want to feel responsible for denying the summit to me and the team. So we unroped and shook hands. Then he went one way and I went the other.

After that I never thought about turning around. I simply continued methodically picking my way upward. To get around the Gray Band I had to work my way left, back into the Great Couloir. Near the top, the Couloir steepened considerably. A small cornice had formed at its edge and I had to pull myself up and over. Now I was on the summit pyramid. A good wind was blowing up from Nepal, and I was torn. Should I continue straight up toward the summit in the full force of the wind, or should I veer to the right and take a longer route along the west ridge where the wind might blow me into the mountain instead of off? I turned toward the ridge and continued working my way between alternating bands of rock and ice.

In all my thinking about Everest I had never imagined a scenario in which I would be heading for the summit alone. Suddenly the immensity of it struck me. I was at 28,000 feet on the north face of Everest, alone, and I didn't even know where in the world I was going! We had studied photos as far as 27,000 feet, but had never talked about the last 2,000. We'd assumed we'd figure it out when we got there. And now here I was with only the slimmest clue about how to get to the summit. To steady myself I ran a continuous checklist in my mind: Memorize the route, look at the landmarks, don't drop a glove, don't trip over your crampons. Drop a glove and you lose your fingers, trip on your crampons and you lose your life . . . *You can do this,* I told myself. *This is what you've spent the last fifteen years of your life preparing for. You just need to put one foot in front of the other for a couple more hours.* And suddenly, with a rush of certainty, I knew I was going to make it.

For the next two hours I walked slowly and mechanically, obsessively scanning the route for landmarks so that I would know how to get down. At one point when I lifted my gaze, instead of seeing the mountain rise in front of me, I found myself looking down into Nepal. Lhotse, the fourth highest mountain in the world, was sitting just over the ridge, a plume of snow blowing off its summit. Two minutes—or twenty minutes?— later I looked up again. This time I was no longer looking into Nepal, but down at the North Col of Everest and the Tibetan plateau. In effect, I was standing with one foot in China and the other in Nepal.

I was at the top of the world.

Back at the North Col I knew Steve Marts was watching me with his camera. I didn't know if he could even see me, but to improve the chances I climbed up on three big snow mounds and waved my ice axe. "Here's your darn movie, Marts!" I yelled, and then I got down to business. First, I took out of my pack a burgundy felt pouch that Wickwire had given me that morning. I took Chris's mouthpiece out and laid it on the pouch and took a picture, then I dug a hole and buried it on the top of the mountain. As I did a pang of anger and regret washed through me. I thought, *What a waste of a good man.* After the mouthpiece I took out a neatly folded red scarf. Marty's mother had sent it to me with instructions to fling it off the summit. I held it in my hands for a few moments and thought about Marty, then I sent it flying down the north face, the side of the mountain that belonged to her, and as I did so I said good-bye.

Then I ate a bit of candy, snapped a couple of panorama shots, and held the camera out at arms' length to get my own summit picture. I was sorry not to have someone else with me to share in the success, but I couldn't dwell on that. It was already 4:00, the hour I had sworn to myself I would go down, regardless of what I had or hadn't done. Wickwire had bivouacked because he had stayed too long on the summit; I was determined not to make the same mistake. So with only three hours of daylight left and a growing sense of urgency, I put on my pack and started to retrace my steps. I had gone only a few feet when it occurred to me that it was silly to carry the heavy oxygen bottle; I didn't need what little gas was left, and I would be able to move faster and more securely without the weight. So I took the bottle out of my pack and was about to pitch it when I realized I should first detach the regulator, the expensive and reusable part of the contraption. For the next few precious minutes I fumbled with the regulator, then hurled the bottle down the Kangchung face. Now I just had to follow my own tracks exactly to get down. With no route markers, they were all I had to get myself back to camp.

Remarkably quickly I reached the Yellow Band. I saw that John had tied our short length of rope to the Australians' rope so that he could rappel down the 200-foot drop. But I had no harness, no carabiners, no belay or rappel device with which to do that. I stood considering the situation, trying to figure out how to get myself down, when I remembered an early climb with Greg and Mike fifteen years before. We were at the top of the Haystack, a 200-foot pinnacle, getting ready to rappel down, and Greg and I were fumbling with a friction device called a brake bar. Mike watched for several minutes as we tried to make the thing work, then finally said, "Look, you guys, you don't need any of that crap," and in a flash he grabbed the rope; wrapped it through his legs, around his hip, and over the other shoulder; and lowered himself smoothly over the edge. That was one of the greatest mountaineering lessons I'd ever had— learn to do things with the least amount of gear—and remembering it now was like meeting myself back in time: Phil the sixteen-year-old kid too fresh even to dream of climbing Everest, meeting Phil the thirty-three-year-old guide who was so cold and tired and oxygen-deprived that his achievement of that dream had not yet fully sunk in. Smiling, I wrapped the rope between my legs, brought it up over my shoulder, and stepped backward over the edge of the Yellow Band.

Now I was home free. From here to camp was little more than a steep downhill walk. I could already see the tent crouched in the shadow of the boulder. I walked toward it, steadily downhill, and to my amazement I saw Roskelley and Wickwire packing up camp.

What are they doing? I thought. *They can't pack up! I'm still up here!*

But sure enough, there they were, getting ready to leave.

Wait a minute, calm down. There's no way they would leave you.

Right, but look! There they go!

Stop it, you dummy. You're hallucinating!

Well, I may be hallucinating, but they're leaving! You're going to have to walk all the way across the north face tonight because there's no more camp!

I began to plan what I would do to get myself across the north face in the dark. I had a headlamp, and the sky was relatively clear; as long as I could read my altimeter and compass I could steer myself in the right direction. I tried to keep myself from considering how beat I was and how more than anything I wanted to walk into that tent, climb into my sleeping bag, and have John and Wick hand me a cup of hot water.

And while I was thinking that, the real Wickwire came walking out of the tent, super 8 camera in hand, filming my return.

When Wick put the camera aside and clasped me in a congratulatory hug I realized that I had actually done it. In his warm embrace I felt myself choke up, but beyond that I was too exhausted to feel much of anything. I just wanted to crawl into bed. I know we radioed down to base camp and ABC, and I know I heard the cheers of the rest of the team, but all of that is lost to me now. I remember simply the hot drink, the enfolding bliss of my sleeping bag, and the reassuring knowledge that I had two good, solid guys who were there to assist me and with whom I could share my thoughts. I drifted off to sleep with the thought that, more than anything, it had been a day of closing circles.

Our friend and PR agent Dan McConnell had lined up a press conference to celebrate the first American ascent of Everest's north side, and as a result we came through customs in Seattle to the flashing of cameras and the battering of reporters' questions. The reporters seemed determined to call my success a "solo" despite my frequent repetition that there was nothing solo about it. It had taken the effort of every member of the team for me to stand on top. Finally one reporter said, "So, Phil, now that you've climbed Everest, what's left?"

What a silly question, I thought. *This isn't the end of anything; it's the beginning.* In my journal on the mountain I had written that Everest was the validation of the way I'd chosen to live my life for the previous fifteen years. "If I summit," I'd written, "it would validate my physical victory over the Crohn's. Maybe then I could put that behind me somewhat." But if I'd seen an Everest summit as the culmination of some essential self-proving effort, that feeling was now gone. Standing in the airport, the skin still peeling off my sun- and windburned nose, I had no interest in putting the Himalayas behind me. If that was because I still had something to prove, so be it. All I knew was that the mountains were there, I was strong, and expeditions were where I felt most alive. This summit would make new opportunities available and I intended to take advantage of them. Nobody knows how long anything will last. I didn't want to look back and regret the chances I didn't grab.

The best part of coming home was seeing my family. They were waiting in the throng of friends and families just outside customs—Dad, in his tan sweater-vest and golf cap, grinning from ear to ear and waving; Mom, looking like she owned the world; my sister beaming. My parents and I had exchanged letters throughout the trip—I always wrote to them when I was away—and all along I had felt them behind me. They were the base from which I operated, the support that made everything possible. But nothing could have prepared me for the overpowering emotion of that homecoming. I hugged Mom and shook Dad's hand, and then he gave me a tight hug. When he let me go he clenched his fist and pumped it in the air. "That's my boy!" he said. And in that moment all the emotion that I hadn't felt before suddenly came flooding out.

What haunted me, though, was something I had noticed about Dad: Something about the way he looked or the way he held himself was wrong.

My parents had invited a few friends to their house and opened a bottle of champagne, and with the steady stream of questions and attention I wasn't able to ask about Dad. But an hour or so into the party Mom took me aside. In the matter-of-fact Ershler way she said, "I just wanted to tell you that while you were gone, Dad had a little stroke. But it was minor and he's going to fully recover."

"Come on, Mom! Why didn't you tell me? Why didn't you send word?" There are ways to get emergency information to climbers. I would have been off the mountain in a minute.

"Your sisters and I decided that there was nothing you could do. He wasn't in immediate danger and you needed to concentrate on what you were doing. Dad wouldn't have wanted you bothered either."

Everything inside me wanted to scream, *What do you mean you didn't want me "bothered"? What do you mean he had a stroke?* I had a million questions, but this was not the time to ask them.

I went back to the party and conversed politely, but the whole time I kept sneaking looks at Dad. Now that I knew what had happened, I could see the stroke's effects. His gait was a little less certain, he seemed tired, and he spent most of the afternoon sitting in a chair instead of tending to each of his guests. Dad never deliberately attracted attention but there had always been something commanding about him, as if the light burned a little brighter over his part of the room. Now that light seemed a little dimmer. How could they not have told me? But as I thought about what my mother had said, I realized she was right. Dad's condition was not life-threatening and there was nothing I could have done. My knowing or coming home would not have improved his situation, but it would have ended the expedition for me, and when I thought about the way he had lit up at the airport, I wondered if maybe my climbing had been the best medicine I could have provided. If the stroke had been worse or Dad had died while I was gone, I would have been devastated. He had always been my hero: naval aviator, recipient of the Navy Cross, boxer and star football player at Duke University. I had always looked up to him, always weighed his opinion heavily, even when I disagreed. Dad had always shown me that he loved me, but his pride in me was something I never took for granted and was continually determined to earn. When he had said, "That's my boy!" at the airport, I had felt as if I could fly. Now my earlier alarm and anger melted into relief. Dad was going to be okay. The world was not rocked; the Ershlers were already on the mend.

During the rest of the 1980s I spent three months of almost every year in the Himalayas. During the summers I guided on Rainier. I was in my thirties, my peers were getting married and settling down, but more than anything I wanted to be able to turn off the lights, lock the door, and walk away. My health was good, there were mountains to climb, and I wanted to be out in them.

I frequently thought about my first relationship with Marty Hoey. I appreciated now that Marty had opened me to the emotional side of life; I was a different and fuller person because I had known her. Before her, I had never acknowledged the part of me that wanted a girlfriend, but her acceptance made it safe for me to date. Now I had numerous relationships—with great women whose companionship I genuinely valued. But I found I couldn't stay with these women any more than I could stay in my apartment. The mountains simply came first.

In 1989 many of us who were on Everest in '84 had a chance to climb the world's third-highest mountain, Kangchenjunga, and building on our Everest success, we became the first American team to summit that mountain from the north. Now I got a burr under my saddle to complete the trio by attempting a north-side ascent of the world's second-highest peak, K2. At 28,250 feet, a scant 800 feet shorter than Everest, K2 has been called "the savage mountain." Its weather is more unpredictable and its routes more unforgiving. I had attempted it in 1987 with a small international team, but atrocious weather had turned us back. Even before we were off the mountain, however, we had begun making plans for a rematch. This time, if we succeeded, I would be the first American to climb K2 from the north, and the first to scale the world's three tallest mountains by their north-side routes.

There would be four of us—Greg Child, Greg Mortimer, Steve Swenson, and me, all planning to go without oxygen—and we spent that spring preparing for our June departure. In late May, a week before I was scheduled to take customers up Mt. McKinley, Mom called. Dad had just fallen in the bathroom and couldn't get up. 911 was on the way.

This stroke was far more serious. Although Dad's body was largely unaffected, his cognitive functions were: He recognized us but could barely speak. I called off the McKinley trip. I considered bowing out of K2 also, but that seemed premature. If I pulled the plug and Dad recovered, I would be unable to rejoin the expedition, but if I waited and he didn't improve, I could cancel at the last minute.

Two weeks went by and there was no improvement. If anything, he seemed to get a little worse. We moved him to a nursing facility where daily occupational and speech therapy did little to help him talk or swallow. Occasional windows of lucidity raised our hopes, but most of the time Dad wasn't there. Then he took a turn for the worse. A series of ministrokes made all that was left of Dad disappear. His brother, a physician, said he wished the first stroke had killed him. Doctors urged us to let them insert a feeding tube and we debated for hours about whether or not to do so. The decision was like being trapped in a hallway with a million doors, each of which opens to a place you don't want to go. Arthur "Mike" Ershler had been a star athlete, World War II hero, devoted husband, and a great father. For him, life on a feeding tube would be no life at all. But how could we choose to end it? Finally I called Dr. Marty Greene, whom I had trusted now for twenty years. He listened for a long while and then said, "Phil, I wouldn't do it." It was the hardest decision any of us ever made.

After that we had little time. My sisters Margaret and Deborah came from London and California, and Dad held his two-year-old granddaughter Katie for the last time. A few days later he began to struggle for breath. Deep raspy noises came from his throat, and Mom and I held his hands. Finally, my mother said gently, "Mike, you can let go." And a short time later, while we were still holding his hands, he did.

Never one for pomp and circumstance, Dad wanted only a basic cremation service that would have placed him in a cardboard box. But I couldn't do that. I didn't mind his being cremated, but I didn't want him going in a cardboard box. So the morning of the service I picked out a casket and we sent him off in that. It was probably one of the few times in my life when I overruled him. He died on June 1, 1990, a few months shy of his eightieth birthday, two weeks before we were due to leave for K2. I had already mentally bailed out of the trip. My sisters were going back to San Diego and London and I didn't want to leave Mom alone. But when I said so, Mom looked at me firmly and said, "Of course you're going. Dad would want you to."

"I don't know about leaving you," I repeated.

"Don't worry about me," she said. "I'm healthy, I have good neighbors, I'll be fine. *Go.*"

So I went. Just as John Roskelley had done in 1984, she cut the ties that held me back.

We said good-bye in her living room. She gave me a tight hug, then stepped back and looked at me as if she were trying to memorize every detail of my face.

"Don't worry, Mom," I said, "you won't have to bury both of us this summer."

She turned and disappeared into the bedroom that had been theirs for twenty-seven years, since we'd first moved into that house when I was thirteen. When she came back, she pressed something into my hand. It was a pair of small bronze wings, the aviator wings my father had earned when he became a Navy pilot. She didn't have to tell me what to do with them.

July 5, 1990

From advanced base camp we could see our entire route: 12,000 vertical feet of snow, rock, and ice rising in a perfect knife-edged pyramid. K2 gives nothing away easily. Everything would be hard: the weather, the routes, the altitude. What I had going for me was the team. Steve and the two Gregs were among the world's most motivated climbers. I felt privileged to be in their company.

Fortunately, the weather obliged us. With uncharacteristic kindness, the mountain gave us a relatively predictable pattern: three or four days of good weather followed by a couple of days of storms. On good days we could fix rope and carry loads to the next camp; on bad days we went down to lower elevation to rest. After two months of this pattern we were in a position to summit. It was late afternoon when we climbed into high camp. The weather had been deteriorating all day. Now the wind was picking up, it was beginning to snow, and the temperature was quickly dropping. The four of us squeezed into a three-man tent and melted snow on a precariously balanced stove in a tiny crevice between us. None of us were firing on all cylinders. We all had headaches, we were all exhausted. Without oxygen, tomorrow morning would be our one and only shot at the summit.

We woke to thick snow and fog. When it hadn't cleared after an hour, we went anyway, Swenson taking the lead, cutting a trail through snow up to his knees. Only a fixed rope left by a Japanese expedition made it possible to consider the traverse. Holding the rope, I wondered, *How many steps will we kick before we trigger an avalanche?* The work was exhausting, and after an hour we were as depleted as if we'd been climbing for half a day. When we reached 26,500 feet the fixed rope ended. Now we were on our own. From here on, with no rope even to tie ourselves together, we would each be doing the rest of the ascent alone. I stopped and took stock of the conditions. It wasn't snowing but the sky suggested that it could start at any moment. No telling what the wind would do. Down below, the flank of the mountain fell away in a sheer straight line. Far below, a narrow glacier ran like a silver river through a rock-strewn valley. I bent my head and dug in again, trying to squeeze every ounce of oxygen out of each breath. The pitch had steepened and I pulled out my hammer to give me a fourth point of contact. Steve and Greg Mortimer plodded on ahead of me; behind me Greg Child brought up the rear. We were 100 to 200 feet apart, but their presence was of minimal comfort. At this altitude, with no oxygen and so little equipment, we were of little use to each other.

We climbed this way for a couple of hours, stopping occasionally to nibble at a candy bar and take a sip of water. The higher we got the more I felt my strength wane. It was becoming harder to move each foot and I could feel myself slowing down. After a while Greg passed me. I looked at my watch: 3:30. Two hours at least to the summit. By that time it would be getting dark and our path down would be all but impossible to see. I looked up again at the sky. How long would the snow hold off? Farther up the mountain Steve and the two Gregs were also looking skyward, but with the distance and the wind there was no way we could talk. The decision to go forward or turn around would be made by each of us alone. I started up again.

Two more times I stopped and reconsidered, weighing the voices that competed in my head. One said, *"Yes, you can make it!"* The other said, *"Yeah, but it'll be luck that gets you there and down again, not skill."* This wasn't the way I'd felt on Everest. On Everest I had known with certainty that the first voice was correct. Now I was far less certain. And if I'd learned anything in the mountains it was to be brutally honest about my abilities and my level of risk.

But how to be honest on an 8,000-meter peak when you're just 600 feet from the summit? At that point, your risk assess-

ment changes. At that point you're willing to risk more. I
thought back to '84 when Roskelley had turned around. He'd
recognized the point at which the risk—for him—was no
longer acceptable. Would I recognize mine? I wanted this summit big time. I wanted it for me, and I wanted it for Dad,
whose wings were in my pocket. But I also knew that I had to
come home from this expedition: If I died it would probably
kill my mother also.

There was no way to signal to the others that I was turning
around, so I merely turned and headed back to camp. Once
there, I started the stove to make sure there would be water for
them when they returned. At around 9:00 p.m. Steve arrived;
four hours later the two Gregs staggered in by headlamp. In an
awesome achievement, all three had made it, setting American
and Australian records.

On the way home I had plenty of time to consider the expedition. I was not sorry I had made the choice I had. I felt bad
that I hadn't made the summit, but I had learned long before
not to second-guess a mountain decision. We make the best
choice we can in any given moment. To question that decision
later is neither fair to yourself nor productive. My feeling about
K2 was now different than it had been in '87. That time I'd felt
we'd never really gotten a shot; this time we'd had a good one.
So I didn't feel the need to return. In fact, I doubted that I
would ever go back to the Himalayas. For the last decade I'd
spent close to a quarter of my life on a Himalayan expedition.
Those expeditions had been extraordinary. I'd seen fabulous
things, spent time with wonderful people, had reasonable success on the world's three highest peaks. But it occurred to me
that I didn't want the '90s to be a repeat of the '80s. I'd had a
good run, I still had ten fingers and ten toes, I'd probably
helped most of the expeditions I'd been on. Most people would
probably say they were glad I'd been on the trip. Now it was
time to do something else: time to devote more attention to

growing our still-fledgling business; time to focus more on guiding, which offered a whole different kind of pleasure from the "me-focused" expeditions; and time, perhaps, to find a relationship that would be as meaningful to me as the mountains. I had no intention of giving up climbing; it was simply the three-month expeditions I felt I could now live without.

On the airplane an hour out of Beijing, I watched the continent of Asia disappear behind us and remembered the closing line of the first book I'd ever read about mountaineering, Maurice Herzog's *Annapurna*. "There are other Annapurnas in the lives of men," Herzog wrote. "We turn the page: a new life begins." I felt that a new life was ready to begin for me. Not entirely new: I would still be climbing. But with the turn of the decade I had the distinct sense that there would also be other challenges, other things to take pleasure from, other kinds of mountains to explore.

July 1992

Phil,
Wednesday night. I could not sleep so I am listening to
"December," sitting on the floor, thinking about you. You and me. I
miss you. Every time I think about you it is with a smile. Sometimes
I wish we could be together more. What a wonderful addition you
have made to my life.

Miss you,
Sue

July 1992

Dearest Susan,
"Happiness is like a butterfly. The more you chase it and chase it
directly, the more it will elude you. So just sit quietly & it will come
& land on your shoulder."
    Thanks for landing on my shoulder, Sue. You make me very happy
& and you still give me butterflies.
    I'm proud of you & I love you.

Phil

4

AMERICAN GUIDE DIES ON MCKINLEY

All my life I've tried to cover up my weaknesses. Maybe that comes from being the littlest, the only girl in a family of boys. I could be the weakest and get left out, or I could try to be strong so they would include me. It wasn't much of a contest. My brothers were wild as animals and I adored them. Mike was a year older than I was, Jerry was two years older than Mike, and Dave was a year older than Jerry. And whatever they were doing I wanted to do too. Since I was so much smaller and couldn't always compete, one of the best ways to be included was to tease them. If we were playing H-O-R-S-E and I couldn't make a basket, I would throw the ball at Jerry's head and next thing I knew we'd have a skirmish. Or I could walk up behind Dave and slug him in the back and within seconds some of them would chase me. I loved the chases. Their legs were longer but I always had an escape route planned. I would run to the bathroom and pull out the drawer so they couldn't open the door and hide until the coast was clear. Then I would do it again. They didn't mind playing with me as long as I played rough like they did. But the minute I cried I was out.

The other way I got their attention was by laughing. I loved making them laugh, and, in turn, I laughed like crazy at everything that came out of their mouths. When Dave got older he sometimes took me on his dates because I laughed so much at his jokes. I'd laugh so hard I'd fall back in my chair and knock over my Coke and he would feel like a big shot in front of his girlfriend. I think I spent most of my childhood trying to make my brothers laugh.

As much as they pummeled me at home, they were my biggest protectors out in the world. If someone even looked at me meanly they would come to my defense. Once, when some tough older girls threatened to beat me up at school, two of them went looking for the girls to show them who they were dealing with. Those girls never even looked at me again.

But there was one way my brothers couldn't protect me. Our father worked at the U.S. Department of Fish and Wildlife, and the summer between first and second grade we moved from Portland, Oregon, to Seattle. On the first day of school my mother introduced me to my new teacher, who was as tall as a giant and had the whitest skin I'd ever seen. I was scared of her and couldn't wait to go home. The next day when I got to school, the teacher was waiting for us at the classroom door.

"Good morning, Susan."

I was afraid to look at her face. "Good morning, teacher."

"What's my name?"

I couldn't remember. So I just stood there, looking at my shoes.

"Do you know my name?"

I thought she might hit me if I shook my head.

Finally she said, "My name is Miss Dammeier," and made me say it back after her.

After that I never forgot her name because it sounded like a bad word.

That afternoon I went home with a stomachache. I had one the next day and also the next. It wasn't just Miss Dammeier. It was also the reading. I had learned to read the year before, but in this school the children read a lot faster. They turned their pages way before I finished mine. I was afraid to tell any-one so I began to turn my pages too, even though I wasn't finished. At night, my brothers and I would sit in the living room to do our homework. I would clown around and distract them until my mother got stern and made us buckle down. Then they would start writing in their notebooks and there would be nothing for me to do but turn the pages of my reader, knowing that all the other children were in *their* living rooms *really* reading. One night I started to cry. The next day my mother went to school. She told Miss Dammeier that I didn't need to be criticized, I needed to be helped, and after that I stopped getting stomachaches and my reading improved. But schoolwork never became an area in which I felt great confidence. It seemed to me that people fell into one of two categories: You were book smart or you were athletic, and I seemed to be the latter. So I squirmed my way through elementary school and lived for 3:00 when I could run back home and play with my brothers.

The summer before fifth grade we moved back to Portland. I was so excited to be going back! After three years in Seattle, Portland still felt like home. Our new house was right near our old one, the neighbors I remembered were still there, and best of all, my parents joined an athletic club just three blocks away. I took one look at the pool (where later my brother Jerry nearly drowned me by seeing how long he could hold me underwater) and the gym, where high school girls were working on a balance beam, and I was hooked. After that I went there every day. Two older boys offered me gymnastics lessons in exchange for (entirely innocent) back massages, and when they weren't there I just went and practiced.

The next four years were idyllic. My brothers, now that we were older, were more willing to include me in their world. They often let me ride on the backs of their motorcycles when they went screaming up the twisty roads of an area called Rocky Butte, vying to see who could lean so far over on the turns that his foot pedal touched the pavement. My oldest brother, Dave, got married, and his new wife moved into our house. When their baby, Jodi, was born we became a household of eight, and I loved the constant buzz of living with so many people. I made a kind of peace with school: I think the energy and discipline required by gymnastics made it easier for me to settle into academics. And every summer I went with my best friend, Rhea Smith, and her family to a lake in eastern Oregon where Rhea and I learned to water ski. I loved the feeling of flying on the water, and as soon as her father let us drive the boat we went out every day. Skiing was the symbol of the freedom that we craved but were not quite mature enough to handle, as we demonstrated all too often. Once, for instance, we dared Rhea's sister to ski naked and she agreed—as long as we agreed to drive the boat the same way. When she got up, we covered up with towels and drove straight toward a boat full of men, while Rhea's sister crouched down and screamed, holding the rope with one hand and covering her body with the other. Rhea and I collapsed laughing, not least because if her sister had thought to release the rope, she would have just dropped into the water!

The summer after my freshman year, my Portland life came to an end. My father transferred within the Environmental Protection Agency, and we moved to Edmonds, fourteen miles north of Seattle. There, instead of a big city high school where the size and diversity made a kind of electricity in the halls, I was sent to a school one-third the size where everyone was the same. Rhea was gone; the gymnastics program was a joke; and my brothers Dave and Jerry had stayed behind.

"Give it a chance," my parents said. "It takes time."

I had no interest in giving it a chance—I was too angry. So I withdrew; I mentally checked out and began the countdown to graduation. Junior year I got an after-school job as a cashier at a Fred Meyer discount department store, and although it wasn't a glamorous job, I liked it. I liked earning money and being in the "real world," and I saw that if I worked hard I could work my way up. Senior year I worked full-time from 2:00 to 11:00 p.m. and began saving up for a car. That spring I bought a used gold Camaro, and the day after graduation I loaded the car and drove down the freeway. Fred Meyer had made me a department manager in one of their Portland stores.

Unfortunately, it didn't take long to see that things were not going to be exactly as I had imagined. The store was in a rough part of town, quite different from the suburban store I had worked at in Washington, and my first week there I witnessed something very disturbing. I happened to glance down an aisle just as a woman ran her ring down a dress, deliberately ruining the fabric. She then took the dress to the cashier and demanded a discount. I was so startled I didn't know what to do. When I reported it to my manager, he shrugged as if to say, "What else is new?" A month later we were robbed again. Two men threw a big raincoat on the floor, dumped an entire rack of clothes on top, then bundled them up and ran out the door. This time the manager chased them, only to be told by the police, "Never chase guys like that. They're armed and dangerous." The other employees shrugged these incidents off, but I couldn't. Perhaps if the other areas of my life had been happier they would have carried less weight, but instead they amplified the discomfort I was otherwise feeling. I loved living with Dave and his family, especially Jodi, whom I adored, but I felt like a fifth wheel. My old Portland friends and I had gone our separate ways; even Rhea and I were no longer as close. I was starting to wonder if I was really meant to be there.

One day, six months into my new "career," I noticed a six-year-old girl hovering over the candy. With her braids and plastic jewelry she looked so adorable I had to smile. About ten minutes later I heard the alarm go off and saw the manager dash out of the store. When he came back in, he was holding the girl by the shoulders. Apparently, her mother had sent her into the store to steal and when she'd seen the manager nab her daughter, she had fled. I couldn't believe it. I couldn't believe that a mother would do that to her child. I couldn't shake the feelings that the incident had triggered.

Just a week or so later my parents came to visit. They had protested mightily when I'd announced my plan to skip college and move to Portland, but after several months of arguing they had given up. Now we talked amicably every week, and I had been open with them about my changing feelings. Over dinner I told them about the little girl. I'm sure my mother could see the sadness in my face, and I think she also sensed an opening.

"Perhaps you and I should take a little vacation," she suggested. "We could drive out to eastern Washington. Maybe see a few colleges along the way."

I probably heard the word "vacation" more clearly than I heard the word "colleges," but I took her up on the offer. A week later she and I drove to Pullman where we visited Washington State University. The minute we arrived I knew I wanted to stay. The sun was shining, there was a fresh sheet of snow on the ground, and—perhaps it was just the contrast with my inner-city experience—everyone we passed looked *happy*. I wanted to be part of that happiness; I wanted the promise the university seemed to hold.

That fall I enrolled at WSU. I majored in business, which suited my long-term plan, and this time, unlike high school, I determined to do well. But my old academic insecurities came back. I seemed to need twice as long to study as other students, and I envied my friend and roommate, Melanie Hedlund, who got straight A's. This time I couldn't check out, however; I'd seen what was available to me without a degree. The only way to make up for my deficiencies would be to work harder, so that was what I did.

During my sophomore year I began dating a lovely man named Gary. He was six feet five, handsome enough to be a model, a terrific athlete, and well on his way to a successful professional career. He seemed to be everything I wanted, and for the next eight years we both worked hard to convince ourselves that we were truly meant to be together. It wasn't until our wedding day that I realized we were making a mistake. I peered through the small window at the back of the giant United Methodist Church in downtown Seattle, waiting for the cue at which my father would walk me down the aisle, and felt a knot tighten in my stomach. My dad assured me it was nerves, but I couldn't entirely believe him. Two years later we filed for divorce. I was overwhelmed with guilt. I had been in my late twenties when we married, I desperately wanted children, and even though I had known in my heart of hearts that Gary and I were moving in different directions, I had let those concerns guide me into making a wrong decision. Gary was a wonderful man and he deserved so much better; because of my own indecision I had stolen several years of his life.

November 3, 1988

It had been a year since my divorce and four months since I had moved from an Operations position at United Technologies to a sales position at GTE. Now, instead of managing a team that helped corporate customers resolve problems with their phone systems, I was selling telecommunications equipment to Seattle's largest businesses. It was my dream job, one I had coveted for years. The sales division seemed so upbeat and the salesmen so confident, and the department was highly valued in the company. I wanted to be part of that energy and prestige. Despite my desire, I had been totally unprepared when my boss, Walt Yaeger, moved from United Technologies to the sales division at GTE and asked me to join him. At that moment my fantasy came smack up against reality. "I can't do that, Walt!" I'd protested. "I've never sold a thing. And besides, almost all the salesmen and clients are *men*."

"You'll be great at sales," Walt had said. "You'll only have two problems: You're an attractive female, and you're short. You'll just have to be tough."

So I had moved to Major Account sales at GTE, where my job was to sell $1 million worth of telecommunications equipment annually. A million dollars! If I hadn't been so terrified I would have laughed. But I was so *proud*. Walt had believed in me, he'd given me the chance of a lifetime, and more than anything I wanted to succeed. Now I walked down Fifth Avenue in downtown Seattle, my new dress-for-success "IBM blue" skirt-suit rustling against my hose, my sales briefcase swinging each time I took a step in my two-inch heels, hoping that the prospective customers I'd just met with had seen the confident saleswoman I tried to project and not the impostor inside.

"Yo, woman! Where's my money!"

Startled, I turned toward the voice. It had come from a huge yellow Cadillac that was driving slowly up Fifth Avenue. The driver was leaning out the open window leering. *At me.*

Oh, no, I thought. Then, *Just ignore him; he'll go away.*

"Where's my money!"

He yelled it louder this time and dozens of heads swiveled in my direction. "I want my money!"

I walked faster, praying that no one on the street knew me, but the faster I walked, the faster he drove.

"Get in the car!"

I kept my head angled toward the buildings until I reached the corner. The light turned red and I stepped off the curb anyway. A car barreling through the intersection honked. I jumped back on the curb and the Cadillac pulled up right next to me.

"I told you, get in the car!"

Everyone on the corner was staring. I knew my face must

be beet red. There was only one thing to do. Looking straight at the sidewalk, I went around to the passenger side and got in the car. "Hiram! Will you stop! What if there's a client out there?"

Hiram Hoed was doubled over with laughter.

"Don't you ever do that to me again! I could kill you!"

Hiram and I had worked together for three years, first at United Technologies and now at GTE. He and our friend John Waechter, who worked with us, teased me mercilessly every chance they got. But they were also my closest friends. We palled around together outside of work, and since I was brand-new to sales, they often gave me pointers. They reminded me a lot of my brothers. One minute they were teasing me and playfully beating me up; the next they were my biggest protectors.

"You can't kill me. Who would teach you everything you need to know?"

I made a wry face.

"Hey, how're you doing?"

"What do you mean, how am I doing? I've just been humiliated in public."

"No, I mean fourth quarter. How're you doing?"

"Oh. I don't know."

"You should know exactly where you are. Add it up."

I did a quick mental tally and came up about $50,000 short of my quota. "Wow," I said, surprised. "I almost made quota."

Hiram looked at me like I had just stepped off the boat. "What do you mean, you *almost* made quota? You can't *almost* make quota. You've got to *make* quota. Or above."

I looked at him, trying to gauge if he was serious; with Hiram it was sometimes hard to tell. But he looked completely earnest. I'd thought the quota was a recommendation, something to aim for, not something I had to hit. I'd simply been trying to sell as much as I could.

As if he could read my mind he said, "You don't get an A for effort in this job, Susie. You get an A for *results*. Ninety percent might have been good in school, but here you need to make a hundred."

We drove back to the office and for the rest of the afternoon his words circled in my mind.

By December it was clear I wasn't going to make it. I'd put many of my eggs in one basket and the basket had a big hole. When I'd first arrived at GTE a manager had helped me make my first sale, to Seattle's largest law firm, Perkins Coie, but then I was on my own. Walt had counseled me to go for the niche I knew and target another law firm, so I'd researched the city's number two firm, Bogle & Gates. If Bogle bought equipment for several of their offices, it could be a million-dollar sale. It would put me way over my quota!

For the next six months I worked that sale almost to the exclusion of everything else, but no matter how persistent I was Bogle didn't buy. They didn't say no—they passed it up and around the chain of command—but they never made a commitment. By September I began to get nervous. I knew I should focus on other sales, but Bogle seemed so close; I really *believed* it would come through. Third quarter ended, and management began to question me. Embarrassed, I took circuitous routes to my cube to avoid them. By early December I could practically hear the dings of the calculators as all the salespeople tallied their sales and hit their quotas. I was still $50,000 down.

One afternoon Walt took me out for coffee. He sat opposite me at the table and turned his coffee cup around and around in his hands. "We're going to have a bit of a reorg," he said. I could feel him carefully choosing his words. "And we thought it might be a better 'fit' for you in the, uh, small-business group."

Small business? But big business was what he had recruited me for! That was where my friends were; that was where I belonged! "What about my accounts?" I said, trying to keep my voice under control.

"You can keep your accounts for now. We just think it would be better if . . ."

I tuned out the rest. I could keep Bogle. I could keep Bogle! They were right, of course: I was no good at sales; it had been a huge mistake to hire me. But I could keep Bogle, and even though all my insecurity told me I would never cut it in sales, a stubborn part of my brain believed that Bogle would still come through. An even more stubborn part was saying, *They think I can't do it but I'm going to prove that I can!*

The following week I turned up the heat under Bogle, and two months later they made the purchase. It was one of GTE's largest equipment sales ever, and I was moved back to major accounts. I had still missed my quota, but I had learned an invaluable lesson: Stick to your vision, never give up, and you'll succeed.

Over the next few years I became more and more comfortable at sales. It turned out to be the perfect job for me: I loved meeting and spending time with clients, I loved helping solve their problems, and I loved the clear, concrete goal that my quota represented because I saw that with hard work I knew how to meet it. If I put in long hours, and did my homework, and formed strong relationships with clients, I could blow that number away. I began to see that I was actually good at sales, and for the first time in my life, I began to feel confident. By the time I'd been at GTE for three years, I had bought a condo overlooking Lake Washington (a top corner unit with a full-on view); I had my own little ski boat (which I could see from my living room window); I had good friends with whom I boated, partied, and skied; and I had more money than I'd ever expected. I felt I had arrived.

The only thing I didn't have was a man to share my life. In the years since my divorce I had dated a fair amount, looking for the one man who might make a loving lifelong partner, but by the time I was thirty-five I had mostly lost hope of finding him. I'd heard of women who found their Prince Charming, but I knew it wasn't going to happen to me. I tried not to dwell on it, but after a long day of work or a party with friends, I would go back to the condo and stare out at the blackened lake and feel empty.

Even harder than not having a partner was giving up my dream of having children. I had *always* wanted children. In grade school I had babysat for free just for the pleasure of playing with the kids, and living with my baby niece had been the greatest joy of my time in Portland. When I turned thirty-four I became obsessed with it, as if my biological clock had begun ticking so loud I could hear it above all else. I talked to friends, Walt, and my parents; I asked them if they thought I could be happy without having children, if they thought I would regret it later. Walt pointed out that I didn't have to be married to have children, and that took a little pressure off. But with every conversation I moved a tiny step closer to acknowledging the truth: that I would probably never be a mother.

In the summer of 1991 I drove my little boat through the Montlake Cut to Lake Union to attend a party given by Northland Communications, a cable company to which I had just sold a telecommunications system. In the process of closing the sale I'd become good friends with John Whetzell, the CEO, and his assistant, Nan Lund, and they had invited me to the company's summer bash on a party boat. I had been there for about ten minutes when John came up to me, beer in hand, and gave me a peck on the cheek. "Hey, Sue," he said with a distinctly mischievous look in his eye, "I met someone I think you'd like."

John and Nan had watched me go in and out of several relationships. I think they both felt determined to find me a real partner.

"What does he do for a living?"

"He's a famous mountain climber and guide." John had just come back from climbing some mountain in Russia. Working out was one of the passions we shared, but I couldn't imagine why he had wanted to climb a mountain. Now it was obvious that the altitude had done something to his head.

"John," I said, laughing, "what could we possibly have in common? I'm a salesperson. I work twelve hours a day. I'd no more climb a mountain than give up my condo."

Apparently John was not dissuaded because five months later Nan called to say that Phil Ershler was coming to the Northland Christmas party and that they had told him about me. So on a cold, damp evening in mid-December I put on my backless little black dress, took extra time with my hair and makeup (just in case), and went. I'd just begun looking for people I recognized when John appeared, wrapped me in a hug, and hollered, "Phil, come over here." A moment later a compact man with dark hair and a trim mustache stepped forward out of the crowd.

"Phil, Sue Burger. Sue, Phil Ershler."

If John excused himself at that moment I didn't notice because Phil had given me a smile that melts ice cubes. Now he looked at me as if I were the only person in the room. He was half a head taller than I and had playful brown eyes that were made more pronounced by the white raccoon mask around them. The rest of his face was a ruddy brown.

"Nice to meet you." We said it at the same time, then laughed.

Like most of the men at the party, he was wearing a navy blazer and dark slacks, but there was definitely something different about the way they hung on his body. It didn't take much imagination to appreciate his muscular build. For the next five minutes we made small talk—how we knew John, what we did for a living, the usual thing. I was surprised, given my powerful attraction to him, how comfortable he made me feel. I was just starting to imagine the rest of the evening (long conversation, close dancing, exchange of phone numbers) when a large jacketless man holding two beer bottles practically inserted himself between us. "You're Phil Er-r-r-shler!" he said, crooning Phil's name as if he were addressing some movie star. The man turned his back to me so that I could barely see around him. "I've been wanting to meet you. I was on Everest . . . well, just a trek to base camp . . . heck of a flight out of Kathmandu . . ." He pattered on and Phil listened politely. Words like "Sherpas" and "Namche Bazaar" that had little meaning to me batted back and forth between them. Finally Phil excused himself and the man moved away.

"I'm sorry." Phil touched my arm. "It's been very nice talking to you. I hope we can talk again sometime." He looked at me with that same room-dissolving intensity, and it took me a second to realize what was going on. He was excusing himself. He had brought a date! And sure enough, as he turned back into the crowd, a stunning woman in a skintight black dress took his arm. *My goodness*, I thought, *what just happened?* I felt as if I'd been caught in an electrical field. I hadn't felt that kind of attraction since I was in high school. And I'd never felt that kind of attraction coupled with such comfort and ease.

The following Monday I went to work early to prepare for a client presentation. Midmorning I picked up my mail and began reading it on the way back to my cubicle. I had just sat down, fully engrossed in a letter, when something clamped itself around my ankle. I screamed and pushed back from the desk so hard that I rolled to the far side of the cube. From under the desk came the sound of deep, sidesplitting laughter. I leaned down for a better look, and there on the floor on hands and knees was John Waechter in his expensive suit. I should have known! The day before, John had stood on his desk in the middle of the office and yelled, "Listen up! I have just been assigned as office manager for the day. You will now do everything I say!" The previous week he'd discovered I was wearing two different high heels and got on the loud speaker and announced it to the entire office. Now he was laughing so hard he was shaking.

"I could kill you!" I started to yell, but by then I was laughing just as hard as he was. "Let's go get coffee." I had been planning to tell John about Phil. John was single, too, and we'd had many conversations about our joint determination never to "settle." We slipped out to the café across the street and I told him about the party. When I got to Phil's name, John practically exploded.

"Phil Er-r-r-shler!" he said with that same iconic reverence the man at the party had used. "I climbed Rainier with Phil! He's a legend!" And he proceeded to tell me the entire story of his climb.

Of course, I listened with a whole different level of interest than I would have the week before. I pumped him for every detail about Phil, and when he told me that I'd find "Phil stories" in lots of mountaineering books, I went right to the bookstore. By the time I got home that night *I* was starting to think of Phil as "Phil Er-r-r-shler!" too.

A week later Nan intercepted a thank-you note intended for John. "Great party," it said in small capital letters, "and tell Sue she can call me anytime. Phil."

"He's interested!" Nan crowed, but my own reaction was mixed. *Isn't that cocky,* I thought, *"she can call me anytime."* Why couldn't he call me? I wrote his number in the back of my Daytimer where it distracted me each time I opened the book. It wasn't as though I needed to call him. I was casually dating someone else—yet another relationship that I knew would be short-lived. The trouble was I couldn't get Phil out of my mind. For the next four weeks I went back and forth— *should I, shouldn't I? should I, shouldn't I?*—until finally I couldn't stand my own indecision any longer. It was 9:00 at night, I was still at the office pricing a data network for a client, and when I could no longer find one more thing to cross off my to-do list, I picked up the phone.

Wait a minute! I put the phone down. *I can't do this!*

But I have to do it. He's obviously not going to call me. It's been four weeks.

But what if he doesn't remember me? What if that woman was his girlfriend?

This was very different from making a sales call. In sales I'd learned never to take rejection personally, but if Phil rejected me it would definitely be personal. Finally I said to myself, *What's the worst that could happen? You'll be embarrassed.* And at that I dialed the number.

"Hi, this is Phil. I'm climbing in Ecuador. Leave a message."

I was so relieved not to actually have to talk to him that I blurted out, "This is Sue. Give me a call," and hung up. I knew that if he never called, I would never call him again.

Two weeks later I was home catching up on bills when the phone rang. "Hi, Sue, this is Phil Ershler."

My heart did three somersaults before coming to rest in my throat. "Oh, hi, Phil. Back from Ecuador?" I tried to sound casual, but probably sounded like a chipmunk on steroids.

He told me about the climb—which, as far as my buzzing brain could make out, seemed to involve a volcano, ancient ruins, and a hot tub—then asked about me. By two hours later my brain had calmed, the sense of ease and familiarity that I'd felt at the party had returned, and we had arranged our first date.

Of course, by the time the date arrived I was nervous all over again. By now I'd heard and read so much about him, it was like dating a rock star. I changed my outfit five times in an effort to look sophisticated-but-casual-but-also-sexy. What did you wear to go to dinner with a mountain climber? Finally I settled on a short skirt and fitted purple jacket, and that must have been fine because Phil's appreciative glance put me immediately at ease. Before we'd even left the condo, we'd settled into that same easy, flowing conversation.

There seemed to be nothing we couldn't talk about. Each topic flowed into the next and despite our obvious differences, we found numerous similarities. We'd both grown up in the Northwest in loving, Rock of Gibraltar families who were still very central in our lives. We both loved our work and took great pleasure in striving to be the best we could be. We both had a glass-half-full approach to life and believed that we could make our lives what we wanted them to be. Despite these concurrences, I was surprised when Phil said, "I just want you to know—I'm not opposed to marriage but children are not high on my agenda." *Whoosh,* I thought, *that's a serious thing to say so early. What's he thinking—that if I say I'm dead-set on children, he'll leave now and not have to pay for dinner?* But behind the surprise I felt a stab of disappointment. I told him I hadn't ruled out having kids, but since I was already thirty-five I had come to think it was unlikely. That seemed to satisfy him because we then went downstairs where, in an old-fashioned display of manners that made me smile, he ran ahead of me to open every door.

Over dinner Phil told me quite a bit about climbing, and afterward, as we entered the condo, he began to illustrate the "rest-step," a way of walking they used in mountaineering. He was so serious about it, and it looked so funny watching him do this deliberate breathing technique in the hallway of my suburban condo, that I started to laugh. "I want to try," I said and asked him to show me again. Then we both rest-stepped down the hallway, noisily blowing out air as if we were blowing up balloons, until the image of what we must look like cracked us up and we both dissolved in laughter. I was still smiling when he left a few hours later.

Two days later I was flipping through my mail in the condo lobby when an envelope addressed in small capital letters caught my eye. Inside was a card.

Dear Susan,

It's a little early for a Valentine's card but it gives me a good excuse to let you know how much I enjoyed seeing you. I hope we get a chance to know each other better. John was right, you are special.
Happy Valentine's,
Philip

I leaned against the wall, let my knees collapse, and said out loud, "Yes, yes, yes!"

Our second date was at the Sun Valley Ski Resort in Idaho. Phil had been invited to the birthday bash of Frank Wells, president of Disney, whom he had helped guide on Mt. Everest in 1983. He said the annual event was always filled with Hollywood moguls and had dangled Clint Eastwood's name, as if I needed extra incentive to go. Of course, I said yes immediately, and then he teased me.

"What kind of girl are you anyway, going on an overnight date with someone you hardly know?"

"Hey, don't get any ideas," I shot back, "I'm only going to meet Clint Eastwood!"

On the airplane, shortly after takeoff, a hand emerged from the seat behind us and tapped Phil on the shoulder. The earnest face of a young man appeared over the seat back.

"Aren't you Phil Er-r-r-shler?" he asked. "Could I get your autograph?"

Phil looked half pleased, half embarrassed. After he'd signed the boy's cocktail napkin he looked at me and shrugged. "Just wanted to impress you," he said. "It's amazing what you can accomplish with twenty-dollars."

The scene at Sun Valley was just as Phil had described: a whirl of skiing and partying. Clint was there, so was Janet Leigh, and I was introduced to more Hollywood producers and deal-makers than I could keep straight. Just to keep up with Phil, I spent the first day flailing down slopes I had no business skiing. I'd wait at the top while he set off in his elegant, rhythmic turns, then launch myself in a heart-stopping straight line, hoping to reach the bottom at the same time he did. By the time 4:00 came and he put his arm around my shoulder and said, "Ready to quit, baby?" my legs were like Jell-O and I was more ready for a nap. But hand in hand we went off to Barsotti's Bar where the minute we walked in the door a chorus of voices began shouting Phil's name. Over in the corner several tables had been pushed together and a group of men, all with that white raccoon mask around their eyes, was waving.

"Hey, Phil! You up here with Wells?"

"Yeah. What are you guys doing here?"

"Came up after the Ski Show in Vegas."

Phil put his arm around me and began the introductions. "Sue, this is Lou Whittaker. Lou and I had a little trip up Mt. Everest in 1984. And Jerry Lynch. Be nice to him, he's my boss. And that's Skip Yowell. Skip finally made his mother proud. Started a little company called Jansport." Phil went around the table, introducing each man with a quip that made him grin. Then it was my turn. "And this is Sue Burger. She agreed to join me up here because she wants to meet Clint Eastwood."

The men laughed and Lou Whittaker motioned for me to sit next to him. "Ershler, we were just talking about Kangchenjunga. You remember the monsoon after we climbed that thing in 1989? Were you the one who told the Sherpas to burn the garbage?"

"Heck no!"

Lou looked at me. "He ever tell you about the leeches?"

I shook my head.

"Well, we'd been on Kangchenjunga nearly three months and we had all this garbage because the Sherpas wouldn't let us burn garbage on the mountain. They said it might irritate the gods and make the monsoons come early. So we waited, and right when we're ready to leave base camp we burn the garbage. Next day, *wham*, monsoon, just like that. So now we get to walk out for a week in the pouring rain and then spend every night picking leeches off each other, like a bunch of baboons grooming each other for fleas."

"Yeah." Phil laughed. "The only redeeming feature was that we all needed a bath."

For the next hour the conversation ricocheted around the table as the men told one mountain story after another. The stories moved from continent to continent, each locale more exotic than the next, and each one larded with good-natured teasing. I was moved by the depth of the experiences and friendships they seemed to have shared, and by how much they obviously liked and respected Phil.

At one point Phil teased Lou about having told him he'd never be a guide. Jerry Lynch laughed. "You were too young, too short. We didn't know what in the world we were going to do with you, but we figured we better hire you anyway.'"

"Yup," said Lou, "and we've regretted it ever since!"

After that, we joined the climbers every afternoon. I loved their company. The jabbing and joking were so familiar to me: It was just what I'd known as a child. But if Phil's friends were familiar to me in that way, they were exotic in another. The people I knew had done what I'd done—followed a traditional career path in the corporate world. But these men—Phil included—had chosen something different. They had followed their passion. Early in life they had found something they loved and had simply gone ahead and done it. For them career and passion were the same. Listening to them talk I had to wonder: What was my passion? I loved sales; in a way, I'd done what they'd done, only backwards. I'd found the job and then realized that I loved it, instead of choosing work in an area I loved. What would it have been like to do it the other way? I'd always valued the security of a big corporation. Now

I wondered if I would have the courage to forgo it for work I truly loved.

By our last day at Sun Valley Phil and I were making out like crazy every chance we got. We were just so darned attracted to each other! Once, when we stopped in the middle of a run, a passing skier hollered, "Get a room!" I should have been embarrassed but instead I felt myself blush with pleasure. A few minutes later Phil skied off and I watched him execute yet another series of graceful turns. *I'm going to marry that man someday,* I thought, shocking myself with both the certainty and the suddenness of that realization.

• • •

John Whetzell and I had been sitting in the hut at 14,000 feet on the side of Mt. Elbrus when he said those immortal words, "Hey, Phil, I know this great gal. I've got to get you guys together." Since John had spent the better part of the climb complaining about women, I found his offer rather ironic, but I answered him politely and then didn't give it another thought—until he called me out of the crowd at his party. Standing next to him was a slim, blond woman with a great figure and a radiant smile who would have turned my head even without an introduction. Instantly, I both remembered and reconsidered John's offer. I walked over to them, all too conscious of the fact that my date for the evening was watching. We only had time for a five-minute conversation but it was long enough to suggest that Sue's personality matched her looks, and when I told her I hoped to see her again I meant it—in the way that I'd hope to see any pleasant, attractive woman. Despite what I'd thought on my way home from K2, I was still very much in the bachelor mode. I enjoyed women, and from my point of view, variety was fine. I'd had a few longish relationships but inevitably the woman would complain about how much I traveled, and we would part ways. One woman had said to me,

"You know, Phil, attendance does count," but if there had been someone out there who could matter to me as much as guiding, I hadn't been ready to find her.

Three weeks after the party I took a climbing group to Ecuador. When I got home, there was a message on the machine: "This is Sue. Give me a call." Who the heck was Sue? I was about to hit delete when I remembered. Two hours later we'd arranged our first date.

When the time came, however, I thought I'd made a mistake. Her condo was in the affluent suburb of Kirkland, right on Lake Washington, her glass-walled living room practically hanging out over the water. The parking lot was flush with BMWs. We might just be a little too different, I thought. My own apartment was pretty "basic," which suited me fine since I was rarely there, and the money I earned went right into the company or into the bank. I was surprised, therefore, when the evening sailed by in easy, unbroken conversation. She was bright and warm, she laughed readily . . . I liked her. And then there was that good-night kiss . . .

After Sun Valley we began to spend most of our weekends together. It wasn't a question of need; we just liked each other's company. Going to the gym, having dinner, sitting in front of the fireplace, reading the Sunday paper—whatever I did was more fun when I did it with her. I had never assumed that I would end up with a climber. What I did want was someone who was independent, passionate, and actively pursuing what she wanted, and Sue was all of the above. Little by little we introduced each other to the other parts of our lives. I met her friends and she met mine; we met and felt immediately comfortable with each other's parents; and every once in a while I'd pull the little card out of my dresser with instructions on how to tie a tie and accompany her to a formal corporate event or to the GTE suite at the Kingdome where she entertained her clients. I'd pour the drinks and play the "corporate spouse" and enjoy the feeling that I was supporting her in her job. I liked watching her at those events—seeing her ease with people and the genuine interest and warmth with which she engaged them. There was an aura of goodness about Sue that I liked being close to.

As the days grew longer and winter slowly moved toward spring, Sue's attention turned to boating. For her, spring meant one thing: the beginning of waterskiing season. She had told me how she and her friends would jump into their boats on Friday afternoons, drive to the middle of the lake, rip off their business suits, put on their swimsuits, and ski until it was time to go back to work on Monday, and I could see in her eyes that she was eager for me to join them. I was game—except for one little problem. I had never been close to water skis in my life and I had no interest in making a fool of myself in front of Sue and her friends. So there was only one solution: Learn to ski *quick*.

"You want to learn to ski in April?" the man at the sporting goods store said when I called looking for an instructor. "It's a little cold."

"I have to be ready for opening day."

I could hear him thinking he had a loony-tunes on the phone, but he gave me the name of an instructor who had his boat in the water and, just as importantly, a dry suit. The following Sunday I met the instructor at a dock on Lake Sammamish at 7:00 a.m. *"Seven a.m.?"* I'd repeated when he'd stated the time. I didn't mind the earliness, or the fact that the day would be at its coldest, but I'd be sleeping at Susan's the night before and I hadn't told her I was taking lessons. How could I get away—and back—without her knowing?

That Saturday I kept her out late. Sure enough, she stayed sound asleep while I crept out of, and then back into, bed. But the following Sunday I wasn't so lucky. She woke while I was getting back in bed and wondered where I'd been.

"Oh, just went for a walk," I lied.

She hugged me sleepily, then opened her eyes and looked at me more closely. "You're wet."

"Oh, yeah, well . . . I walked through a sprinkler."

"Oh." She lay back down and immediately fell asleep.

I didn't like lying but I hoped telling her the truth later would exonerate me.

The third week I told her I would be getting up early to help a friend move. When I climbed back in bed and she questioned my wet hair, I told her it was sweat. My fourth and final lesson was on boating season's opening day, the day Sue and her friend Kathy Hasson had planned to teach me how to ski. I managed to sneak out and back without detection, and a little after 9:00 a.m. Kathy sprayed her garden hose against the window to wake us. We dressed and went downstairs. Halfway along the dock I accidentally dropped a ski glove.

"How come your glove is wet?" Sue asked when she picked it up.

"Oh, I, uh, dropped it in the water."

She gave me a look that seemed to say, "You think you're going to be able to ski when you can't even hold on to your gloves?" but tossed it back to me and ran on down to the boat.

As we headed out onto the water, Sue, Kathy, and their friend Jim decided that they should ski first so I could watch and get some pointers. (For all the instruction they gave me I might still be sitting in the lake.) When it was finally my turn, I flailed around in the water letting them correct me and then yelled, "Hit it." The boat took off and I stood up. I saw Sue grin with surprise and pride. The boat did a wide turn around the bay and I hung on. After three or four minutes they dropped me off at the dock. Sue and the others crowed over my success, for which they took full credit. Then I said, "Hey, you guys are such good teachers. Show me how to do this on one ski." They guffawed—no one slaloms on his first day!—but I persisted, so they agreed. I put on the slalom ski and pretended to flail around again, and then once again, I got right up. Sue's face registered shock and then delight. I waved and, grinning like a kid, she waved back. When Kathy started to steer the boat to-

ward the dock I made a loop with my hand to show that I
wanted to go around again, and this time I took the slalom ski
back and forth across the wake. In the back of the boat Sue was
practically jumping up and down, but Jim was saying something to her and shaking his head. We finished the loop and
Kathy dropped me at the dock. After they'd parked, Sue
jumped out and gave me an enormous hug.

"You're amazing!" she cried. "That was incredible!"

Jim looked at her sardonically. "Sue, he's skied before."

"No way! He told me he hasn't and he wouldn't lie."

"Come on, Sue. No first-time skier gets up on one ski and
cuts back and forth across the wake."

"Well, Phil does," said Sue, almost pouting. "He's a natural
athlete. And he read a book!"

"Well, I want to see a copy of that book!" said Jim, and I
practically burst out laughing. It would have been a good moment to tell them the truth, but I wanted to hold on to my secret a little longer.

That evening, Sue had her parents over to the condo. I liked
her parents a great deal. The first time I'd met them, I'd shaken
her mother's hand and said, "Mrs. Ellerman, a pleasure to meet
you," and she'd looked me right in the eye and said, "My name
is Mary." Nothing extra. It had reminded me of Frank Wells
telling me that the first time he'd called me he'd gotten my answering machine—"This is Phil Ershler, leave me a message"—
and he'd known right at that minute he could work with me.
That's the way Mary is, too, I thought, *no formalities, straight to the
point.* Now I listened to Sue go on and on about my skiing, and
I knew I couldn't let her deceive them. So I confessed. Sue
threw a chair cushion at me, I grabbed her and gave her a kiss,
and we all had a good laugh. But that was the last time I ever
tried to put one over on Sue.

. . .

On May 9 we celebrated Phil's forty-first birthday at the Salish Lodge, an elegant little hotel that overlooks Snoqualmie Falls, half an hour's drive from Seattle. Phil was about to leave for three weeks on Mt. McKinley, his first long trip since we'd been dating, and while I'd known for months that he would be going and part of me was looking forward to the time alone, his imminent departure also felt like a huge loss. In the three and a half months that we'd known each other my life had taken on the aura of a fairy tale, complete with my own Prince Charming. For much of each week I continued the single life I loved—working hard, seeing John, going out with girlfriends—and then every weekend Phil would be there to come home to. He joked (paraphrasing Meryl Streep in *Out of Africa*) that we might not be much good at saying good-bye but we were great at saying hello and, indeed, the hellos were rapturous. For the first time in my life, I felt I could tell a man anything. I felt wrapped in unconditional love.

Now, as we sat on the floor of our room in front of the fire and toasted each other with champagne, Phil grew serious. "Once I'm on the mountain we'll have no contact," he said. "So no news is good news. Okay?"

"Okay," I answered. It didn't occur to me to worry. Phil had guided for years. Why would I worry about Mt. McKinley?

Seven days later I found out. I was lying in bed watching the news when an announcer broke in with a news flash: "A forty-one-year-old American guide and several others have died on Mt. McKinley." I sat straight up. *This is it*, I thought. *This is how it happens. I'm not his wife, not his family; no one will call me. I find out on the evening news.* I began to sob. I didn't know what to do or whom to call so I called my family and friends. I did everything I could not to cry into the phone and they did everything they could to console me, but nothing they said was any help because none of them could tell me he was alive. I hit the remote over and over, desperate for more information, but all I could find were black-and-white movies and a religious talk show broadcasting to people whose lives were still intact. Finally I fell asleep and slept fitfully until dawn when a Canadian goose honking on my balcony woke me up. I ran downstairs for the paper and there it was on page one: "American Guide Dies on McKinley." I skimmed the article feverishly, looking only for the name of the guide. ". . . worst storm in ten years . . . record snowfall . . . lip of the crevasse collapsed . . ." Two paragraphs down I found it. "The guide's name was Muggs Stump." It wasn't Phil! It wasn't Phil! Farther down in the article they listed the seven other climbers who had died. I read each one twice to verify that none of them was Phil. But even in my relief I could not feel unadulterated joy. Phil was still up there in the storm, and somewhere other families' pain was just beginning.

The next few days passed in a whirl of work—my sanctuary when I am stressed. I listened to the news and weather obsessively. The storm did not improve and it seemed that each day another death was reported on the mountain. I repeated Phil's words—*no news is good news*—like a mantra and finally, on the eleventh day, I got a card.

Dearest Susan,

The bad news is that the weather's been rough. The good news is that the forecast is looking better. I'm still hoping to get home early in June.

I miss you. You must be good for me. I feel as strong as ever and I haven't exactly trained hard for the last month. You've been a great addition to my life and I want you to know how much I care for you.

I'll stay safe and smart and I'll be anxiously awaiting our hello. I think you're great.

Love, Philip

All the tension of the last few days dissolved.

Two days later he returned. The group had found a "sweet spot" between two storms, and all three of Phil's customers had made the summit.

Later that summer Phil went off to Rainier, and then to the highest peaks on other continents, but I didn't worry about his safety. I saw the McKinley experience as a fluke, a once-in-a-decade storm, and I knew that Phil had handled it safely. He would do the same if such a thing happened again. People who knew I was dating a climber would say, "But it's so dangerous!" and in the back of my mind I acknowledged that it was, but I didn't dwell on it. It wasn't my nature to worry. And each time Phil came home safely, any reason for worry diminished. There was only one other time when I feared for his safety.

The following November Phil flew to Antarctica to lead a climb on Mt. Vinson, the tallest peak on that continent. He promised to be back by December 12 so that we could attend the annual Northland Christmas party at which we had met the year before. By December 8, however, I hadn't heard from him. By that time he should have been off the mountain and back in a place where he could get to a phone. Why hadn't he called? When I still hadn't heard from him two days later I became frantic; it wasn't like him not to call. *No news is good news,* I reminded myself over and over again, but repeating the mantra did me little good. There was no way Phil could make it home now in time for the party, and there was no way he would miss the party unless something terrible had happened. That night I had dinner with John Waechter. I held it together throughout the evening, only mentioning briefly that I was worried about Phil, but as he dropped me off at my condo I burst into tears. I hated having him see me cry, but he held me close and said, "You don't need to worry. Phil is the safest guide out there. He's just delayed by weather." When my sniffling had subsided he said, "I'd like to have someone care that much about me."

John was right. The next day Phil called from Punta Arenas, Chile. They'd spent an extra week on the ice waiting for the weather to clear so a plane could come and fly them off. He'd had no way to contact me and he was super-apologetic about missing the party.

That June Phil asked me if I wanted to ski down from Camp Muir. The fact that Camp Muir is the base camp for Mt. Rainier, that it sits at 10,000 feet elevation, was apparently not an issue. "It's no big deal," Phil said, "just a hike up and then a nice long ski down." He made it sound so simple that I said, "Sure." So one Sunday we drove up the dizzying switch-backed road to Mt. Rainier. We rounded bend after bend, first one side of the car then the other hugging the mountain while the ground fell away in steep ravines on the opposite side. Spidery waterfalls glistened through hundred-year-old trees. Around one bend, the entire mountain rose before us and I gasped. My whole life, Mt. Rainier had been a postcard image on the horizon, sometimes there, more often not, appearing and disappearing almost like a figment of my imagination. But this mountain, rising ahead of me, was as solid and monumental as the earth itself.

"Welcome to my office," Phil said, and I thought, *Office indeed. This is his* world.

The trail from Paradise wound upward through snow. Phil pointed out avalanche lilies poking up through the white but it was hard for me to fully appreciate them. With the added weight of the skis, my backpack straps were killing my shoulders and my lungs were screaming. What Phil had neglected to mention about our "little hike" was that it started at 5,400 feet where there was less oxygen per breath than at sea level. But I was determined not to make him wait for me, so I kept my head down and my eyes on the snow. At 7,000 feet we stopped for a break.

"You're doing great," Phil said. "How do you feel?"

"Terrific," I answered. In addition to feeling like I was dying, I was getting light-headed from the altitude.

Phil gave me a squeeze. "Almost halfway there. From here on up, it's just a two-mile staircase."

Oh, just a two-mile staircase! Why did I not feel relieved?

After what felt like eternity, but was less than two hours on my watch, Phil stopped and pointed up. "That's Muir."

I felt a surge of joy. "Where?"

He pointed again at a cluster of tiny dots.

"Oh," I said bleakly. "I thought those were rocks."

For the next forty-five minutes I looked up frequently to see if Muir was getting closer, but no matter how long we climbed, the dots remained the size of peas. "It's not getting any closer," I complained.

"Yup," said Phil, "that's the joke about Muir. It's like walking up a down escalator. You keep walking and it never gets closer."

I didn't think it was a very funny joke.

Finally, five hours after we'd left the parking lot, we arrived. I felt as if my lungs were about to explode and my legs would never move on their own again. I collapsed onto the snow and a cabin girl brought us sandwiches and Kool-Aid. Gradually, as we sat and ate, my heart stopped pounding and my breath returned. The view was spectacular: above us, the glaciers and ridges of the upper mountain; below us, the vast snowfield we had just walked up. In the distance Phil pointed out the jagged snowcapped line of the Tatoosh Range, but I was too exhausted and worried about the ski down to really appreciate it.

After lunch we strapped on our skis and made the descent. It was, as Phil had said, a nice long ski down, and by the time we reached the parking lot I could barely lift my legs to get them in the car. I snuggled down in the front seat of Phil's Mazda RX7, exhausted, and it hit me: I had done it. I had actually climbed to 10,000 feet and skied down! Phil pulled out of the parking lot, and I had a vague awareness that he was talking. ". . . next time . . . all the way to the . . ." Before he reached the end of the sentence I was asleep.

A month later I joined one of Phil's guided trips to the summit. This time the stakes would be higher. It wouldn't be just Phil and me; there would be twenty-two other climbers and five more guides. What if I couldn't keep up? What if I couldn't handle the glaciers? Or the altitude? I spent most of the climb to Muir worrying, and by the time we arrived, I had a pounding headache. After dinner, we gathered in the bunkhouse for a pre-summit review. I listened as Phil explained the schedule and the importance of drinking, things he had already told me. Then he held up an ice axe. Around the room people's heads nodded as if they'd actually held such a thing before—and then it dawned on me: These people had all had training! When the session was over I took Phil aside. "Phil," I said, pointing to the axe, "shouldn't I know what to do with that?"

He looked at me, looked at the axe, then looked back at me. "Nah," he said. "If you fall, I'll stop you. You wouldn't be able to stop yourself anyway."

By 7:00 p.m. we had turned in for the night. Seeking privacy, Phil and I had unrolled our sleeping bags on the low, flat roof of the cook shack, and within seconds he was out. But I lay in the dark unable to sleep. The murmur of other climbers, the bobbing of headlamps, Phil's snoring, the mountain's fine pumice blowing against my face, the press of millions of stars overhead, fear, and exhaustion all made it impossible to settle down. When Phil woke me at midnight I felt like I had barely closed my eyes. The temperature was 32 degrees. The last thing I wanted to do was get out of my bag. *I could be home in bed*, I thought. *What possessed me to come up here?*

For an hour and a half the camp was like a Chinese fire drill conducted in the dark: guides scurrying around helping clients, boiling water for oatmeal and coffee, reminding everyone to go to the bathroom—"It's a whole lot harder to do it with your harness on and with an audience at 13,000 feet!"—gathering ropes and crampons, checking everyone's gear; clients scrambling to get themselves and their gear together exactly the way we'd been taught. By 1:30 we were standing on the glacier, roped four to a team. Phil moved off, and in the light of my headlamp I watched the rope spool out behind him, then felt it go taut. That rope was like a leash and a life preserver rolled into one. On the one hand it would protect me if I fell. On the other, it committed me to going forward. There was no turning back now.

The first leg of the climb was like an exercise in cold, discomfort, anxiety, and frustration. We were climbing the Cowlitz Glacier, a lumpy field of snow and ice pockmarked by exposed rock. I was fine on the ice where my crampons bit securely into the surface, but when we got to the rock, it was like walking in boots with high heels; I could barely keep my balance. And there were a million things to think about: Keep the rope on your downhill side, keep it taut but don't pull! Keep your ice axe in your uphill hand, don't catch your crampon in your gaiter! Breathe out through your mouth in rhythm with your step! But I could barely breathe at all and . . . what rhythm?

After forty-five minutes that felt like two hours, Phil called out that we were coming to a ridge with potential rockfalls. "Don't do the ostrich thing," he warned. "If you hear a rock, look up so you know how to react." He'd told me a story about a climber who had been hit in the jaw by a falling rock and almost died because his partners had had difficulty keeping his airway open. Somehow the idea of looking up offered little security against such an occurrence. We moved forward, this new terror at least effective at making me move faster.

By the time we took a break I had begun to develop what might be called a rhythm and I was actually beginning to think

I could do it. But as soon as we stopped, my confidence seeped away. The chill infiltrated my down parka and all three sub-layers and I was bathed in my own icy sweat. My legs trembled as if they were still climbing and my feet and shins were blistered from my rented boots. My stomach had turned to liquid. Despite my protests, Phil forced me to eat half a peanut butter and jelly sandwich and take a few sips of water. "You have to eat," he said. "You'll need it for the Cleaver."

Disappointment Cleaver is a prominent knife-edged ridge about halfway to the summit. I had been dreading it since I'd first agreed to the climb. There are numerous stories about how the Cleaver got its name. One has it that a group climbing it in a whiteout thought they were at the summit only to find, when the clouds broke, that they still had 2,000 vertical feet to go. Others say it's because so many people make it that far only to turn around. I got my first glimpse of the Cleaver shortly after the break. "Look up and to the right," Phil called. He'd been narrating our climb all the way along and I'd passed up every viewing opportunity, thinking that if I so much as moved my eyes off the trail I'd lose what little ability I had to propel myself forward. But this time I did look up. The sky was beginning to lighten and there to the right, emerging from the gray, was a dark, sharp ridge angling upward at 35 degrees. Small dots of light, the headlamps of other teams, were inching along its spine. *We're not going to climb that*, I thought. But the panic in my stomach acknowledged that we were.

"This next section's going to be a little more difficult," Phil said in what I was coming to recognize as his tendency toward understatement. He told us to coil up the ropes so we could walk close together; to minimize the chance of triggering rockfalls on each other. Phil was about three feet in front of me and I considered putting my arms around him and letting him simply drag me up, but instead I stayed right on his heels, trying to put my feet exactly where he had put his.

Unlike the glaciers we'd been crossing, the Cleaver was exposed rock with patches of ice, snow, loose rock, and dirt; by following Phil's footsteps I was able to step in areas that were relatively flat and clear. Suddenly one step landed awry. The back of my crampon hit a high spot, leaving the front tines in the air, and when I leaned forward to transfer my weight I almost pitched forward head over heels. Instantly I planted my other leg, but my foot skidded in loose scree. I felt myself start to tumble. Then suddenly the rope jerked and I was hoisted back to standing.

"You're doing fine. Just take it slow."

My chest and arms stung. My adrenaline was pumping.

"I've got you. Just step where I step."

I remembered a story Phil had told me about eleven customers who had died in a freak avalanche at a spot just below here in 1981. They had been at a break, resting, and a wall of snow had collapsed on top of them. They hadn't even made it this far. Cautiously, I moved my left foot back onto solid rock. Behind me I could hear the men shifting on the rope. In front of me Phil waited, his hand on the rope that was taut against my waist. I stepped forward onto a section of flat rock and we continued slowly upward.

After an hour and a half the ground flattened considerably and turned again to ice and snow. We had topped the Cleaver. We all dropped down on our packs too tired even to find our snacks or talk. Phil came over and put his arm around me. "You're doing great," he said. "The sun's coming up; you'll be amazed how your spirits lift."

"I don't know, Phil. Maybe I should go down." Around us the guides were forming new rope teams, separating the customers who would be turning around. Phil had reminded people that they should continue only if they were sure they had the strength to get to the top *and* back down.

He looked me pointedly in the eye. "You don't quit when

you hit a rough patch at work, do you?" He watched me patiently as if he already knew what I would do.

A few minutes later we started up again. The path was less steep now, and less exposed, and indeed, the mountain began to lighten. The Ingraham Glacier sloped away behind us, and up ahead the mountain rose in a jagged patchwork of dark and light. At one point Phil stopped and yelled something, pointing over my shoulder, and when I turned and looked, there was the orange ball of the sun, so huge and close I thought I could touch it. After that, my spirits did lift. The temperature rose and in the warm morning light, the entire mountain took on a luminous rosy glow. It was like being present for Genesis, like witnessing the dawn of civilization. By the time we got to the third break at 13,400 feet, we were just 1,000 feet from the summit and I knew I could make it. Phil reminded us to stay clipped into the rope while we rested—"If you fall while looking for your M&M's you're gone"—and before we had a chance to get cold again we were off. Now, as if he could smell the summit, Phil picked up the pace. *Not so fast*, I thought, *we're attached by a rope!* Contrary to all etiquette, I pulled on the rope and he turned around. I was embarrassed that I'd done it, so I looked innocent, but when he started up again, he went at the same pace. So what choice did I have? I tugged the rope again. This time he slowed down. For the next half hour we climbed steadily, one foot in front of the other, and occasionally, for whole moments, I was able to simply feel the work of my body without judging it as being good or bad or painful. At one point I looked up and realized that where earlier there had been endless white, there was now blue sky. Instantly my pace quickened. *This must be what Phil felt earlier,* I thought. I had the desire, though not the power, to run. A few moments later we were there: over the lip of the volcano, looking down into the crater, which spread before us like a giant bowl, filled with snow.

One by one the other rope teams joined us and we broke into whoops and hugs of congratulation. Phil coiled up the ropes and I grabbed people's cameras, taking summit shots of every climber. When Phil finished, he took me by the hand and pulled me aside. "You made it, baby," he said. Then he whispered something I had longed to hear. "I love you."

February 1999

Dear Susan,
I remember a trip I did to Vinson in '92 when I took your picture there and wrote your name in the snow. Then, in '98 I took you instead of the picture. You have become such an important part of my world. Each day we're together is just one more reason for me to celebrate. I love you, Sue.

Phil

May 1999

Seven years, Seven Summits, guess our lucky number is seven. I loved you from that day in Sun Valley, though even on that day I had no idea one could love another this much. We have what many people search for, wish for, strive for. You are my partner, my mentor, my hero, my love,

Forever,
Sue

5

SEVEN SUMMITS

Just a week after Rainier Phil asked me if I wanted to climb Mt. Kilimanjaro, the highest mountain in Africa, where he would be leading a climb in September. "Sure," I said, "and then let's fly to the moon." But Phil said, "It's not that hard, just a little physical on summit day." So I agreed. I had liked the Rainier climb. Despite the discomfort and fear and difficulty, I had loved the challenge and exhilaration and the triumph of standing on top. I had loved it for the same reason I loved sales. I had set a goal—*worked, worked, worked* to achieve it—and it had paid off with an unequivocal, tangible reward. And I had loved doing it with Phil. He had made it very clear to me that he didn't care if I climbed; that was not a requirement of the relationship. But I wanted to climb for him: I wanted to share that part of his life.

September 18, 1992

It had been years since I'd taken a vacation. The travel I'd once hoped to do, which had propelled me right out of college to work for a year as a flight attendant, had long ago gotten lost in my enthusiasm for sales. But now here I was, standing in the airport in Nairobi, Kenya, swatting away flies the size of malted-milk balls with my crisp new passport, waiting for a customs inspector to give me my very first stamp. Compared to Phil's passport, which was as thick and dog-eared as a family Bible, mine was a pristine and skinny thing, but turning its pages I felt I was holding a ticket to something I had dreamed of but thought I had given up.

The Nairobi airport was like no airport I'd ever seen. It was an old brick building with cracked windows and a few dim fluorescent lights. Wooden fans overhead sat motionless as if they were powerless to stir the thick air. Some of our bags were placed on an ancient groaning carousel; the rest were dumped in a pile on the floor. While Phil helped the customers retrieve the gear, I went to the bathroom. In the stall where I expected to find a toilet was an ancient porcelain bowl embedded in the floor with two worn footprints painted beside it.

Outside, we piled into two vans for the six-hour drive to Marangu, Tanzania. Ten minutes out of the airport, however, the vans came to a stop. Cars were lined up on both sides of the road and through the open windows, over the roar and honking of Nairobi traffic, came the sounds of drumming and children singing. We got out to investigate. We had walked about 100 yards when we saw dozens of schoolchildren in blue and green uniforms lining both sides of the street. A tall man in a long purple robe was dancing up the road between them, and behind him walked a man in a Western suit waving to the crowd. Phil made a questioning gesture to the man standing next to him, and the man nodded vigorously. "Pray-zee-den! Pray-zee-den!" It took a moment to understand. The man walking before us was Daniel arap Moi, the president of Kenya.

The road to Marangu was long, straight, and teeth-jarringly potholed. All around us the ground stretched away in a sere, beige sheet, broken here and there by tiny acacia trees casting feeble circles of shade. There was no sign of a town or settlement, yet narrow paths crisscrossed the landscape and occasionally we'd see a woman walking with a brightly wrapped bundle on her head, or a bare-chested man running. Where were they coming from? Where were they going?

At the border the vans stopped. A crowd of red-robed Masai women and children swarmed against the windows, thrusting their hands inside, calling, "Pleez! Pleez!" and waving beaded necklaces, bracelets, and little figures of polished wood in our faces. Right outside our window a young mother held an infant who was almost completely concealed by her robe. Like all the women, she was very black, her hair shaved close to her scalp. Rings of beaded necklaces circled her neck, and long, beaded earrings pulled her earlobes down into exaggerated pendants. With her free hand she dropped a thin leather bangle into Phil's lap. "How much?" he asked. She held up four fingers. "No way!" Phil held up two. The woman shook her head and held up three. Phil waved as if he would never consider such a price, then handed her four dollars. She smiled and they clasped hands. Now other Masai swooped to our window. This time I did the bartering. Following Phil's lead I rejected the original price only to give each vendor exactly what she wanted. By the time the vans pulled away our laps were full of trinkets. When I looked back through the rear window, they had all sat down in the dust, like so many brightly colored parcels, and were waiting for the next car to arrive.

As we got closer to Marangu the landscape began to change. Gradually the barren savannah gave way to low green hills, and rows of banana trees and shrubby, red-beaned coffee plants appeared in small stands on either side of the road. Through the open windows came the smell of damp earth. We were approaching the rain forest. By the time we reached Marangu, the world around us had transformed.

Marangu was a settlement of scattered farms and houses carved out of the rain forest. Phil had arranged a tour, and the next morning a lean man in his mid-thirties with a shriveled leg and a crutch made from a straight stick came to take us around. Phil introduced him to us as Abby. Abby led us along paths of deep red earth and down steep trails to see the area's numerous waterfalls. As Phil extended his hand to clients, Abby bounded past them, his useless leg hanging, the crutch perfectly doubling as a second leg. As we rested by the side of a stream he told us he had had polio as a child because his parents hadn't gotten him a shot. Back in the village we walked past tiny "farms"—really just small plots of land— where colorfully turbaned women bent over bean or coffee plants. From behind one-room houses made of cinder block or mud and branches, children stared, or if they were bold, ran out to greet us. Through the open doorways and glassless windows we could see the spare interiors and swept dirt floors. Of course, I knew that much of the world lived without bathrooms, kitchens, and electricity, but the difference between knowing and *seeing* suddenly became stark. For the first time I had the sense of being terribly American. I felt embarrassed at how much I had taken for granted, and a tremendous sense of gratitude.

At the end of the tour Abby took us to see the school. Phil had told me about the school. On his first trip through Marangu three years before, he had hired Abby for a tour and when they reached the school, the two of them had had an idea. Contrasting the lack of classroom supplies with the relative wealth of the customers, they thought, What if Phil's customers were given the opportunity to buy desks for the school? For $20 each, the school could commission desks from local craftsmen and have money left over for supplies, and each client could make a material difference in the lives of Marangu villagers. On the spot each customer had forked over $20 or more, and eight days later when the climbers returned from Kilimanjaro, the desks were sitting outside the school, each one proudly bearing the name of the donor. Since then, each group of climbers had continued the tradition. Now Abby led us down a long dirt driveway to a one-story cinderblock building. In the front "yard," painted rocks had been arranged in an outline of Africa. Fifty children in white shirts stood in a line in front of the school, and in front of the children were ten long wooden desks, each bearing stenciled letters:

TRUST FUND MARANGU AND INTERNATIONAL MOUNTAIN GUIDES
DONATED BY

followed by the donor's name and home city.

Now Abby cleared his throat, and in a voice he apparently reserved for making formal presentations, said, "My brother, these are your desks."

Everybody clapped and Phil took pictures, and within minutes the group began digging out their wallets. Phil took out his wallet too and said something quietly to Abby. I think he meant to surprise me later with a photo, but I could overhear him. He'd asked Abby to make a desk that said "Sue."

The following day we drove to the Machame entrance of Kilimanjaro National Park to begin our climb. This time, instead of starting in the dark at 10,000 feet and cramponing through ice and snow, we set out in the full light of a tropical morning and hiked on a well-worn path through thick, sun-dappled forest. Overhead, the occasional monkey rustled in the moss-covered trees, and up ahead of us ran our Chagga tribe porters. Unlike on the climb to Muir, where I'd had to carry a heavy pack, here the Chaggas would carry our gear.

Phil had told me that climbing Kilimanjaro would be like going from the equator to the Arctic in five days and, indeed, it was true. By the second day heather and wildflowers had replaced the lush canopy of trees, giant "chandelier" plants towered over the trail, and for the first time our heads were exposed to the tropical sun. By the end of the third day the temperature had dropped to near freezing. The climb itself was way less steep than Rainier but the relentlessness and altitude made it hard, and I watched in amazement as the Chaggas ran barefoot or in flimsy sandals up the uneven path, fifty pounds of gear balanced on leaf or cloth "donuts" on their heads. On our fourth day we made it to Barafu, high camp at 15,000 feet. Camp was pitched in a barren spot where the wind dropped the chill factor below freezing, and for the first time I began to feel anxious. I was higher than I'd been on Rainier, my head ached from the thin air, and I couldn't get warm. I'd heard about people who were physiologically incapable of going above a certain altitude. Would I be one of them? At dinner I had no stomach for the Chaggas' meat and rice, and when it was time to lie down I tossed and turned in anxious, altitude-induced discomfort.

We were roused just before midnight to begin the ascent to the summit, the 4,000 vertical feet that Phil had famously described as "a little physical." The ground was loose scree so that each step was one step up, half a step down as the rocks slipped and settled. I consoled myself by thinking that hard as it was, it was easier than climbing the Cleaver in crampons and a harness. "Pole, pole," the Chagga guides called in Swahili as if we had any choice but to go slowly. At the first rest stop I put on my down jacket to conserve body heat while we stopped, but even after we started up again I was too cold to take it off. I took some small comfort from the fact that Wilson, our lead Chagga, was also wearing a parka and mittens.

For the next seven hours we pushed upward. When I felt I could go no farther I thought, *Is this really all you can do?* When the sun rose and a band of orange spread across the horizon my spirits lifted, just as they had on Rainier, and even though Phil had stayed back to help the climbers at the rear, I caught up with Wilson. When he began a bouncy little two-step, I did the same, and right behind Wilson, I danced my way to the summit.

Back at the hotel the whole team gathered around four pushed-together tables. We drank cold Cokes and laughed, swapping stories about the climb. I had grown close to these people. From a group of strangers we had become intimates; together we had each pushed ourselves beyond our "edge," gone someplace we hadn't thought we could go. I understood why Phil felt so bonded to the people with whom he climbed, and why climbing changed people's lives. As I sipped my Coke and watched Phil laugh with the customers and the Chaggas, I thought that no Coke had ever tasted so good; no other Coke would ever have that much meaning.

I thought back to the GTE retreat center at which I'd stayed just three weeks before. There had been white linen on the tables, and men had been required to wear jackets to dinner. What a contrast from where I was now! I liked that contrast. I had loved the luxury at the center, and here, despite the discomfort, I had loved sleeping in a tent. Each experience intensified the other, made me appreciate it more. Remembering the retreat center made me realize that in the last ten days I had rarely thought about work, and when I had, it had not been with the same single-minded focus I had back home. *My goodness, Sue,* I thought, *there's a whole world outside of work! What you've been missing!*

• • •

The "true summit" of Kilimanjaro is called Uhuru. It is the highest point on the crater rim, and while the weariest climbers often stop when they reach the crater, most trek that final 400 feet. From where I was walking at the back of the line, I had a good view of our whole team going the final mile, and right up there at the front, right behind Wilson, was Sue. I could see her keeping her eye on him, just as I'd told her to, stepping exactly where he stepped in the narrow places where the trail approached the crater's edge. I knew from climbing with Wilson before that his steady pace would accelerate as he got closer to the summit, and I hoped that Sue could keep up. And sure enough, as he accelerated, Sue stayed right on his heels. When there were only about 200 feet to go, Wilson began the little shuffle that was his traditional "summit dance." I looked away for a moment to check on another climber and when I looked back, I had to laugh. There was Sue in my purple down jacket, her hat tipped low on her head, the pants she had borrowed from me 6 inches too long for her legs, mimicking Wilson's step.

What a trouper! I thought. She wasn't just in tune with Wilson; she was in tune with everything we'd been doing—from sleeping in tents, to not taking showers, to eating food unlike any she'd ever tasted. She hadn't minded getting dirty, she'd been willing to sweat, she hadn't needed everything to be just the way it was back home. And she hadn't needed a disproportionate amount of my attention. In the past I'd shied away from inviting girlfriends on my climbs out of concern that their presence would detract from my focus on the customers. But Sue had intuitively understood that the customers came first. Throughout the trip, she'd played the same role for me that I'd played for her at the Kingdome, smoothing the way for me and my clients. One of the clients had joked, "Phil, you make us feel secure, but Sue makes us feel like rock stars!" And I knew that was true. Quietly she had made herself my partner.

Watching her dance up to the summit I felt a rush of exhilaration. It wouldn't have been a deal-breaker if she hadn't taken so well to the trip, but she *had,* and that made a tremendous difference in what was possible. It opened up a chance for me to give. I would never be rolling in money; if she wanted a house on a lake I would never be able to provide it. But what I *could* give her was the ability to see the world in a special way. I thought back to her pleasure at seeing the singing children, her delight at bartering with the Masai, her respectful interest in Abby and the Chaggas. The fact that she was open to those things, that she appreciated them, meant that there was a world of experiences we could share. It meant there were unlimited places to which we now could go together.

That night we camped at a place called Horombo. It was our last camp; tomorrow we would spend the night in the hotel. Sue and I were lying in our tent reading when I felt a familiar, and unwelcome, sensation: cramping. This was a surprise; I hadn't had any Crohn's issues in a while. I lay there trying to focus on my book as the pain in my stomach intensified. Finally, when I couldn't find any way to make myself comfortable, I got two Tylenol-with-codeine tablets out of my rucksack.

Sue looked up from her book. "What's the matter?"

"My stomach's bothering me a little. I'll be okay."

I hadn't told Sue about the Crohn's. She knew I had some digestive problems. Despite my effort to disguise them, she'd watch me pick at food and hold my stomach after meals from time to time, but I'd mostly deflected her questions and she hadn't pressed it. It just wasn't something I talked about. There were people who had known me my whole life who still had no idea. My attitude had always been, there's nothing you can do that will make it better for me so why should I burden you with my problem? But that had begun to change with Sue. I'm not one to say "I love you" hastily and when I said it to Sue on Mt. Rainier it was a declaration of commitment. For six months now we'd been learning about each other, growing comfortable with each other, building intimacy. When I said "I love you" it was the beginning of saying, "Will you marry me?" and that meant that Sue needed to know.

As the codeine took the edge off the pain I closed my book and turned off my headlamp. A few minutes later she did the same. "You know," I said, rolling over to face her in the dark, "I have a little issue that you should probably be aware of." She turned to face me and I told her about the Crohn's, ending with, "It's under control, but it's always going to be there."

She sat up in her sleeping bag. I could feel her getting energized, her eagerness to ask me a lot of questions. "Well, isn't there a way we can fix it or make it better for you?"

"I'm already doing everything I can." My tone must have told her I didn't really want to discuss it further.

"Well," she said matter-of-factly, "it doesn't change anything for me. It's way too late for that. I'm already in love with you so we'll just have to deal with it together." And with that, she snuggled up against me in her sleeping bag and went to sleep.

Shortly after we got back from Kili I realized I had been thinking about something all wrong. For some time now I had been casually looking to buy a house. I knew exactly what I wanted: something in the Cascade foothills just beyond the suburbs, with easy access to the city and direct access to my mom; someplace where the neighbors weren't right on top of me and I could see the mountains out my window. But after Kilimanjaro, I realized there was a flaw in my thinking. If I wanted Sue to be my partner, I needed to think in terms of a house for both of us. And that promptly changed everything.

There was no getting around the fact that Sue and I wanted different things. I wanted rural; she wanted close to town. I wanted rustic; she wanted more amenities. I was a financial tightwad; she was willing to spend. The issue had all the makings of our first real tug-of-war. To start the negotiations I suggested North Bend, a town thirty miles east of Seattle. Sue said it was too long a commute.

"Okay," I said, "how about the Sammamish Plateau, ten minutes closer in?"

Still too far. "Let's try Kirkland," she suggested, the suburb where her condo was.

"Too close," I said, "not to mention out of our price range." We hadn't even looked at anything yet, and already we were disagreeing.

The Realtor showed me a great lot right near Lake Sammamish that I thought was a perfect compromise. Sue talked to the Realtor about Kirkland.

"Why don't I just buy the next-door condo in your building?" I teased.

She looked at me eagerly.

Finally I had to admit that Sue had a legitimate point. I would be gone nearly half the year while she would be commuting daily. I needed to give on the location. "All right," I said, "you go out with the Realtor and find us something in Kirkland." I thought there was no way they'd find something in our price range.

But one day, she and the Realtor drove me past neatly landscaped suburban homes to an overgrown lot on a corner. In the middle stood a dilapidated shack.

"Sue," I said, "I've known dogs with nicer houses than that."

She rolled her eyes. "Look down there."

I followed her finger and there, maybe ten blocks away at the bottom of the hill, small white triangles were sailing across a sea of blue: Lake Washington. I looked back at the lot. It was a good size and sloped upward to a knoll about twenty feet above the street. I could easily imagine how we could site a house. I looked back at the lake. It wouldn't be visible from the windows, but driving in or walking out to the mailbox we'd be staring right at it. *Heck,* the tightwad part of me thought, *we'll have a great view when we're driving home and we won't have to pay for it!* I looked at Sue. "Susan, I don't know how you did it, but I think this could work."

She grinned. "Well, you should know not to underestimate me by now."

That Christmas, 1993, we stood a little Christmas tree in the fireplace of the half-built house and decorated it with tinsel. Rain watered it through the unfinished chimney. On New Year's Eve we were sitting in the living room of the condo toasting each other with champagne when I got an inspiration.

"Come on," I said, pulling Sue to her feet, "bring the champagne."

I grabbed a headlamp and bundled Sue into the car and we drove over to the new house. In the light of the headlamp the tinsel on the tree sparkled. We had no electricity and no music, but in our new living room we danced.

By the summer of 1994 I had hatched the plan for our engagement. That fall Sue would be accompanying me when I led a Himalayan trek in Sikkim, a once-independent kingdom that was now an autonomous region of India. On the way in I was planning a stop at the Taj Mahal and I thought, *the Taj is the epitome of a person's love; what better place to get engaged?* So I asked Phursumba, a Sherpa friend who had been living in the States for many years, if he could help me with the arrangements.

"No problem, Sah'b!" Phursumba assured me. "From airport in Delhi to Taj Mahal one hour and half, two hours most. We meet you at airport, we have bus take you right to Taj Mahal, you spend the night, we drive you back next morning, you catch flight to Bagdogra, from there you drive to Darjeeling for your trek. No problem!"

So the itinerary was set, Phursumba made the arrangements, and when we boarded the plane in Seattle, I had a diamond ring in my pocket.

The bus had been crawling through the congested streets of Delhi for close to an hour when it became obvious that there was no way we would make it to the Taj in two hours. An hour later, when we were still in the Delhi outskirts, I could see we wouldn't make it there before dark. *Man, I hope it's open at night,* I thought, *because we have a plane to catch tomorrow morning.* At 7:00 p.m. we pulled into the parking lot. It was pitch black. No sign of the Taj anywhere. We piled off the bus; the driver went to investigate, and I got a sinking feeling in my stomach. But a few minutes later the bus driver returned looking unconcerned. "Taj Mahal close at six-thirty," he said, "but no problem! You come with me!" We piled back in and he drove us a short distance to another building where two women in saris ushered us into a room filled with curios of the Taj. In the center of the room stood a 4-foot replica of the building. Delighted that the bus driver had wangled a special entrance for us, we sat down on the benches that lined the walls. The two women brought us cups of tea which, after the stifling heat of the bus, we drank gratefully. The two women smiled at us and pointed at the model, and smiled some more and pointed. Respectfully we all got up and admired the model for a third and fourth time. And gradually we understood: We weren't getting a special tour of the Taj; we had been brought to a curio shop to purchase souvenirs!

The next morning our flight left from Delhi at the crack of dawn, but we were not on it. We had slept for four hours at our hotel near the Taj, then left at 3:30 a.m. for the drive to the airport. The return trip took even longer than the Taj-bound trip: We sat for hours without moving. Even in the middle of the night the temperature was 75 degrees. *Hour and a half no problem!* Phursumba's voice rang in my head. It was the only time in my life that I've wanted to wring the neck of a Sherpa. Finally we flew to Calcutta instead of Bagdogra, spent the night in that city where the poverty was wrenching, then the following day made our way to Darjeeling for the beginning of our trek. We'd lost a day of our climb, my customers had spent a dozen hours in the sweltering heat of a bus, and I had lost my chance to propose at the Taj Mahal.

I began rethinking my game plan. *Don't push it,* I said to myself, *the right time will come.* I stowed the ring deep in my pack, and within a few days I had a plan. Our trek was taking us toward the east face of Kangchenjunga, third-highest peak in the world. I'd summited the mountain from the north in 1989. As we walked I thought, *One of these days we're going to get a view of the east side of that mountain, and when the sun rises it's going to light that thing up like Sue's first sunrise on Mt. Rainier.* I began asking

Gombu, my good friend and Sherpa guide, when we would get the view. On our twelfth day Gombu gave me the high sign. The next morning I woke Sue early and in classic Sue mode, she didn't want to get up. We were at 13,000 feet, it was freezing cold, she didn't want to get out of her bag.

"What, are you planning to come back to Sikkim next week, you can see the sunrise on Kangchenjunga then?" I needled.

Finally she put on her down jacket, her hat, and her headlamp and followed me onto the trail. I walked fast—this was "Taj Mahal II" and I didn't want to blow it. I was timing it so we'd arrive just as the alpenglow was beginning. I scurried along for a few paces, then turned to make sure Sue was on my heels. She was there—but so were all the customers! I didn't want an audience for my proposal! I urged Sue to walk faster— which wasn't easy given her early morning where's-the-coffee? condition—and finally we got to a crest in the trail where the view of Kangchenjunga opened up before us. It was just light enough that we could make out the bulk of the east face. Sue and I stopped and the customers pulled up behind us. I moved us farther on. Like lemmings, the trekkers followed.

"Hey," I said to them, trying to sound gentle, "why don't you guys hang here for a bit?"

They took the hint and I led Sue about 100 yards away to the next rise in the trail. By now the light was growing and Kangchenjunga was getting a pinkish glow. I hugged Sue to me and we watched as the alpenglow deepened. Just when it was at its height I pulled out the little box with the ring. "You know, so much of the last decade of my life was tied up here in the Himalayas. Expeditions were always the number one thing. But now my life has taken a turn. Now you're the focal point and . . ."

Sue began to cry. I had opened the box and the sun was refracting off the diamond's facets. "Oh my," she said through her tears, "I missed the words. Are you asking me to marry you?"

"No," I said, "that's a friendship ring."

"Great," she said, "I can't wait to see the real thing."

. . .

In June 1995 I found myself sitting in the shotgun seat of a tiny Cessna 185 flying low over the glaciated summits of the Alaska range. Every one of them was higher than Mt. Rainier; in the lower 48 each one would have been a national park. Phil sat in the seat behind me, sardined by backpacks, sleds, and climbing gear, providing color commentary as if I could hear him over the head-rattling roar of the engines. In what had seemed, until just before takeoff, like a perfectly reasonable idea, we were about to climb Mt. McKinley.

The plane touched down at 7,000 feet on the southeast fork of the Kahiltna Glacier. The West Buttress rose above us in near-vertical ice and rock ridges. I had to crane my neck to see the top. "I'm screwed," I said to the mountain. It was obvious that Phil had way overestimated me. I'd barely made it up Rainier, which was only 14,000 feet. This one was 6,000 feet higher.

Pulling a loaded sled, Phil came over to where I was standing. I took one look at the sled and for the first time I got what he had been telling me for the past eight weeks, that this was an *expedition*. It wasn't an alpine climb like Rainier or Mt. Elbrus in Russia, the tallest mountain in Europe, which we had climbed almost a year earlier, where you climb up and down in a day. It wasn't a supported climb like Kilimanjaro, where you have porters carrying your supplies. It was a two-week we're-all-we've-got expedition, and not only was it higher, colder, longer, with less oxygen and requiring greater technical skill, but for the first four days I would be skiing uphill dragging a 50-pound sled. "Phil," I said fighting down panic, "I don't think I can do this."

"That's what I thought the first time I saw it."

"No, this one is *really* over my head."

"It looks big, but—"

Suddenly my panic exploded as anger. "Why did you get me into this? You've way overestimated my ability! You—"

"Whoa," Phil said. "Calm down." He put his arms around me and I could feel my heart hammering against his chest. "You don't have to climb the thing in a day. We're just going to climb a little bit today and then we'll sleep. And then we'll climb a little bit more tomorrow and then we'll sleep some more. And finally, one day, we'll be in a position to reach the summit." He kissed the top of my head. "It's just like eating an elephant, one bite at a time."

But what if you're not sure you want to eat the elephant at all?

For the first four days we did nothing but slog upward on skis pulling our sleds. My pack dug into my shoulders, the sled harness dug into my hips, and my feet got blistered from sliding back and forth in my boots. We were not far from where Muggs Stump had died three years before, or from where Chris Kerrebrock had died in 1981, or from where a young woman had fallen into a crevasse in 1983 and died while her team was pulling her out. I spent much of the time imagining what would happen if I went down. On the fifth day we reached 14,000 feet and the McKinley base camp, and it was like coming upon a little civilization. A cluster of colorful tents sat in a cul de sac at the far end of the glacier, horseshoed by the West Rib and West Buttress of the mountain. Off to one side, un-walled, undraped, was a toilet and on the toilet was a man. *Oh my goodness,* I thought, *this is where we're going to . . .*

We were on our way up to high camp when I lost it. We had stopped shortly before, in what Phil said was the most diffi-cult section of the climb, because I was exhausted. John Waechter and another friend, Andy Lufkin, who were accom-panying us, were physically stronger than I was and I fretted about being the weakest link. Phil calmed me down and forced me to eat and drink, but when we started up again I could feel that I was still too cold, too tired, and too miserable to really climb. Phil had told us to maneuver ourselves around the rocks in such a way that, if we fell, the rocks would act as a belay, catching the rope and breaking our fall. But I was feeling lucky just to get one foot in front of the other; I couldn't worry about the rocks. I picked up my left foot and suddenly, for the second time that day, my crampon stayed behind. *Crap!* I put the foot back down and it slid backwards on the ice. No traction. I managed to tighten my leg and stop the slide, but when I stepped again the same thing happened. I couldn't even step down long enough to fix the darn crampon! Legs splayed, I dropped down in the snow and began to cry.

"What's going on?" Phil must have felt the rope stop. He was around a knoll and couldn't see me.

Behind me Andy called, "I think Sue's having a little problem."

Phil walked back to where he could see me. "Sue, can you walk a little way with one crampon?"

I didn't think I could since I'd done such a bad job of it already, but I got up and by digging my left foot sideways into the slope, I managed to plod uphill, dragging the crampon behind me. When I reached Phil, I took it off so he could fix it. John and Andy came up behind me. I didn't want them to know I'd been crying, so I tried to wipe away my tears with my frozen mitten. Then, for some reason I thought of Tanya Harding, the figure skater, who after a bad start in the free-skate program at the 1994 Olympics, hoisted her skate on the rink wall and cried to the judges that she needed to start over because her lace had broken. To save face I held up my crampon and said, "I need to start over!" and they all got the reference and laughed.

With my crampon fixed we continued to climb, and to my surprise, I now found the climbing easier. Having released my stress by crying, I think I now had more energy for the climb. At home it took a lot to make me cry: fear about Phil, or a major disappointment at work. But when I was climbing, my emotions seemed to simmer just below the surface. I was so drained, so out of my comfort zone, so intoxicated by altitude, it took very little to bring on tears.

Two days later we prepared to leave high camp for the summit. It was a spectacular day, clear and sunny, perfect for summiting, and John, Andy, and Phil were raring to go. I, unfortunately, had just gotten my period and had terrible cramps—ordinary cramps times five because of the altitude. Phil knew I was embarrassed, so he said to the others, "You know, the weather's so nice, we've got lots of food and gas. Let's just enjoy McKinley today and go on up to the summit tomorrow." They were disappointed, but what could they do? That night it began to snow. It snowed all night, all the next day, and all the day after. Not only could we not summit, we could hardly go out of our tents—which was probably a good thing since even over the howling wind I imagined I could hear John and Andy cursing the fact that we'd delayed. Thank goodness they didn't know why! Of course, we had nothing with us—no books, no cards, no pencils and paper—because we'd gone as light as possible to high camp. So we spent the whole three days yelling back and forth between the tents, quizzing each other on trivia. "Who was secretary of defense under Bush?" "What battle turned the tide of the war in the Pacific?" The game ended when Phil yelled, "What year did women get the vote?"

"1942, during World War II!" yelled back John.

"No way!"

"Yeah, it was! I saw the posters!"

"You sure you want to go with that answer?"

"I'm so sure I'll bet you a round of golf at Pebble Beach!"

"Whoa, John, you don't want to go there!"

But John did, so they made the bet. As soon as we got home Phil e-mailed John an encyclopedia entry stating that women got the vote in 1920. John *had* seen the posters; he just had the wrong war!

Finally on the fourth day the weather cleared and we took off for the summit. The route was painfully steep and exposed, and as I shouldered into the wind, I already longed for the first break. When it finally came, my pack, which was practically empty, felt like it weighed a ton and I felt that familiar despair: *I can't do this.* But each of the guys took some of my things, and being relieved of that little burden somehow made me feel 50 pounds lighter. Suddenly I felt I could fly! I practically ran the rest of the way to the top.

Shortly after we got back from McKinley I was promoted to regional sales manager. I was thrilled. I had been the manager of the education market for almost three years, and in that time we'd grown the department from $1 million to $17 million. I had loved working with my team, coaching them to reach the goal, and even more fulfilling than our numbers was that in my last year as manager, every member of my team made it to President's Club, the reward for GTE's top sellers. But once we had the education market sailing smoothly, I had begun itching for a new challenge, and now, in addition to education, I was asked to take on all major markets: financial services, high tech, health care, and the top accounts in the Northwest region. My quota would soar to $50 million.

I was ecstatic—but I saw a potential hurdle: I was planning to join Phil on his guided climb of Aconcagua, the tallest mountain in South America, which meant that just four months into the new job, I would be leaving for a three-week vacation. I'd just come back from three weeks on McKinley and didn't think they'd be happy about my going away again so soon.

To grease the skids, I sent my boss a copy of *The Seven Summits*, a book by Dick Bass, Frank Wells, and Rick Ridgeway describing Bass and Wells's quest to scale the highest mountain on every continent. McKinley and Aconcagua were two of those summits; perhaps if my boss read about them, he'd be a little more sympathetic to my climb. A week went by and then another, and I never heard from him about the book. Then I saw him at a corporate function and he handed it back to me without a word. *Way to go, Sue,* I thought, *he hated the book and now you have to tell him you're climbing one of those mountains!* I waited a week and then called for a meeting. I knew he wouldn't stop me from going, and I knew I'd work my butt off before I left so there would be no decline during my absence, but I hated having to start my new job by asking for special treatment.

For the first few minutes of the meeting we made small talk. I told him how excited I was to be in the position and we briefly discussed my strategy for maximizing sales, but then I had to tell him. "I need you to know," I said, "that even though I've just arrived, I actually have a vacation scheduled. I'm going to be climbing Aconcagua, the highest mountain in South America, for three weeks in February. But I'll have everything lined up to operate smoothly while I'm gone." I could hear the self-conscious edge in my voice; I hoped it didn't make me sound defensive.

"Say again?" he said.

"I'm going to be climbing Aconcagua, the highest mountain in South America. But my teams will be ready and—"

"Aconcagua . . ." His brow furrowed. "Isn't that one of the mountains in that book you sent me? Whoa, those guys had spunk, didn't they? You gotta hand it to them. Don't think I could do that." He paused and looked at me. "Did you say you're climbing Aconcagua?" He looked me up and down as if he were trying to detect a climbing harness under my jacket.

I nodded.

"That's right . . ." He was putting two and two together. "Didn't you just climb McKinley?"

I nodded again.

"And now you're going to do Aconcagua. That's the one down in the Andes. The one where in '83 Frank almost fell into the river. Yeah, and on the first trip, didn't Bass summit via the Polish Glacier?" He rattled off details from *The Seven Summits* that I'd completely missed in my own reading. "Hey," he said suddenly. "Can I ask you a couple of questions?"

For the next ten minutes he didn't say a word about work; he just wanted to hear about climbing. When he heard that Phil had climbed Everest (and was, in fact, the same Phil who had helped guide Bass and Wells on several of the climbs featured in the book) he practically asked for his autograph. Finally we stood up and I moved toward the door.

"So, Sue," he said, "just one more question. You've done Elbrus and McKinley, and now Aconcagua. You going to do all Seven Summits?"

I smiled. I hadn't verbalized the thought to anyone, but in the back of my mind I was already hoping that we would. Since Phil's friend and client Dick Bass had first done it in 1985, fewer than thirty others had succeeded. I had no idea if I could really do it—much more experienced climbers had tried and failed—but I loved goals and that was a big one.

I was halfway to the door when he stopped me again, his voice a little firmer now, as if he had just remembered the reason for our meeting. "Sue, before you go you better have all your ducks in a row."

I assured him that I would.

"And . . ."

I expected him to ask me to call or e-mail from South America.

"You better come back here safe."

For the next four months I worked like a dog. Phil was gone much of the time so I went in early and stayed late; I did everything-*plus* to make sure my teams were set up for my absence. To tell the truth, it wasn't that different from how I normally worked. What I hadn't told my boss was that climbing had actually *improved* my performance. I'd found there was no way I could carry on at work, prepare for absences, *and* train for a climb while keeping up my previous bad habits. So in the last few years I had stopped partying, cut way back on wine, and begun working out religiously every day. The result was that I had more hours for work, and more energy to work with.

About a week before we left for Aconcagua my period was late. I told myself it was because I'd been working out so much, or because I was nervous about the trip, but when after several days it still hadn't come, I took a pregnancy test. I had done that once before, the first year I'd known Phil, and that time, while I'd waited anxiously for the result, I had inwardly hoped it would be positive. That was before I knew about the Crohn's, before I understood why he had said with such certainty that having children was not on his agenda. He didn't want to take a chance on passing the disease on to them, or risk complications from his medications. Waiting for the test results, I didn't carry my hope to its logical conclusion, to the fact that if I were pregnant he and I would need to work out our conflicting feelings. I just felt again the yearning to have children, which I had hoped I had put aside.

This time things were different. To my great surprise, as I sat in the bathroom and waited for the color on the little strip to change, the feeling that welled up inside me wasn't *yes*, but *No! Don't let me be pregnant!* I couldn't afford to be pregnant. If I were pregnant everything would change: Phil, the climbing, the dream of the Seven Summits—none of that would be possible if I had to care for a child. I sat on the edge of the bathtub opposite a photo of us on Mt. McKinley and thought, *What happened to that yearning?* I realized I hadn't thought about it in quite some time. I did an internal sweep, looking for the feeling. Across from me, the two of us smiled out of the photograph, framed in our climbing gear against a backdrop of snow and sky. Inside me I found love, and happiness, and a surprising amount of contentment. But I didn't find a deep desire for children. Somehow, when I wasn't looking, the yearning had gone away.

· · ·

Aconcagua has a reputation for cold, windy summit days and I could see that today would be no exception. When we got up at 2:00 a.m. the wind was already gusting at 20 miles per hour and the temperature was in the single digits. I got out of the tent quickly to get the clients ready, get the stoves going, and get the water heated for breakfast. It was going to be a long hard climb, 4,000 feet in altitude, and I wanted everybody to have the best possible shot. When I went back to the tent twenty minutes later Sue was still in her sleeping bag.

"I'm not feeling well," she said. "I have a stomachache and a headache."

Altitude and nerves, I thought. I remembered a similar moment on Mt. Elbrus. We woke up in the sleeping hut the morning of our summit climb and Sue felt completely trashed. Her head was pounding and she didn't think she could move. I'd suggested she stay at the hut. We were going for the experience, not for the summit, and I only wanted her climbing if it was going to be fun. But Sue had said, "Well, I can stay here and feel like crap or I can climb and feel like crap. If I'm going to feel like crap I might as well go." After a little bit of climbing she began to feel better, which hadn't surprised me. Sometimes movement is the best medicine for altitude ills. Now I wondered if a similar thing might happen here. "Why don't you just stay here?" I suggested. "I only want you to go if it's going to be fun."

The next time I went back to the tent she was fully dressed, boots on, ready to go.

Right out of camp the climbing was difficult. The summit

of Aconcagua is a killer, even for the strongest climbers. The trail is made of loose rock that makes good technique imperative. You have to plant your foot strategically, keeping your weight directly above your foot so that you compress the rock instead of causing it to slide out underneath you. And you have to concentrate on breathing, taking two or three breaths per step, to increase the oxygen in your blood. When clients reach the top they usually drop down on their rucksacks and put their heads between their knees. They don't even have energy to snap pictures.

Sue, on the other hand, was walking around taking summit shots for the customers. I watched her in amazement. We were at 23,000 feet, almost 3,000 feet higher than McKinley, and she wasn't sucking pond water! She was up, taking care of my customers, thinking about *their* experience, fully being my partner!

I'd had a good idea even before Rainier that Sue would do well in the mountains. It's my business to evaluate climbers and make determinations about how much they can do, and I'd had more confidence in her than she did when we did that first climb. But what I hadn't known was how much her climbing would bring us together. Each of our climbs—and particularly the expeditions—was such an intense experience. We were thrown together twenty-four hours a day, all the experiences of life compressed into a short, finite period. As a result we shared everything: meals, thoughts, sleeping, physical distress, worrying, rejoicing . . . It could easily have driven us apart. Days on end in a 6- by 6-foot tent can challenge even the strongest relationship, but we were so well suited that it drew us closer instead. Every time Sue had one of her little breakdowns—which I'd started to think of as "Sue moments"—we broke through to a new level of trust. Each time she worked through a limitation, or learned a new technique, or overcame a fear, we learned about working together. And as much as she leaned on me physically, I leaned on her emotionally. She brought so much goodness to our climbs—with her warmth, her kindness, her sense of humor, her optimism, and her drive—that she made everything better for me and for my clients. In all my years of mountaineering I'd had amazing partners and incomparable experiences. But as wonderful as those experiences were, climbing with Sue was better. Even more fulfilling than standing on top of Everest was climbing with the woman I truly loved.

• • •

Two months before we left for Aconcagua I learned that I'd been named GTE's Regional Sales Manager of the Year. It was an incredible honor; I felt I'd reached the pinnacle of my career. But with the honor came an obligation: I would finally need to learn to play a decent game of golf. I was to accept the award at the President's Club retreat in Bermuda, and golf would be an "encouraged" part of the activities. Golf was deeply embedded in the GTE culture; it was a way we were expected to entertain clients. I'd attended a few golf events, but I'd always ridden in the cart or just attended the dinners. Now the day of reckoning had come: The company higher-ups would be there, and they would expect me to join them on the links. I told Phil we needed to learn how to play.

"*We* don't need to learn," he answered, "*you* need to learn."

"Oh, come on, Phil. You'll love it."

"I need to learn to play golf like a moose needs a hat rack. But if that's what you want, set it up."

So the two of us took lessons, and all that winter, night after night, we went out after work and hit balls. My right hand, the one without the glove, got colder than it ever did in the mountains. By the time President's Club came around in April, we were both starting to feel confident. In all our practice, however, we had never stepped on a golf course to play.

We had been in Bermuda for barely a day when the golf schedule was posted. Just as I'd feared: Phil and I were scheduled to tee off with Tom White, the president of telephone operations—who I knew was an excellent golfer.

"Don't worry," Phil said as we walked over to the course, verbally rehearsing everything we'd learned. I, at least, had proper clothes: long tan shorts and a white top. Phil was wearing short shorts that looked great on Rainier in summer but were definitely not regulation golf attire. "We just have to get a good shot off the first tee. Just keep your head down, don't take your eye off that ball, and swing for the fences."

Oh boy, I thought, *what pressure!*

When we got to the tee there was a gallery of about fifty people watching. I tried to save face by telling Tom that neither of us had played before, and he politely told us not to worry. *That's what you're saying now,* I thought. Phil teed off before I did. He smacked the ball right down the center of the fairway. *Yes!* I jumped up and down. But when my turn came I felt the pressure even more. I bent over the ball, recited all the elements of proper stance, and prayed, *Let me at least hit the ball!* Incredibly, I hit it right down the middle too. Tom looked at us and raised his eyebrows as if to say, "Yeah, right, you haven't played before!" But neither of us hit another worthwhile shot the rest of the round.

That fall, October 1996, we got married in a small ceremony at Salish Lodge—the same place where we had said our good-byes four years earlier, before I thought I'd lost Phil to Mt. McKinley. It was funny to recall that time, and all the unexpected places our relationship had taken me since then. When it was time to sign the marriage certificate, Greg Linwick and John Waechter signed as our witnesses, Greg as best man and John as my "maid" of honor. Then Greg, who is not generally prone to poetry or to deep expressions of emotion, recited a toast he had written:

What brings these souls, their lives to share,
And draws our joyous witness bear?
I cannot presume to speak for all,
But what I hear as common call
Is not the lure of strenuous pace
To some high, remote, majestic place,
But two in whom each other see,
Love, respect, and honesty,
And magnify in one another
Enthusiasm for life unlike any other.

The only thing I could have added was that—unexpectedly and against the craziest odds—we had each found our soul mate.

If getting married made me think back to the beginning of my relationship with Phil, it also prompted me to look forward to my future with GTE. The job as regional sales manager was everything I had hoped it would be. It offered new challenges and variety, great customers and colleagues, even a corner office. My team and I were riding high, having surpassed our $50 million quota. But I could also see that I had gone as far as I could go. If I wanted to advance in management my only option was to move to GTE headquarters in Dallas, and that was something I was unwilling to do. I was mulling this dilemma in the back of my mind when I was recruited by my own competition. It just so happened that my brother Dave was working at U S West and knew Bill Waters, the director of sales for the Northwest. Bill told Dave that he was getting tired of losing sales to me and my teams, and Dave told him to call me. So Bill called and made me an offer that included prospects for advancement, and on the last day of 1997 I moved to U S West with the same title I'd had at GTE.

I had been there for six months when Bill invited Phil to the company to make a presentation, which was something

Phil did from time to time: Companies (usually those of his customers) would bring him in, and he would show slides and describe his climbs. Inevitably audiences were wowed. They found the climbing exotic and unimaginable, and at the same time it inspired them. Invariably people would come up afterward and thank him for giving them the courage to pursue their dreams. Watching him, I'd often thought that I'd like to make presentations that encouraged people to pursue their dreams. I had always been too busy to take the idea seriously, although my favorite part of my own job was working with my teams, helping them clarify and reach their goals.

Now I sat in the back of the room as Phil wrapped up his presentation. He ended with a quote from Robert Frost: "My object in living is to unite my avocation and vocation as my two eyes make one in sight." As I listened I thought back to that day at Sun Valley when I had first met Phil's climbing buddies, and remembered my revelation about how they had turned their passion into their career. Suddenly I felt a twinge of regret. For more than twenty years my work had been challenging, fun, rewarding—everything I could have wanted in a career. In the last few years, however, I had become ready for a change. I wanted time for travel, time for climbing, more time to spend with Phil. I didn't want to stop working, or even working hard, but I wanted more balance in my life. And I wanted to turn my passion into my career.

• • •

In June 1998 I led a climb to Mt. McKinley. My assistant was a twenty-one-year-old guide named Chris Hooyman. I didn't know Chris well, but I had worked with him half a dozen times on Rainier and knew he was exactly the kind of guide I wanted with me: outgoing and enthusiastic, a strong climber, and great with the customers. He was also excited about climbing McKinley, which he had never done, and I was excited about taking him there for the first time.

We had been climbing for four days when a back problem forced one of our customers to go down. We decided Chris would take him, and I told Chris that he could stay down if he wanted to. The three remaining customers were strong; there were other guided parties in the area; I could manage on my own. But Chris wanted to climb, and a day later he rejoined us at 11,000 feet. In the following days, all five of us summited.

On the morning of June 6 we headed down from high camp at 17,000 feet. Our route would take us down the West Buttress, a steep exposed ridge with a drop of 2,000 feet on the right-hand side. Spirits were high; we were looking forward to the hot showers and cold beer that were forty-eight hours away. As we picked our way down the ridge, however, the wind picked up and I began to get uneasy. The wind would make it hard to keep our balance on the narrow trail, and I didn't want to take a chance on someone going over the edge. So Chris and I huddled and decided the safest thing was to go back to 17,000, reestablish camp, and wait another day. The next morning conditions improved, so once again we broke camp, roped up in a five-man team, and headed down. I went first, picking the route and setting protection, and Chris walked in back, watching the clients. I was feeling good: The weather was decent, the team was strong, and in the unlikely event that someone fell, Chris and I would be strong enough to stop him.

Ten minutes into our descent the wind picked up—exactly what had happened the day before. I leaned into the mountain away from the exposed drop and began to wonder if we should turn around again. I had just draped a sling over a horn of rock, put a carabiner on the sling, and clipped the rope to the carabiner so that the rock would hold us if we all fell, when the man behind me slipped. I turned. He was lying on his belly in ice axe arrest position, but with his heavy pack he was having trouble getting up. He was 25 feet behind me, but because I was holding the belay, I couldn't go up to help. A second later I heard a scream, and out of the corner of my eye I saw a form hurtling down the buttress. *Good thing I just put in this running belay because if that person doesn't stop himself at least I've got him,* I thought, and braced myself for the tug. But it never came. Puzzled, I looked up toward the rest of the team. The spot behind the last customer was empty. At the side of the trail, halfway between where Chris had been standing and the fallen customer, Chris's ice axe was stuck pick down in the snow in perfect ice axe arrest position.

I stared at the empty spot. Chris had unroped to help the customer and gone off the side of the mountain. I wanted to look for him immediately, but I couldn't; first I had to get the clients to a safe spot. So I turned us around and headed back to 17,000 feet, where we could reestablish camp. It was too windy, and we moved too fast, to talk. At the campsite I got them started setting up the tents, then grabbed extra rope. When I got back to the spot where Chris had fallen, Kyle Hillman and Jeff Ward, two other Rainier guides, had already set an anchor and were tying ropes together so I could rappel down the slope. The weather had deteriorated badly and the visibility was next to nothing; unless Chris was within 25 feet I wouldn't be able to see him. I went over the edge and down 400 feet, but there was no sign, so I jumared back up. While I'd been down, Kyle and Jeff had gotten more rope and now Jeff and I went down together. As we approached 600 feet, the wind became so fierce that we got knocked around just hanging on to the fixed rope. After twenty minutes we went back up. In those conditions, searching more would be pointless. We'd come back tomorrow when we hoped the weather would be better. But we both knew without saying it: There was no way Chris could come out of this alive.

The storm raged through the night. The wind and visibility were so bad that people got lost at the campsite. A man from another team staggered into our tent and stayed because he couldn't find his own. In a way I was thankful for the wind. With the customers stranded in their own tents I was spared the anguish of talking to them. I knew that was wrong—I knew they needed me now as much as they ever needed me while climbing, but I was too lost in my own torment to help them with theirs.

By early morning the weather had improved and the wind had died dramatically. My good friend Romulo Cardenas, with whom I had long guided in Ecuador, went with me back to the site. We rappelled down to the end of the rope, 600 or 700 feet below the trail, and although visibility was good, we saw no sign of Chris so we jumared back to the top. Park rangers and another guide would come with more rope, which would permit them to search farther, but we had done all we could do. Now we needed to get the customers down.

Five days later the customers and I were in Talkeetna getting ready to drive to Anchorage for the flight home when word came that a search helicopter had spotted Chris's body on the Peters Glacier, 2,000 feet below the trail. The Park Service needed someone to identify the body, so I put the customers in the van and waited in Talkeetna. I hadn't known Chris well when we began the climb, but two weeks sharing a tent will bond two people. We'd had a lot of time to talk, a lot of time to discover all the ways we were alike and all that we had in common. Opening the body bag was the most painful thing I had ever done. I had always thought that no climbing death would ever be harder than Marty's, but I was wrong. As close as I had been to Marty, she and I had been equal members of a team. But on McKinley I was in charge. And although I told myself a thousand times that there was nothing I could have done, I couldn't absolve myself of guilt.

Back in Seattle I met with Chris's family. I had never met the family, but I knew from our conversations in the tent that it was a lot like mine—loving, supportive, close. They were very kind to me. There was no hint of blame. They wanted to hear the facts of the accident, what Chris had been thinking, how he had been the day before, and I tried to tell them everything in detail. They showed me a letter he had written in which he said how much he liked guiding with me, that I treated him like a partner, not an underling; that we'd equally shared responsibilities and chores. It pleased me to read that, to see that my feelings for Chris were returned, but it only heightened my grief.

A week later the family held a memorial. People came from all parts of Chris's life: friends from Stanford where he went to college, from his high school in Seattle, from the cycling team he'd raced with and the outdoor education program for which he'd volunteered. They offered personal stories and reflections of their time with Chris, and several read poems that Chris had written. Almost all the poems had been written in the wilderness. One was printed on the inside cover of the memorial program.

My Choice
I chose the hard life
One of toil and strife,
But I loved every minute for sure.
I loved the tall cliff
And the bottomless drift
Because I found life's only cure.
I found that hard work
Is where success lurks
And that sweat is my special path.
It's the river that flows
To where I will go
And, well, a few might laugh.
But I know it's true
Because I found a clue
On the bounds of what some call insane.
I call this place home
And it's where I'll roam
Until He comes and smothers my flame.

Until that sad day
All I can say
Is that I love the man I became.
    By Chris Hooyman, age 16

• • •

When Phil got back from McKinley he looked like a refugee. He had a lost look in his eyes, and he seemed perpetually on the verge of tears. He couldn't concentrate on anything; the details of putting together his next trip—things he'd done hundreds of times—eluded him, and he had trouble sleeping and eating. When he took his shirt off he was all bones. His partner George Dunn acknowledged that Phil was the worst person this could have happened to because of how responsible he would feel. We spent long hours talking, and I must have told him a thousand times it wasn't his fault. He would repeat it back, but in his heart I knew he didn't believe it. The sensible part of me said he just needed time, but I didn't see how he would ever be able to be happy again.

Gradually, as the weeks went by, we talked about it less. Phil led several climbs on Rainier that summer and prepared for a November climb of Mt. Vinson, the tallest mountain in Antarctica, where I would accompany him. By early fall, however, I noticed that he was hunching over after meals. Each time I asked about it, he told me he was fine, but I knew he wasn't. He was having a flare-up. Phil didn't like to burden me with his health problems, and I knew he would tell me more only when he felt I really needed to know. By October his skin had turned an ashen gray and he had no energy. He went to see Dr. Marty Greene, his gastroenterologist, who told him he had anemia and put him on iron. Within a few weeks he seemed visibly better.

On November 18, 1998, we left Seattle for Antarctica.

*   *   *

Antarctica! Just getting there was an adventure—flying first to Punta Arenas, Chile, the very tip of South America, and then, in a C-130 cargo plane, 2,000 miles farther to Patriot Hills, just 600 miles from the South Pole. I'd seen pictures of the endless ice and the midnight daylight, and I was eager (if a little nervous) to see them for myself. I was also excited because Vinson would be our fifth of the Seven Summits. I had told Phil my hope of doing all seven and he'd rolled his eyes the way he does when he thinks I'm chasing a pipe dream, but after Aconcagua, I didn't think it was that unreasonable. He himself admitted that I'd done fine at 23,000 feet, and he said he believed I could climb higher. Kosciuszko in Australia, he'd said, was "a walk in the park." That left Everest. Phil didn't even have to roll his eyes at that one. He just looked at me for a long second and went right back to what he was doing. I didn't take that as a no. He was *almost* as goal-oriented as I was, and I just had a feeling that by the time we knocked off Vinson and Kosciuszko, he might warm up to the idea.

On November 25 we landed on the ice at Vinson base camp. It was like landing on the moon. There was no vegetation, no color, no living creatures—nothing but ice as far as the eye could see. We set up our tents—bright spots of color in the all-white world—and Phil taped a photo over the door of his tent at the same base camp in 1992 with a photo of me in a bikini pinned above the door. Now he'd brought the photo-of-the-photo back to where he'd shot it. It was funny to see me in a bikini in the middle of all that ice, and it gave us all a good laugh.

From day one the conditions were difficult—windy and bitter cold. If I put on enough layers to stave off the chill I sweltered as soon as I began to climb, but if I omitted a layer in anticipation of the heat, I froze as I tried to walk. At "night"—which looked identical to day—Phil taught me to put my down parka under my sleeping bag on top of my two foam pads, but even so, the cold infiltrated my bones and I woke up freezing.

As we climbed higher onto the mountain and the view opened up to the lowland below, we found ourselves looking out over vast fields of fog broken occasionally by snow-covered rocky crags. But it wasn't fog; it was ice, flat and unbroken to the horizon. Back in Punta we had heard about a Japanese man who was trekking from the edge of Antarctica to the South Pole, toe- and fingerless from frostbite, dragging a sled that weighed 400 pounds. It was eerie to know he was out there somewhere in all that ice. On Thanksgiving Day we used a saw to cut blocks of snow and built ourselves a kitchen. Phil cooked turkey stew out of a can, and we made long, detailed, mouthwatering lists of all the foods we could have been eating with our families.

Despite the discomfort, Antarctica was magical: otherworldly, pristine, and *silent*. Other than the wind and the crunching of our crampons, there was no noise. When the wind abated and we stopped for a break, I thought I had never been in a place of such peace.

On day seven we climbed to high camp. Along the way we passed a perfect pyramid of a mountain.

"You know what that's called?" Phil hollered over the wind. "Sue's Pyramid!"

I laughed.

"It's true," he said. "Since 1992 that's what I've told all my clients. There are at least fifty people in the world who think it says that on the map."

During the climb I had a lot of time to think, and what I mostly thought about—what I had been thinking about tirelessly since Phil's U S West presentation—was the idea of moving into public speaking, the idea of building a career in which I helped inspire people to achieve their dreams. Sometimes the idea seemed completely viable. My team members had achieved sales goals far in excess of what they'd imagined, and when I first started in sales I hadn't believed I could sell a thing, yet here I was, a top performer. I thought businesses might find me credible enough to talk to their employees. And then there was my success at climbing. Who ever thought I could climb enormous mountains? Yet, with Phil's coaching, I had. I knew that women without my business background had parlayed success in the mountains into corporate speaking careers. So wasn't it reasonable to think I could do the same? But, invariably, I'd get that far in my thinking and then the other side of my brain would kick in. *Get real, Sue,* it would say, *you've spent over twenty years getting to where you are; would you really walk away from your career?*

On December 3, in a twelve-hour day, we reached the summit of Vinson. The sun was so strong that with all the heavy breathing, I burned the inside of my mouth on the reflection from the ice. But who cared? We'd made it! We'd stood on the top of the bottom of the world! The next day Phil pushed us relentlessly to get back down and I thought, *Jeez, Phil, what's your hurry?* But when we got to Patriot Hills we just made it on to the Hercules flight to Punta Arenas. The group behind us had to wait a week for a break in the weather. The heater in the plane malfunctioned and it was the longest, coldest all-night flight, but I curled up in my down parka and laid my head on Phil's shoulder, warm with pleasure. We'd done Vinson. Now there were just two to go: Kosciuszko and Everest.

• • •

Mt. Vinson was a turning point in my thinking. Sue had mentioned the Seven Summits numerous times and I knew she was set on doing it, but I had serious reservations. For one thing, I was not certain of her ability. Aconcagua had persuaded me that she could handle high altitudes, but there was a difference between 23,000 feet and 29,000, and if Sue thought Everest was going to be anything like Aconcagua, she had another think coming. For another thing, I had put the Himalayas in the rearview mirror back in 1990, and my thinking hadn't changed since then. Plus, I wondered if Sue really understood what was involved in pulling an Everest expedition together. The time, the money, and the logistics required to outfit and support a climbing team for three months in seriously inhospitable conditions on the other side of the world were not something you took on lightly. There was also the matter of responsibility. If I took Sue and a few others to Everest I wouldn't be just one of the climbers, I would be the guide, and as good as Sue and I were together in the mountains, I didn't want to be dealing with her three brothers if anything happened! Underneath the joke, it was no laughing matter.

Nevertheless, I couldn't help but notice that I seemed to be putting the ducks in a row. I had traded professional favors to get Sue on the $16,000 flight to Patriot Hills so we could climb Mt. Vinson, and less than a month later I made sure she joined me in Australia for a climb of Kosciuszko. I wasn't thinking Everest—well, I was thinking maybe we'd just trek in to base camp—but you never knew what might happen. And, *just in case,* I didn't want some anticlimactic "walk in the park" to be number seven.

By the time we came back from Kosciuszko, Everest was a done deal in Sue's mind. To bring me around she put John Waechter on me. John had also done six of the seven summits, most of them with us, and was as determined as Sue to climb Everest. He and Sue had a little competition going; there was no way one of them was going to get there without the other. They hammered me every chance they got, and every time I said, "Forget it. It ain't gonna happen." But inside I could feel myself soften. I could see for myself the biggest reason to do it: I needed to do it for Sue. One of the founding principles of our relationship, the one I had learned when we bought the land for our house and that had subsequently gotten us through other difficult decisions, was the practice of asking, "To whom does this matter more?" In this case, it was clear that Everest mattered more to Sue than it did to me. I could see how much she wanted the summit, and next to that, my desire not to do it paled. How could I not make it happen?

So in May 1999 we began officially pulling an Everest expedition together. We solidified the team: Sue, me, John, and Andy Lufkin, who had climbed with us on McKinley. We planned the financing, secured the permit, and I arranged for Sherpa support. We began the negotiations and planning that would enable us to be gone from March through May of 2000, and we all began serious, systematic training. None of us had any reason to suspect that everything was about to go wrong.

Phil, wrestler in training, age 15

Phil and his good friend and climbing partner, Greg Linwick, late 1970s

Marty Hoey has the biggest
tombstone in the world
(JIM WICKWIRE)

"My father, Arthur Ershler, the man who taught me how to be a man"—*Phil*

"It was my honor to carry Chris Kerrebrock's trumpet mouthpiece to the summit of Mt. Everest in 1984"—*Phil*

"Getting my ticket punched: my self-portrait on the summit of Everest, 1984"—*Phil*

Phil returning to high camp from the summit of Mt. Everest, 1984 (JIM WICKWIRE)

Phil greeting his mother, father, and sister, Margaret, on his return to Seattle from Everest, 1984 (MIKE BAINTER, SEATTLE POST-INTELLIGENCER, NOVEMBER 1984)

Phil working his way up the
icy north side of
Kangchenjunga, 1989
(GEORGE DUNN)

"Growing up with three older brothers taught me how to survive. David, Roy (Dad), me, Mary (Mom), Mike, and Jerry Ellerman"—*Sue*

"My good friend Nan Lund led me to John Whetzell who introduced me to Phil"—*Sue*

"My boating life before Phil"—*Sue*

"Sue" on the summit of
Vinson Massif in
Antarctica, 1992

Phil's clients generously
donate desks to the Chagga
school children in Tanzania

Sue sharing a drink
with our climbing
friends, Sasha and
Igor, in Russia, 1993

Dick Bass, the first person to climb the Seven
Summits, and Sue in Antarctica, 1998

Sharing a great view on Aconcagua, 1996
(ANDREA FAVILLI)

Together on the
top of the bottom
of the world,
Antarctica, 1998
(Andrea Favilli)

John Waechter, Andy
Lufkin, and Sue descending
the summit ridge of Mt.
McKinley, 1995

Looking down on "Sue's
Pyramid" in Antarctica. What
looks like clouds is actually ice—
as far as the eye can see, 1998

Celebrating Phil's 400th climb of Mt. Rainier with Everest legends
Nawang Gombu and Jim Whittaker, 2001

Our 2001 Everest team, Phil, Sue, John Waechter, Greg Wilson, and Charlie Peck
(CHARLIE PECK)

Memorials dedicated to lives lost on Everest

Our *puja* altar and the Khumbu Icefall, Everest, 2001

Looking down to America! Everest, 2001
(CHARLIE PECK)

Phil's frozen eyes, Everest, 2001

Phil climbing above the "bottomless
hole," Everest, 2002

Crossing the final
crevasse before Camp 2,
Everest, 2001
(CHARLIE PECK)

Climbing Sherpas
Dorjee and Dawa,
upon returning to
high camp,
Everest, 2001

Turning our backs on a dream,
Everest, 2001
(CHARLIE PECK)

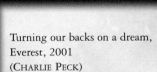

The dream came true:
the summit of
Mt. Everest, 2002

Relief after descending
the Lhotse Face,
Everest, 2002

"Phil Ershler, my
mentor, my hero,
my guide"—*Sue*

Sue sharing the moment with three Nepalese school girls, 2002

Another dream realized: signing the board at the Rum Doodle, Kathmandu, 2002

The wedding of our friends in Ecuador, Romulo and Patricia, 2005 (JULIAN LARREA)

October 1999

Dear Susan—
Not exactly the way we expected to spend our third anniversary. I promise, I will make this up to you.

You've been incredible. I never could get through this without you. When I said "no regrets" last month, I meant that I didn't regret anything I've done in the way I've lived my life, especially that I met & fell in love with you.

You're my rock & *my* mentor.

Love,
Phil

October 1999

Phil,
"Sunshine *always* follows rain" and (as George Dunn says) "good weather *always* follows bad." Our good healthy times are just ahead. We are *still* on a roll, just hit a bump temporarily.

I love you so much!
Sue

6

EVEREST DREAMS FADE

That whole fall of 1998 before we left for Antarctica I was exhausted. I spent a large part of each day dozing, unable to get out of bed. I passed it off as too little sleep, a long season on Rainier, lingering stress from Chris's death, but underneath I had a feeling it might be something more. If Sue hadn't been going on the climb, I might have ignored those symptoms, let someone else guide in my place, waited for the exhaustion to pass, but she was excited about going and I was excited about taking her, and I needed to make sure I was in a position to do so. So I went in for an exam with Marty Greene. Dr. Greene listened to my symptoms, ordered blood work, and suggested a colonoscopy. When I mentioned that I had been having trouble eating, he also recommended an endoscopy to make sure the opening between my stomach and small intestine hadn't narrowed. "That's fine," I joked, as if he were going to use the same tube for both exams, "just make sure you do the endoscopy first!" As usual, I didn't tell Sue; I didn't want her to worry.

I was waking up after the exams when the attending nurse asked me who was driving me home. I told her I planned to sit around for a couple of hours until the anesthesia wore off and then drive myself. "I don't think so!" she said. We were "discussing" my transportation when Marty walked by. "No way, Phil!" he said when he heard the conversation. "I'll take you home with me." So he took me to his house and over dinner explained what he'd seen. My stomach was healthy but my colon was badly inflamed. He adjusted the medication I was already taking and suggested I schedule two infusions of a new drug for Crohn's. Two days later he called with the results of my blood work: I was seriously anemic. He didn't have to tell me what that meant for Vinson. With my red cells so depleted, there was no way I could take Sue to Antarctica. Dr. Greene put me on iron and said that if I didn't feel better in two weeks he would authorize a transfusion, upping my red cells by adding a pint of new blood. After two weeks I wasn't exactly 100 percent, but I was confident I could get by without a transfusion and would do okay on the mountain.

"All right, but I want you back in January," Marty said. "I want to check your blood and take another look at your colon."

By the time we got home from Vinson I was feeling almost back to normal. We'd had a good climb. Sue had done great, and it was easy to think that the bad times in the fall had been just another flare-up. But I couldn't completely shake the suspicion that something else was wrong: Things had been too bad for too long. When I went back to Marty in January, the follow-up colonoscopy confirmed my fears. It revealed cell changes known as dysplasia, a precursor to cancer.

"You really ought to think about an elective resection of your bowel," Marty said. "Get the diseased portion cut out. You'll lose a few feet of intestine, but it's not doing you any good anyway. We can piece the rest of you back together, and you'll have enough left to have reasonably normal bowel function." He told me about a patient with a similar situation who ignored his advice—and then came back two years later when it was too late to do much for him.

Either way, I was looking at getting cut. The demon in whose shadow I had lived for thirty years had awakened.

"I'll do it," I said, "but not till after Everest." I figured colon cancer grew slowly; I had plenty of time. And for the first time in months, I was feeling fine. How could I choose to get filleted?

"Get it done now," Marty countered. "You're fit; you'll

bounce right back. In six weeks you'll be healed and still have six months to train before the climb."

I wanted to believe him. But call it sixth sense, or maybe just my old fear of the slippery slope, I didn't trust it would be that easy. For thirty years I'd had reasonable success at beating down the disease. I had been strong and active and had achieved many of my dreams, but in the back of my mind I had always known that my will and my luck were ultimately no match for time. I knew the usual course of the disease meant I would probably get cut and cut again, and I was afraid.

Marty knew me well enough not to insist, but as the winter progressed and I led my usual South American climbs, he stayed on me, urging me to have it done *now*. Finally I went for a second opinion. I trusted Marty implicitly but I needed someone to tell me that I could at least wait until after Everest. I didn't get what I wanted. The second doctor was more direct and even less willing to listen to me talk about the Himalayas. "Heck," he said, "you probably already have cancer—just not in the sections they biopsied." Unlike Marty, who had known me for so long, he wanted to remove my entire colon, probably leaving me with a colostomy bag, to prevent a recurrence. He wanted to protect my life at the expense of my lifestyle, not understanding that, for me, they were one and the same.

I dreaded telling Susan. I hadn't told her about the dysplasia or Marty's recommendation because I didn't want her to worry, but now that surgery was unavoidable she needed to know. I hated laying that on her. I wasn't worried about her reaction; I knew she would understand. It was my own feeling I was dreading. I hated letting her down. All my life I'd tried to be physically and mentally strong for others. Perhaps it was a male thing, perhaps I'd spent too much time in macho Latin America, but she was my wife and I wanted to be strong for her. I didn't want to be a burden. On an even deeper level lurked a darker fear: if I became the one who needed help, would I ever stop being helpless?

One evening in July I sat her down on the couch and told her I had "a little issue" I had to deal with. I described my conversations with Marty and my decision to go ahead with the surgery. I kept my tone light, as I had in the tent on Kilimanjaro, because that helped mask my discomfort. When I got to the end, Sue looked me right in the eye.

"Well, we'll do whatever we have to do," she said simply. "You've beaten this thing before and now we'll beat it together."

I appreciated that word "we."

Shortly after, I took her with me to see Marty. He showed her pictures and explained the issues, and on the way home we discussed the timing. I was still thinking about waiting till after Everest, but Sue was adamant. "We're going to Everest," she said, "but you're getting this done first." So we scheduled the surgery for the middle of August, seven months before we planned to leave. Three days later I told John and Andy, assuring them this wouldn't jeopardize our climb. But underneath, I was far less certain. The surgery had brought into focus what I had probably been feeling for a while without admitting it. I would need to be *stronger* than I'd been when I summited Everest in '84 because in addition to getting myself up the mountain, I would need extra reserves to help Sue, John, and Andy. A climber's performance declines between ages forty and fifty and I would be forty-nine, and Chris's death as well as my own health had reminded me that I was not invincible. Perhaps more than I wanted to admit, my confidence was badly shaken.

• • •

I was surprised when Phil took me to Marty Greene's. He had always been private about his health issues, like a dog going into his den to lick his wounds, and I respected that. That was the way he needed to be. So in July when he asked me to go with him to Marty's I felt I was being admitted to the inner sanctum. After seeing Marty I got scared. He showed us pictures of Phil's colon—most of it was red and shriveled and useless—and although he was confident they could remove the diseased part and preserve enough to keep Phil functional and active, he ran through the litany of things that can happen during major abdominal surgery. Afterwards I couldn't stop myself from running the "what ifs" in my head: What if there's not enough left? What if there are complications? What if he needs a colostomy bag? What if he can't climb? What if he can't guide? The thoughts were so terrifying that I put them away. No sense going there now.

Driving home from Marty's, Phil said, "I don't want anyone to know."

"I know."

"No," he said, "I mean no one. Not even your friends."

"Not even my friends?" I looked at him, startled. "What am I supposed to tell them when they ask how you are?"

"I don't care what you tell them. They don't need to know."

His tone was so brusque, so uncharacteristically angry. I knew how much privacy meant to him, but how could I not tell my friends? "But Phil . . ."

"This isn't their business. They don't need to know."

I turned away and looked out the window. Mt. Rainier was visible in the distance. From here it had a picture-postcard flatness, none of the freezing, heart-pounding reality it had when I'd climbed it. How could I argue? It was his body, his health. I had to respect his wishes. I traced the contours of the mountain with my eyes, trying to pinpoint familiar landmarks, and as I did I thought of something that had happened that first time I climbed. We had stopped at our highest break and were all sitting on our packs trying to catch our breath, when one of the customers leaned over and threw up. I didn't know then that people often throw up at that spot because of the altitude, so I was surprised when, instead of offering solace, Phil said, "There! Don't you feel better now? When I get that stuff out of my system I'm ready to go!" "Phil," I whispered, "shouldn't we do something?" But he had answered, "Nope. If you treat a person like an invalid they'll become an invalid." At the time I'd thought that was pretty hardhearted. What I realized now was that he had been talking about himself.

We drove for a while in silence and then another thought occurred to me. "We have to tell our parents."

"No."

"Phil! We have to tell them."

"It will only worry them. They don't need to know."

"They're our parents!"

"When they need to know, they'll know."

And when will that *be?* I thought. *When it's all over! That's not fair to them.* "Well, we at least need to tell Fran," I said. I knew if push came to shove, I *would* tell my parents, but we couldn't not tell Phil's mom.

He didn't even bother to answer. He just stared hard at the road.

Twice more in the next few days I tried to persuade him to tell his mom. Both times I met the same stone-faced refusal.

Fortunately, once Phil decided to go ahead with the surgery, he scheduled it quickly. *Good,* I thought, *the sooner, the better. Once it's over, I'll be able to talk to someone about it.* But as the day approached, I couldn't wait. I had to tell my parents. After Phil, they were my major support system, and I needed them to know. "Hey," I said when I got them on the phone, "I just wanted you to know—Phil's going into the hospital for a few days, no big deal, just elective surgery. He's going to have a portion of his colon removed, and he'll be out in about five days." I realized I was minimizing it to them just as he did to me—and probably for the same reason: I didn't want them to worry. They empathized, reminded me that my aunt had had the same surgery just a few years earlier, and managed to make it seem almost routine. Of course, I swore them to secrecy—I knew they would never tell anyone—and afterwards, if part of me felt a twinge of guilt about "betraying" Phil, the larger part was glad I had done it. Sharing it made me feel less alone.

Two days later we were driving to the hospital when Phil took my hand. "You know," he said, "you're probably going to need some support through this. It's okay if you want to tell your parents."

. . .

When I woke up in the recovery room I hurt so badly. That should have been my first clue that things would not go as smoothly as we'd hoped. I had expected to be in pain but this was a whole different level from what I'd expected. Up in my room they hooked me up to morphine-on-demand. Each time I pressed the button the machine shot morphine into my IV, and this time, unlike when I was sixteen, I didn't hesitate. I would have used more if the machine had let me. Over the next few days the pain didn't quit. Sue brought me a pillow that we'd bought in India, and I lay with it pressed against my stomach. The constant pressure was the only thing that took the edge off the aching.

The day after the surgery they got me up to walk. Sue pushed the IV and I leaned on her and the pole. Bent over like an eighty-year-old man, I made it halfway down the hall and back. My vision of walking out of the hospital forty-eight hours after surgery crumpled. The following day they urged me to do two laps around the floor. I pushed the pole through one whole circuit, then took a shortcut through the nurses' station back to my room. I heard Sue telling the nurses that I really *had* climbed Everest. If I'd had a sense of humor I might have laughed. The next day, and the next, and then the one after that I made the same painful circuit of the seventh floor. All around me, old men recovering from similar surgeries were walking upright, pushing their IVs, doing better than I was. That should have been the second clue that something was wrong, but we just assumed that this was the normal course of healing.

. . .

When they wheeled Phil up to his room on the seventh floor he seemed to have tubes everywhere. He was drenched with sweat, his face was tight with pain, and even when they started him on morphine, the pain didn't subside. I mopped his forehead with cold washcloths, one after another. That evening Dr. Steven Medwell, the surgeon, came in. "Good news," he said. "We didn't see any signs of cancer. We'll get the pathology report in a few days but the organ looks clean."

Cancer? Phil and Marty had never said anything about cancer. "I didn't know they were looking for cancer," I said when Dr. Medwell left.

"Yeah, well . . . that's always . . . a possibility," Phil said, his words clipped as if it were hard to speak through the pain. "Good to know . . . it's not an issue."

I spent the first night of Phil's hospitalization sleeping on a cot in his room. The second night he urged me to go home to get a better night's sleep. I promised to be back first thing in the morning. The next morning I got up at dawn, did a quick run, then drove over to the hospital. When I entered the room Phil looked at me with glassy eyes.

"The doctor came by earlier," he said in a flat voice. "I have cancer."

"But—"

"They think it's contained."

He couldn't have cancer! They hadn't seen any signs of cancer!

"They still need to get the final pathology on the lymph nodes."

I needed to get out of there. I couldn't let him see me cry.

He needed me to be strong, not to upset him and make things worse. I ran out into the corridor past nurses wheeling breakfast carts and into the elevator. On the first floor I wove through the crowd until I found a secluded alcove. There I curled up against the wall and sobbed. No! There can't be cancer! How could I have left him alone to hear that by himself? When I thought I could contain myself I called my parents, but the minute I heard my mother's voice I fell apart again. Finally, I pulled myself together and said, "He's got cancer," and then I couldn't talk again.

"I'm so sorry, Sue. I'm so, so sorry." There was nothing else for her to say. But she held me with her voice until I was ready to go back upstairs.

Phil lay in bed, his eyes still glazed.

"What does it mean?" I asked. What I thought was, *Please, please, don't let him die!*

He told me the doctor had said it had probably not spread beyond the colon and that there was a good chance they had gotten it all, although there was no way to know for sure. They had sent the pathology report of his lymph nodes to an outside expert and were waiting to hear back. I held Phil's hand and swallowed my tears.

Three days later Phil was released. I walked next to him as the nurse wheeled him to the entrance, and as I looked at the corridors and the lobby that had become so familiar, I realized that I was not saying good-bye, but rather making a plan. I was plotting where I would eat in the future, which running paths I could take to vary my run from the hospital entrance, how perhaps I could find a conference room where I could work for extended periods. I was so happy and relieved that Phil was going home, but inside some quiet voice already knew that we would be coming back.

We settled Phil at home as best we could—the pain was still unremitting—and he was sitting on the couch when Marty called. The lymph nodes were clear. As far as they could tell, they had gotten it all. There was no guarantee it would not return, but for now there was nothing else he needed to do.

Phil had been released with instructions to walk as much as possible. Fortunately, the weather was good and every day he went outside, the Indian pillow clutched to his stomach, concealed by a jacket draped over his arm. But he could barely make it around the block before the pain became so intense that he had to go back inside. When he'd been home about a week we went to his mother's house for dinner. He still had not told her about the surgery and now, as he hobbled up the steps, I thought to myself, *What is going through his mind? He's walking like an invalid; does he think she's not going to notice?*

Sure enough, Fran opened the door, took one look at him, and said, "What happened?"

"I had a little surgery," Phil said.

She swept him with her eyes—his bent posture, the pain-tightened face—and her own face filled, first with fear and then, for the first time since I'd known her, anger. But then to my horror, she looked right at me. "What were you thinking?" she practically hissed. "He could have died in there!"

I wanted to die myself. How many times had I told him? I love Fran; she is one of the warmest, most loving women in the world, and she and I have always been close. Now it killed me to feel I had betrayed her. "I promised him I wouldn't say anything," I said feebly.

She turned and looked at Phil. For the first time, I heard her speak to him in anger. "Why didn't you tell me?"

"I didn't want to worry you."

"I'm your mother!"

He baby-stepped into the house. I was almost afraid to follow.

In the living room Phil settled himself on the couch, grabbing a pillow and pressing it to his stomach the way he did at home. He tried to make it look as if the pillow were a fashion accessory rather than a lifesaver, but Fran obviously could see the truth. She opened her mouth, but before she could utter a word he told her about the surgery. He minimized it, of course, leaving out any mention of cancer and downplaying his persistent pain.

When he finished she looked more concerned than angry. "You know, I can handle these things," she said, looking at both of us. "You don't need to protect me."

Phil nodded in a way that said we had reached the end of the discussion.

Fran got up to serve dinner and I went into the kitchen to help. Contritely, I pulled out the serving spoons and carried dishes to the table, feeling about two feet tall. I thought she would chastise me for not telling her, but instead she pumped me for more information, wanting to hear the details she knew Phil would never supply. Phil had told me under no circumstances to mention the "c" word, so I told her as much as I could without mentioning cancer. I listened through her words for signs of her continuing anger, but she seemed to hold no ongoing grievance toward either me or Phil. Just before we called Phil to dinner she said, "I wish Phil wasn't afraid to tell me these things. Not knowing doesn't protect me."

"I told him that, Fran! I told him to tell you. But you know your son, you know how he is. He didn't want *anybody* to know."

"I know," she said. "Grin and bear it. Just like his father." She gave me a resigned smile.

Driving home I replayed every aspect of the dinner, looking for clues that our relationship was intact. I knew Fran still cared about me; after that unfortunate beginning she had been nothing but warm, but I prayed there would be no long-term scar. One thing I knew for sure, I would never go through that again. I looked over at Phil. In the late-summer twilight, there was just enough light in the car for me to read his expression. Despite the pain it seemed relaxed, as if he were relieved that the secret was out. "You know," I said, "if something like this ever happens again, we're telling her at the beginning."

"I don't think so!" But despite the fact that his gaze never left the road, a tiny smile lifted the corners of his mouth and eyes.

"Bite me," I said, and we drove the rest of the way home holding hands.

On September 3, Phil's ninth morning at home, I woke up to the sound of groaning. I rushed to the extra bedroom where, for greater comfort, he was sleeping. He was lying in the bed with his legs pulled up, holding his stomach. There was no way this was normal postoperative pain. "I'm calling 911."

"No."

"Then I'm calling Dr. Medwell."

"It's too early."

"Phil, I'm not waiting until eight-thirty to call someone." I ran to the other room, got the surgeon's number, and dialed. The after-hours service answered. I described the situation and finally, after ten minutes of anxious waiting, Medwell called.

"I know Phil can tolerate pain," he said. "If he's feeling that bad you better bring him to the office now."

With shuffling steps, we got Phil into the car. As I wove through the early-morning traffic he clutched the pillow and rocked back and forth, moaning. In the waiting room he pulled me by the sleeve and rasped, "Get . . . me . . . drugs!"

I went up to the receptionist and asked for pain medication.

"I'm sorry, but you'll have to wait for the doctor."

"We can't wait! You see how much pain he's in!"

She looked at me apologetically. "We really have to wait for Dr. Medwell."

When the doctor arrived he examined Phil for about five minutes, then told me to take him to the hospital. At Emergency an attendant loaded him into a wheelchair and wheeled him away.

When I found him on the seventh floor he was sitting on a bed in a private room, doubled over, arms pressed hard across his stomach, screaming through gritted teeth. It was an animal sound—as if you had taken an animal and twisted off its leg. He took one look at me and said, "Susan, get me drugs!" I ran out into the hall and cornered a nurse, who told me they had already ordered morphine. When I went back to the room, Phil was staring into the mirror opposite the bed, still making that horrible scream, staring at his own face as if trying to find some connection with another Phil who was not in such intolerable pain. Twice more I ran into the hall looking for the morphine, and finally a nurse arrived with an injection. But the first injection didn't touch it. It took a second, and then a third, before he began to get relief.

By that time, Dr. Medwell, Marty Greene, and a second surgeon had arrived. Phil was too out of it to pay attention, but I listened as they huddled. ". . . intestinal blockage . . . adhesions . . . relieve on its own? . . . surgery? . . . too risky . . . lose part of the small intestine . . . but he's a mountain climber . . ." I didn't understand the specifics but I could follow the thread. Phil must have a blockage or adhesions somewhere in his intestine, and while surgery would be the best treatment, the risk incurred in operating nine days after his previous surgery was high. But if they didn't operate, he might lose a major portion of the small intestine, and if that happened he couldn't climb. I listened, feeling numb and powerless, and screaming inside, *Please, please, please, don't make him unable to climb!* Finally they agreed: They would take him back to the operating room that afternoon.

"How do you do the surgery?" I asked.

"We just go right back in on the same incision," Dr. Medwell answered.

I felt my own insides twist. We had just spent nine days protecting that incision, doing everything we could to help it heal.

The doctors left, and I sat with Phil as his pain partially subsided. We were making the right decision; that seemed certain. But something else seemed equally clear: Things were not going the way they were supposed to. All the fear I had carried since my first visit to Marty's, and that Phil had borne since who-knew-when, came and sat with us in that room. In the overwhelming face of it there was very little to say. At one point I held his hand and said, "I don't care what you say. I'm calling both our parents."

This time he didn't argue.

. . .

Going into that surgery was like going into a tunnel I had chosen to enter, but from which I didn't know if I'd emerge. I held tightly to Sue's hand. I was scared.

There were still so many things I needed her to know. I needed her to know that no matter what happened, it would be okay. That we had done everything we could have. That we had shared everything there was to share. That we had been there for each other at every turn and that nothing was left unsaid.

I squeezed her hand three times. *I . . . love . . . you.* "No regrets," I said.

The rest was out of our hands.

I woke up from surgery and I was in pain—*normal* pain. I felt the difference immediately. This time things had gone *right*. Apparently my small intestine had twisted on itself and was strangulating—six more hours and it would have died—but they had successfully untwisted it and it would now be able to heal. They moved me back to the seventh floor, and the next day I took my first walk. I did a complete circuit of the hallway. For the first time in three weeks I felt my optimism return.

The following afternoon I was clicking around the TV stations when the resident who had assisted Dr. Medwell came to check my incision. He poked at it for a minute and then his face wrinkled into a frown. "Looks like this has gotten infected. We'll have to open it back up." And before I could even ask a question he pulled out what looked like a wire snip and began popping the staples that held my outer layer of skin together. From the corner of my eye I could see my abdomen slide open from below my belly button to just beneath my sternum. Underneath, the stitched-up wall of muscle and connective tissue was red and pulpy.

"Now we need to clean this out." As if he were gutting a fish, the resident stuck his thumb into the incision and ran it up and down between my skin and the underlying layers. Sue left the room and I looked away, every shred of optimism extinguished. The resident finished gutting me, washed his hands, and started to walk away.

"When do you sew this back together?"

"Actually, we need to leave it open to heal from the inside. We'll pack it with moist dressings that will get changed several times a day."

They were going to leave me wide open! I didn't even disguise my anger. "How long is this going to take to heal?"

"Six weeks or so."

"Oh crap!" I said just under my breath. Then I pounded the remote button and killed the TV. My future had become clear as mud; I was never going to get better.

The day before they were to release me a nurse came in and announced that it was time for me to shower.

No way! I thought. What was the point of taking a shower when I was tumbling down the slippery slope?

She removed the dressings so that my abdomen was wide open, my innards exposed to the world. "Come on," she said, "let's get you up."

I didn't move. I thought if I so much as budged, my guts would spill out over the floor.

"Here, I'll help you," said Sue, leaning in to support my upper body.

The nurse left, closing the door.

Sue looked at me with those tender but determined eyes. "It'll be okay, Phil. We can do this."

Reluctantly I let her put my arm around her shoulder and draw me to my feet. I kept both hands clutched to my stomach to catch my organs as they fell. Slowly we hobbled to the bathroom where she propped me against the wall while she ran the water. In the full-length mirror I saw my body: white, shrunken, open like a can of sardines. A shell of a man. Sue stepped into the shower with me and gently sprayed me with the hand hose. The water ran into and out of the incision.

"We can do this, Phil," she said softly, "we can do this."

It took everything I had not to cry.

. . .

The hardest thing, even harder than seeing him so sick, was seeing him so depressed. It was like Chris's death all over again, and it was difficult for me not to be pulled into his despair. But I couldn't go there. If I got demoralized, it would only reinforce his hopelessness. I needed to be positive for both of us. So I spent all my time in the hospital, cleaning him up, handing him water, helping him to the bathroom—and all the while I reminded him that he would get through this. In my heart I believed that. Perhaps it was my innate optimism, perhaps it was denial, perhaps it was the fact that I could see the situation more objectively, but I believed that we would kick this thing, whatever it threw at us.

In the meantime, it gave me enormous pleasure to be helping him. Helping him eat, washing him down, lifting his legs into bed: Each of those little tasks filled me with a tremendous sense of closeness. I felt the way I imagined a mother must feel about her newborn infant—that my life had taken on a different purpose. Not only was I in love with Phil, but I was in love with being needed. It was a new and intimate way to be together.

After the second surgery I had given up the idea that we were going to Everest, but when I said that to Phil he said, "There goes your dream," and looked at me morosely.

"Who cares?" I answered. "We'll go next year." I didn't really think we would. I believed he would climb Rainier again, and probably other mountains, but not Everest. He had been so beaten up I didn't see how he could do it. But I was okay with that. All my priorities had changed. All that mattered now was Phil.

Even without the Everest climb I continued to run daily. Now it wasn't training: it was an outlet for my stress. Pounding the pavement, block after block around the hospital, I felt I was pounding out my anxiety. My other outlet was work. The hospital had been very kind to me and given me a spare conference room to use as an office, so I set up my computer and spent several hours every day immersing myself in business. The concreteness of data networks and sales figures and the camaraderie of people outside the hospital were such a relief from all the uncertainty upstairs. I felt a little guilty focusing on something other than Phil, but I needed that time away.

The irony of Phil's illness was that it had come at a time when my career was skyrocketing. On January 1 I had been promoted to director at U S West. I'd been able to create my own team, and now together we were responsible for providing broadband data networks to the company's biggest customers. It was exactly the position I had moved to U S West for. And then, just a few months after the promotion—a few months before I went with Phil to Marty's—several members of my team and I had won the President's Club again. It had seemed that in every way Phil and I had reached the top: We had the jobs of our dreams, we had our growing partnership and marriage, we were cruising toward Everest . . . And now *this*.

One night Mimi Bemis and several of the other directors who reported to me came and took me out for a drink. It wasn't long—maybe an hour and a half—but it felt so good to get away. We drank wine and I told them about Phil and we got a little teary, and then they started telling stories about work and we began to laugh. It had been so long since I had laughed! When it was time to go I hugged each one of them, but the gesture seemed inadequate. They hadn't needed to come; they had come because they wanted to. In my absence they were working harder than ever to keep everything running smoothly, and now, in their free time, they had come to show me they cared. Out on the sidewalk I must have said a million thank-yous, but I don't think they really understood how much their generosity meant to me.

• • •

Nine days after my second surgery the hospital sent me home—laced up like a football. I was wearing an adhesive bandage that was tied with a shoestring around my middle, and twice every day Sue was supposed to untie the bandage and change the dressings. Each day a nurse would come at noon to clean the incision. It was almost more than both of us could stomach. But at least I was going home, and I knew if I was ever going to heal it was going to be in my own house. I had gotten great care in the hospital; despite my recalcitrance, the staff had been kind and responsive. But for me, home was the place for mending.

Almost immediately I began to feel better. The combination

of lying in my own bed, surrounded by my own things, and eating food prepared by Sue or one of our mothers, was like an infusion of a wonder drug. Within the first few days, my remaining pain subsided and I began to feel a sense of the future return. Sue was my guardian angel. She rarely left the house, working from home, leaving only to go to the store. Even in the evenings she refused to go out with friends, insisting that she wanted to stay close to me. I wasn't exactly good company since I spent most of the time sleeping, but I was glad she was there. She was my biggest reason to get better.

By the time I'd been home a week and a half I was feeling faint traces of the Phil Ershler I knew. I didn't have any stamina or muscle tone—I got winded going up the stairs—but I had started to gain back some weight and I could move around the house like a mostly self-sufficient human being. So when Sue was invited to an early Halloween party I urged her to go. She'd played nursemaid long enough. She needed to get out.

But she was reluctant. "It's too far," she said. "It'll take too long to get there and get home."

"Go," I said. I could see that she wanted to and was only resisting out of concern for me.

So finally she went, promising not to stay too long. I assured her I would be fine.

That evening I was sitting in the kitchen eating a chocolate ice cream bar when I happened to glance down at my shirt. Right smack in the center was a brown stain. *You slob,* I thought, *dropping ice cream on your shirt!* But as I looked more closely I realized it wasn't chocolate. I lifted the shirt. Underneath, the bandage was also stained. Feeling sick about what I was about to find, I unlaced the bandage and pulled up part of the dressing. It was soaked with brown. "Crap!" I said out loud—*literally.* I went upstairs, took the rest of the dressing off, and with the hand shower rinsed off the incision. Within seconds, the clean tissue refilled with brown. Intuitively, I knew: My colon was leaking through the wound. I grabbed the phone and called Sue on her cell. "Darn it, Susie, why don't you have your phone on!" I growled to her recording. "Get home right away. I'm leaking." Then I dialed Dr. Medwell. Once again, it was after hours. The answering service paged the doctor and after a few minutes an unfamiliar surgeon called. When I described the situation he peppered me with questions. "How are you feeling? Are you in pain? Do you have a fever?"

"No, no pain. No fever."

"Okay. Then just keep changing the dressings and come in Monday morning."

"Monday? Not sooner? What about peritonitis?" Between my first aid training and my college biology major, I knew the dangers of fecal matter leaking into the abdomen.

"No fever, no pain: You don't have any signs of infection. Just keep it clean and come in Monday."

I hung up and felt my recovery leaking away.

On Monday morning Sue took me back to Medwell's office. He cleaned the wound and pulled the two sides apart. By bending my head I could see the hole in the wound where the brown ooze was coming out. "You've developed a fistula," he said. "That's an unnatural opening between two organs—in this case between your large intestine and your skin."

"Crap," I said under my breath. "So now what? Another operation?" I could barely say the "O" word.

"Not sure we want to open you up a third time. There's a chance we can get this thing to heal on its own."

I felt a bit of cautious optimism. "What does that involve?"

"Well, we have to give that intestine a chance to heal, and that means we have to keep things from going through there. So we'll put you on TPN, total parenteral nutrition. You'll get a catheter in your vein and we'll feed you intravenously. Nothing by mouth for six to eight weeks."

I looked at Sue, who looked as if she were trying to get her mind around what we had just heard. "Let me get this straight.

For the next two months I'm going to be hooked to a machine and I can't eat a single thing?"

"Or drink either."

I swallowed the rage that was rising inside me. "What are the chances this thing will close on its own?"

Medwell looked as if he wished the phone would ring right now. "Probably about fifty-fifty."

"And if it doesn't?" I already knew the answer.

"Well . . . then . . . we'll probably have to go back in."

I crushed the information sheet he had given me into a wad.

That afternoon I checked into the hospital yet again. The old seventh floor. A nurse inserted a PIC line into my arm, a thin tube that threaded its way from below my elbow up to my shoulder and then down into the big vein going into my heart. All my nutrition would get dumped in there. They showed me how to take care of the PIC line, and how to empty and reattach the colostomy bag that Dr. Medwell had plastered over the wound with an adhesive "donut." I hoped Sue was paying attention because I wasn't. I was too pissed. That night Marty Greene came by to visit. We stood talking at the foot of my bed and I thought, *What in the world is going on here? I'm standing up, I'm not hurting, we're having an ordinary conversation. I'm finally feeling* better *and now I'm back in the hospital again!* In my ears I could hear the wind whistling down the slippery slope. Earlier that day they'd brought me the "informed consent" papers with the list of possible complications. As I'd read it I'd thought back to the first surgery and the list I'd signed then: risk of infection, risk of intestinal blockage . . . "The risks are small," Medwell had said when I'd asked about the likelihood. Now I thought, *Yeah, small—except when they happen to you.* I was checking off every one of them.

The following day they sent me home. A visiting nurse came and taught me how to hook the end of the tube to the food pump, and a short while later a delivery arrived with a week's supply of liquid-nutrition bags. I threw them angrily into the refrigerator. That night Sue took the first bag out two hours before bedtime to let the liquid warm, and mixed in the supplemental vitamins to make what she cheerily called "Phil's formula." I growled that she could joke because it meant she didn't have to cook, then I took the pump and the bag to bed. *What a sight,* I thought as I climbed the stairs: *emaciated me, in my boxer shorts and bathrobe, hooked to this pump and bag, a colostomy bag hanging off my stomach* . . . The next morning, instead of going to the kitchen for my usual cup of tea, I carted the pump and bag to my home office and watched the last cc's of "Phil's formula" drain out into my vein.

Despite my bad attitude, I slowly began to feel stronger. Each week they upped the size of the bags, and bit by bit I began to gain weight. The small amount of pain that was left disappeared completely. For the first time in two months I was able to walk without the pillow clutched to my stomach. Cautiously, I took myself for walks around the block. It was good to be outside under my own power, feeling the fresh air. Soon the one block became two, and then two became three, and then one day I thought, *I bet I can walk all the way down to the lake.* So with the IV tube rolled up under my sleeve I walked the long hill down to Lake Washington and back up. It was slow, and on the uphill I was breathing as hard as I sometimes did on the route to Muir, but when I got to the top I thought, *There is a light at the end of this tunnel. I know how to exercise, I know how to motivate myself, I know how to put myself back together.* All I'd needed was control.

Six weeks after the second surgery I bought an elastic exercise band and started doing some moderate upper-body exercises in the house. At my next checkup I asked if I could go to the gym. Dr. Medwell looked at me with an expression that was equal parts humor, encouragement, and caution and said, "Just don't overdo it." So with the tube still rolled up under my sleeve I began lifting weights and walking the treadmill. My performance was feeble; I was a little embarrassed. It reminded me of coming home after the early Everest expeditions when we had each lost 20 or 25 pounds and the first days in the gym I could do so much less than I'd done before I had left. But I persisted. On December 2, almost eight weeks to the day since the PIC line had been inserted, I began to notice that the colostomy bag, which I'd had to empty every day, was no longer filling. A week later the PIC line was removed. The fistula had closed.

On December 11 Sue and I went to the annual Northland Communications party. The Northland party had always been a kind of marker for us, a celebration of our years together, but this year it had added poignancy. I knew I wouldn't have been there without Sue. On the most practical level she had been my nurse, my chauffeur, my caretaker. She had changed my bandages, listened to the nurses when I couldn't, learned what I was unwilling to learn. But more than that, she had been my *partner*: the partner who wouldn't let me quit. No matter how bad things got she never adopted my despair, never stopped saying, "We'll get over this, too," never stopped providing the motivation for me to get better. That attitude was as necessary to my recovery as going to the gym. I knew it wasn't easy for her. Sue is an optimist by nature but I knew that more than once she had gone away to hide her tears. By never giving up in front of me, she had kept me from giving up.

I thought about how many times I had snapped at her when I was too angry and demoralized to appreciate her efforts. I thought about how much grief I'd caused her by preventing her from talking to our friends and parents. I felt, all over again, my guilt at having dragged her into my health problems, at having been less than the perfect provider. Sue didn't need a provider: She was more than capable of taking care of herself; heck, she could make more money than I could. But I *wanted* to take care of her. And I didn't want to be the one who was needy.

A short time into the party we found a quiet corner and, as we always did, we toasted each other and marked our unofficial anniversary. More with actions than with words, we told each other how much we valued our years together; then I repeated what I had said to her before, but that I needed her to hear again, "You know, I never could have made it through all this without you."

Sue laughed. "Oh, yeah, you could have. All those nurses couldn't wait to help you!"

But I was being serious. "You didn't sign up for this."

"I'm married to you, Phil. It comes with the territory."

"Yeah, but I thought we took that part out of the wedding vows—that part about 'in sickness and in health.'"

Her face went suddenly stern. "Don't say that! I don't want to hear that. I love you, and it's part of the relationship."

"Well, I just didn't think that was part of the dea—"

Before I could finish she punched me in the chest (being careful, I noticed, to strike above the incision). "Knock it off. Everything that happens to us is part of the deal. It's all part of the deal."

"Okay, okay." I grabbed her hand. "Let's go back to the party." I didn't want to get hit again.

• • •

Even before the Northland party, I had begun working primarily in my downtown office. Phil didn't need me anymore—at least not in the same way. Once he started working out in the gym he became pretty self-sufficient. He could get around by himself, fix his own meals, work from his home office. He didn't need me to change his bandages, or help him shower, or help with the other little tasks of daily living. It was such a relief to him! He had hated being taken care of. But to my own surprise, I missed it. I was so happy for him, and even relieved to be able to go back to working my crazy hours, but there was also an element of loss. I had loved that extra bit of closeness.

*   *   *

In mid-December I went on my first business trip since Phil's original hospitalization. I had a long flight back East, a time I usually used to catch up on paperwork or read. This time I felt my thoughts wander. I'm sure it was the combination of knowing that Phil was finally healing and I was able again to go out of town for my own work, but for the first time since August I found myself thinking about my own career and, once again, thinking about becoming a motivational speaker. It had been so far from my thoughts during Phil's illness that I was surprised to find a new urgency attached to the idea. It was as if the events of the last three months had injected it with a higher level of purpose. *Suppose you got sick and were going to die?* I thought. *How would you feel about your life? Would you feel fulfilled?* Phil could look at his life and say he had truly done what he'd wanted, but I wasn't sure I could say that. All the changes of the past eight years— the climbing, the travel, the relationship with Phil, the *opening* of my self and my world—had punched a hole in what, until then, had seemed like a perfectly satisfying life. Now it was harder to feel that I was using my life in the most fulfilling, most beneficial way. It seemed that I could continue to do what I was doing, helping my own teams achieve their goals, or I could reach out to people all across the country who—in business or in life itself—believed their dreams were unattainable; people who allowed their fears or insecurities to stop them. If I could reach a fraction of those people, if I could encourage them to do what they thought they couldn't, I would feel that I had done something truly worthwhile. Could I really make a difference in people's lives? I didn't know. But for all of my insecurity, I now realized, I didn't have a choice. I'd followed the current road as far as it went. Somehow I would have to muster the courage to set out on the next one.

For some time we had been talking about taking Phil's body out for a test drive. He was consistently feeling good; he was spending an hour a day on the treadmill and bench-pressing 200 pounds; he was ready to get out and see what he could do. So on December 31 we decided to hike up Mt. Si, a 4-mile, 3,200-foot climb—usually way too puny for Phil—but it was a half hour from the house and was where I went regularly to train.

"You know what I've been through," he said as we drove to the trailhead. "We're not running up." Usually I timed myself and tried to beat my own record.

"I know," I answered. To myself I thought, *you're not going to run but I am!* This was my one and only chance to beat him!

We set out at a slow pace. It was a cold gray day and the bottom of the mountain was shrouded in fog, but it felt so good to be outside on a trail with Phil. I could almost pretend that the whole last five months had never happened. I walked leisurely in front, and the crunching of his boots behind me sounded like a wordless prayer of thanks. A little way up, the trail steepened. I leaned into the hill and breathed in and out more deliberately. Behind me I could hear Phil's steps on my heels. "How're you doing?"

"Fine."

"Sure we're not going too fast?"

"Just keep walking."

We moved on up the path. On either side, the towering firs were covered with wet lichen. Underfoot the ground was spongy. Since Phil was staying right behind me I figured I could pick up the pace. He matched his pace to mine. "Gosh, Phil, you're doing great!"

"Yeah, yeah, yeah."

"You sure you're okay?"

"I'm fine. Just keep walking."

A little later I picked up the pace again—and once again he stayed with me. *Man,* I thought, *he's amazing.* So I speeded up again, and then again, and every time he matched me. Soon I was climbing Mt. Si as fast as I ever had, and Phil was still on my heels.

We were almost at the top when a thought occurred to me. "Phil," I said, stopping and turning around, "what have you been doing at the gym?"

He shrugged. "Weights, treadmill, a little step mill."

"Step mill! Since when do you work out on a step mill?"

"Since I haven't been able to climb."

I looked at him suspiciously. "You never mentioned the step mill."

"No? Well, you know . . . We started talking about this little hike and I just figured I'd start getting ready."

"Phil! You trained for the training hike! You never told me!"

He got a sly grin on his face, bent his knees, and put both hands out in front of him as if he were holding a waterskiing tow bar.

"You cheater!" I said, and began to pummel him in the chest and arms, careful to avoid his stomach. But he grabbed my hands and pinned them behind me, and then what could I do but let him kiss me?

Up at the top we looked out over what, on a clear day, would have been a panorama of Seattle and its suburbs. Dense clouds obscured all but the nearest peaks, but we didn't care. We raised our water bottles and bid good-bye to 1999, a year we were happy to see the end of. On the way down, with Phil still on my heels, I couldn't help my mind from racing. He's going to climb again! He's going to guide again! Maybe . . . "Hey, Phil," I called, "Everest in 2001?"

"Sue," he said behind me, "just keep walking."

September 2001

Sue:
I'm in Arusha and it's about 2 in the afternoon. I wanted so much to call you but it probably doesn't make any sense to wake you up in the middle of the night.

Keep up the training, lover. We're going to be ready for that thing and there are going to be no regrets. Be ready for some walking when I get home.

I really do miss you when I'm gone but I like missing you. It only confirms that I got lucky and made a very smart choice. I have very little left to wish for (maybe a new large intestine). Thanks for filling in all my gaps.

I think I'm going back to the hotel and take a nap. I want to dream about a very special woman. Her name is SUE.

Love,
Phil

February 2002

Phil,
If we get up Everest, what a testimonial for your skills as a guide . . . getting a plain old non-mountaineer up all Seven Summits. I will write you a letter of recommendation ☺

Love,
Sue

7

FIRST COUPLE IN HISTORY
CLIMBS THE SEVEN SUMMITS

When we got back from Everest in June 2001 I felt lost. Phil left for Ecuador, and then for Russia, and I worked twelve-hour days—mostly to keep myself from stewing about the situation. How could I have used that word "failure"? It didn't matter that I had been talking about myself; he'd heard it as if I were talking about him, and it killed me that I had caused him additional pain.

One morning at the end of July I went out in my sweatpants and slippers to get the Sunday paper. As I walked back to the house I could hear the phone ringing. It was Phil, calling from Amsterdam where his flight had just landed from Moscow. I was so excited to hear his voice that I could hear my heart hammering in my ears. He gave me a quick summary of the trip, and I told him about the crazy schedule I'd been keeping. In the background I could hear the airport PA system announcing flights. I wanted to tell him what I'd been thinking, how sorry I was, how much the trip *wasn't* a failure, but I was afraid to reopen the wound on the phone. While I was trying to decide what to do he said, "You know, you better order that Suunto."

It took a moment to register. The Suunto. The altimeter watch that, early in the expedition, we had agreed I would need if we ever went back to Everest.

· · ·

When I left for Ecuador after Everest I was boiling. Many of the clients knew I'd been on Everest and asked about the climb. I smiled and said, "Good trip," then changed the subject. I didn't want to think about it. But it was in my mind whether I wanted it or not: sitting at the Balcony unable to see a single thing, all because I'd been too stupid to clear my exhalation hole.

My friend Romulo and I led the clients on a one-day hike up the ancient volcano Pasochoa, and then on to Cotopaxi where we spent the night at the hut at 15,500 feet. When we roped up at 1:00 a.m., the sky was filled with shooting stars. I liked climbing Cotopaxi. With its steep crevassed glaciers and impressive crater, it reminded me a bit of Mt. Rainier. Perhaps it was that, or maybe it was talking with Romulo in the hut, or just the fact that long climbs provided a good opportunity to think, but as we moved up the mountain, I replayed my argument with Sue in my mind. I didn't feel differently about the trip—there was no way that trip was a failure—but little by little I could see it from Sue's point of view. I would have gone back till the cows came home if I hadn't made it in '84. That was how Sue felt—but she didn't feel it for herself, she felt it for the two of us together.

I could feel myself softening, but that didn't mean I was ready to commit to going back. Just like the year before, she still didn't get the magnitude of what she was asking, the level of work and responsibility involved in pulling off an expedition. It was late June already, for Pete's sake. If we were going to go again in 2002 we'd have to go in March. It was already time to pull all the pieces together: the planning, the training, the committing to Everest above all else . . . Was I ready to go there? Not yet. If I was honest with myself I wanted her to stew a little bit. I was opening up to her desire, but I was still pissed.

After Ecuador I left for Russia to guide a group on Mt. Elbrus, and it was while I was on Elbrus that I realized my mistake. I hadn't listened. Sue hadn't said the *trip* was a failure; she'd said *she* was a failure because she hadn't met her own expectations. But *I* felt like a failure, so I'd heard it as if she were talking about me.

Suddenly I realized how much I missed her. I missed her laugh; I missed the way she runs around and snaps a million pictures when we reach the top. But more than that, I missed the way we were together. Suddenly, it became the clearest thing in the world to me: We had to go back. Back to Everest, yes, but more important, back to each other. I remembered what Everest was about—a representation of all we had built together—and realized that, inadvertently, I had shortchanged it. The whole time we were planning the expedition—maybe even the whole time we'd been climbing—I'd actually had no expectation of summiting. Given the odds and my medical history, I'd thought that going there would be enough. But I'd been wrong. We'd gotten to 1,400 feet from the summit, and if the weather had cooperated—if I hadn't been stupid enough to freeze my eyes—there was a good chance we would have made it all the way. Well, we *could* make it all the way. Now I knew that—because I was strong enough and Sue was strong enough, and because that's the kind of thing we can do together. I remembered joking before we left for Everest that the worst outcome would be to have a good climb and not make it, because if that happened I knew where we'd be spending the spring of 2002. So I guess I'd known all along that we would be going back. What I knew now, though, was that we would be doing it with a vengeance.

· · ·

The minute Phil told me to order the Suunto I saw it. I saw it as clearly as if I were looking in the pages of an album: the two of us in our big hooded suits, goggles on, masks dangling, standing in the brilliant sunshine on top of the world. It wasn't like the image I'd carried last year, which was always fuzzy, a little out of focus. This image was crisp and shiny. Real. It was as if I'd been granted a glimpse of the future.

I threw myself in gear. Almost immediately I put together a training regimen: ninety minutes daily of working out at the gym, running, or climbing my office building's thirty-two flights of stairs with 30 pounds of kitty litter in my pack. Weekends I hiked, hard. My goal was to complete 100 hikes with a total vertical gain of 300,000 feet. I began to read everything I could get my hands on about endurance training and high-altitude physiology, and I mined everybody I met who had been to Everest recently for pointers. When I read in a book called *Endurance Sports Nutrition* by Suzanne Girard Eberle that low ferritin stores can be a problem for endurance athletes, I had my ferritin levels checked and, sure enough, they were depleted. I went on supplemental iron and my energy surged; my runs and workouts seemed way shorter. There were dozens of factors that could affect our ability to summit—weather, avalanches, illness, unexpected delays, political turmoil, the presence of other teams—and over most of them we had no control. But what I did have control over was my own performance, and I didn't want to be the factor that made us turn around.

Now that a year had passed, I could see what a long shot our '01 climb had been: Phil fresh out of the hospital, me a Himalayan neophyte. I could see what neither of us had admitted the year before: that for all our hope and effort, we hadn't really believed we would succeed. But *this* year . . . This year Phil was healthy; I knew what to expect. Why couldn't we reach the top? It was still a long shot to be sure: Our odds were still only about one in ten. But that just drove me to work harder. I determined to "train like an Olympian." I had no pretensions of being an Olympic-class athlete, but it was a way of motivating myself even more.

Coincidentally, I was frequently traveling to Denver at that time because my company was based there, and Denver was just 70 miles from the U.S. Olympic Training Center in Colorado Springs. On one of those trips it occurred to me that I could stay an extra half day and visit the center. Despite my training slogan I had no idea of what it meant to train like an Olympian, and I thought if I immersed myself in that world for a little while, I might learn some useful tools. I took a notebook, prepared to write down how many hours a day they trained, what they ate, what they did to stay focused. What I actually learned was something far more abstract, and infinitely more helpful.

From the moment I entered the complex I was in awe. Large brick buildings connected by lawns and sidewalks gave it the feel of a college campus, but any sense of sedentary study vanished the minute I stepped inside. In the Visitor Center, a short film showed clip after clip of skiers, skaters, divers, curlers—all smashing records, besting their own best, bowing their heads to accept a medal. Already I was hooked. I followed a tour guide to the gymnasium where gymnasts and wrestlers were busy training. Behind the grunts and thuds of the athletes and the exhortations of their coaches, I imagined I could hear the Olympic theme. I knew it was just the power of association, but I felt a thrill of excitement: It was as if the theme were being played for *us*, as if just my being here, in the presence of such dreams and dedication, in the place where the work happened to make the dreams come true, was enough to burnish our climb with a bit of Olympic gold.

My last stop was at an open-air rotunda where wall panels displayed quotes from past Olympians. I made a slow circuit, reading each one, writing many in my journal.

Athletics is all I care for. I sleep them, I eat them and I try my level best to do them as they should be done—Babe Didrikson Zaharias, track and field, 1932.

I learned to win by losing—Jeff Blatnick, wrestling, 1980, 1984.

Success is a journey, not a destination—Bob Beamon, track and field, 1968.

The voices of the athletes rang off the walls and I felt as if I were in their presence. Their voices filled me with possibility, and a sense of limitless power. Over and over, in different ways, they said the same thing: It isn't just the training regimen that counts—superb physical conditioning is a given—it is also the *attitude* that makes these accomplishments possible. It is the willingness to hurt, the ability to push through your limits, the determination to go back and back and back until you achieve your goal. It is the total mental and physical commitment to the dream. I walked out of the rotunda and knew that I had just learned the most important lesson of my training. What we had lacked in 2001 was the *belief* that we would succeed. But we would make up for that in 2002!

As I had for previous climbs, I posted our summit goal ("29,035'!") on a sticky note on my computer next to my annual quota, and every time I worked out I recorded my activity. When I took my logbook to the gym Phil would laugh and say, "Why do you need to write it down? You know whether or not you did it." When I came home from a hike and entered the number of vertical feet I'd climbed, he'd say, "Well, let's see, I've made 500 Rainier attempts; each one was 9,000 feet; that's 4½ million vertical feet!" But I liked tracking my progress. Every weight lifted and every vertical foot climbed was a step toward that 29,035. And underneath his teasing, I think Phil appreciated my dedication.

The hardest part about training was not the workouts, but my schedule. To fit the training in around work, I went to the office early and left late so that I could go to the gym or climb the stairs at lunchtime. (It took a few weeks just to get over the embarrassment of riding the elevator down with my pack and gym shorts on and smelling like old socks, while at practically every floor the elevator stopped for people going out to lunch.) When I traveled, my assistant, Ann Dehn, booked me into hotels that had a gym or running path nearby. It worked well for melding training with my corporate life, but it came with a price. I had to put the rest of my life on hold. When I wasn't working or working out, I was falling into bed exhausted, and the things I'd previously counted on for pleasure—seeing friends, reading the Sunday paper, playing the occasional game of golf—disappeared onto a list of activities I looked forward to doing again when this whole crazy Everest dream was over. Even time with Phil came with a price tag. Since I was gone most weekends pursuing my "100 hikes," we scheduled Friday night workout dates: 90 minutes in the gym followed by going out to dinner. If he had any romantic aspirations after dinner, I was usually too sleepy to even notice.

The stress of constantly working—one way or the other—was tiresome but not daunting. But as the fall wore on I began to feel a different kind of tension: a conflict between the training and my job. If I was really going to stand on the summit with Phil, I needed to give my *all* to Everest, and I couldn't give my all as long as I was giving so much to the job. I had faced a similar problem in 2001, and the company had graciously granted me a three-month leave of absence, bringing in my own former boss to do my job while we climbed. As a result I had actually worked *harder* before I left to make sure things were prepared for my replacement, and on the mountain my attention was split because I e-mailed and called the office from base camp. But this time I couldn't afford those distractions. We wouldn't be doing Everest a third time.

"Quit your job," Phil said.

Quit my job? We talked about it endlessly. The idea of quitting sent a shiver up my spine. I had imagined I would quit my job eventually—to pursue my dream of speaking—but that was a long way down the road, after I'd eased into speaking while still doing sales. I'd never considered quitting cold turkey. How could I? My job was important to our financial security. We loved the perks. We needed the health insurance.

"We're not talking forever," said Phil. "Just till after Everest. We can manage for a while."

I couldn't bring myself to do it. From my very first job at Fred Meyer, I'd been working my way up the ladder, and now I was a vice president responsible for hundreds of millions in revenue. How could I give that up? "What?" Phil would say. "You think when we come back you'll never get another job?" It wasn't that; I knew I could get another job. But there was no guarantee that I'd find as senior a position. And, as if the successful grown-up Sue were still staring down the young, insecure girl, I wasn't yet ready to let go of the title.

That November Phil left to guide a climb on the Mexican volcanoes, Ixta and Orizaba. I had done those climbs with him the year before when we were training for Everest, and while he was gone I went hiking with two friends, Wynne Leon and Jill Jones, whom I had met on that climb. We spent the first part of the hike laughing about our "Mexican escapades" (which had included a night of post-climb reveling in which we'd actually managed to get kicked out of a bar) and then settled into a brisk, heart-pumping rhythm. One of the things I loved about hiking with Wynne and Jill was that after our initial laughter and conversation we walked fast, often too fast to talk, and as a result we had long stretches without conversation. I used those periods, as I did my solo hikes, to work through my thoughts. Now as we walked, my mind wandered from my Ixta climb with Wynne and Jill to my first trip to the volcano in 1997. It had been many months since I'd been on a mountain, and being at altitude again, feeling the burn of hard work, and relishing the bonds that came from living and climbing so closely with others had reminded me of how much I loved climbing. Even as my stomach began to roil and my head to ache, I felt privileged to be there.

At camp, Phil made tuna and noodles for dinner, and despite the queasiness in my stomach, I took a few bites. Instantly I knew it was a mistake. I ran behind a rock, threw up, and then retreated to the tent. That night the vomiting wouldn't stop. Every hour, like clockwork, I climbed over Phil and the other guide who was sharing our tent to get outside, until finally they moved me next to the door. It wasn't until early morning just before Phil's alarm went off that the vomiting subsided. Phil urged me to stay at camp that day to get some rest, and for a few moments I considered it. But how could I stay when everyone else was going to the summit? So I went, and once I got climbing and breathing deeply, I began to feel a little better. My stomach still felt like Jell-O and my head still pounded, I was still dehydrated and exhausted, but as I got into the rhythm and began to anticipate the summit, I felt the surge of determination that I always felt to make it all the way. Three hours later I stepped onto the summit ridge and when I turned around, the Mexican landscape spread out in a rose-colored plain as far as the eye could see.

Climbing now with Wynne and Jill I remembered that determination and the exhilaration of standing on top, both undiminished by my having been sick. Maybe because I was missing Phil, who was on Ixta right then, or maybe because of the mountain air and the satisfying burn in my chest and legs, it hit me how much I wanted us to stand on top of Everest together. In that moment I understood that there was no job decision to be made. Two days later I told my boss that I would resign at the end of the year. Starting on January 1, 2002, I would have a new job to focus on: fulfilling our dream.

*   *   *

From January to March I did nothing but train and pack, train and pack. It was as if everything besides Everest had ceased to exist. In my single-minded focus, it didn't occur to me that everyone close to me might not feel quite as excited about the climb as I did, so I was surprised when on March 19 I got an e-mail from Linda Hasselstrom, my brother Jerry's significant other. "Just between you and me," she said, "Jerry is really worried about this. We've talked it up, down, and sideways, and there isn't a darn thing *you* can do. But in case he hasn't mentioned it lately, he sure does love you." In our family that was the equivalent of standing on a rooftop and shouting out your feelings. I felt a huge flood of love for them—along with a twinge of guilt—and realized that there was something I needed to tell them. That evening I wrote my parents and brothers a letter and put it with our wills.

> *To my family,*
> *If you are reading this letter then something happened on the climb. Do know that I would not have traded this Everest climb and these last ten years of adventures for forty more years of a normal life. I would not have been happy living that way. I achieved everything I could have hoped for in life. I am very lucky. Please do not be sad; smile because I had so much more than one deserves: the best family, husband, friends, and these incredible experiences.*
> *Love, Sue*

The next day my parents came to drive us to the airport. They handed me a small box wrapped in delicate Chinese paper. Inside was a necklace with a beautiful jade charm meant to afford protection against harm. I promised them that I wouldn't take it off until we returned. On a last-minute impulse I gave them the only two items I still had from childhood: a polished rock that a doctor had given me when I was hospitalized at age eight, and a key chain with my name on it from the same year. I didn't know if I was doing it because I feared I would not be back, or because I wanted to assure them that I *would* be back by giving them my treasures for safekeeping.

Just before we left the house I took one last look at my e-mail. I laughed at myself while I did it. Here I was, going off for three months to a part of the world where my normal, e-mail-dependent life would be completely irrelevant, but I still couldn't resist that early morning check-in. As it turned out, I was glad I did it. My "quote of the day" had just arrived in my in-box.

> *Forget past mistakes. Forget failures. Forget everything except what you're going to do now and do it.*
> —William Durant, founder of General Motors

"Where do you want to go for dinner?"

It was our first night in Kathmandu and it was a totally rhetorical question. Phil knew perfectly well where I wanted to go: to the Rum Doodle! The Rum Doodle is a climbers' and trekkers' restaurant and everyone who summits Everest signs his or her name behind the bar. We'd gone there in 2001 and I'd seen all the signatures—Sir Edmund Hillary, Tenzing Norgay, Jim Whittaker, Phil Ershler!—and I'd felt terrible that I hadn't been able to sign. This year my name was going up on that wall!

Mark Tucker, a friend and guide from IMG, came with us. Tuck had summited Everest in 1990 but never signed the board. Now he was almost as excited as I was. We made our way from group to group, catching up on news, getting reports on Everest; then after dinner we went up to the bar so Mark could sign. The wooden boards on the wall were crowded with signatures—looped and straight, cramped and sprawling, an international gazetteer of names. The bartender handed him a black felt marker and pointed to the place where he should sign, and with a blushing, boyish shyness, he added his name and the date. When he had finished, all of us near the bar broke out in applause.

Phil gave me a squeeze above the elbow. "In three months that'll be you."

"And you! Aren't you going to sign again?"

He looked at me as if I were crazy. "We're going to stand on top together and we're going to sign the board together. I want the world to know that I climbed this mountain with my wife."

I felt myself flush with pleasure.

The next day we left Kathmandu for the flight to Lukla, an airstrip 35 miles from Everest base camp. There we began the trek that took us, over the next twelve days, along the pedestrian highways of the Khumbu valley. Beside the trail, men plowed fields with long sticks pulled by yaks and women tossed handfuls of seeds into the furrows. In some of the same villages we'd visited the year before, residents served us milk tea in white enamel cups and presented us with *katas*, white ceremonial scarves. We shopped in the open-air stalls in Namche Bazaar, the commercial center of the region, and watched the sun rise on Ama Dablam as the chants of the Tangboche monks rose from the monastery that clings to the side of the mountain. On our tenth day, with two days still to go before arriving at base camp, we hiked a series of steep switchbacks where our breath grew short and our pace slowed. Around us the terrain had grown rocky and arid; at 16,000 feet, little grew. Up ahead, snow-covered peaks offered a preview of our destination. I was just starting to wonder if all my training would really make the climbing easier when I heard the familiar flapping of prayer flags. The sound was coming from over the crest of the hill, just beyond my field of vision. Instantly, I felt a tightening in my stomach. It was the *chortens*, the memorials to those who had lost their lives on Everest. I remembered them from the year before when they had overwhelmed my confidence with fear. A few minutes later we rounded the hill and came into a narrow valley. There they were, in long parallel lines: more than a hundred neat stone pillars, tiered like miniature temples, guarding the memories of those who had died. Instinctively the group grew quiet, our arrogant belief that we could climb this mountain suddenly shredded.

Who was I kidding? Many of the people remembered here were far better climbers than I; what made me think that I would fare better than they had? And why was climbing this mountain so darn important? Was I really willing to risk my life? Oddly enough, I had never really asked myself that question. Now, as if the *chortens* had thrown me a challenge, I felt a need to explain my behavior. I moved on through the valley, in and out of the mist that was drifting across the valley floor. The monuments appeared and disappeared as if they were carved from smoke. I was climbing Everest for Phil; that was foremost: for everything he had done for me, everything he had given me, everything we had done and become together. But that was only part of the story. I also wanted to climb it for myself. I wanted to do one *spectacular* thing in my life: something that made up for all the times I hadn't achieved, all the times I'd *believed* I couldn't. I had always been the kid who had the potential but never used it: I had the intellect for reading but didn't act on it, I had the athleticism for gymnastics but didn't pursue it. I'd squandered dozens of opportunities because somehow, inside or out, I'd let something tell me no. Now I wanted Everest *because* of everything that told me no. I wanted something that would prove to me and the world that I *could*, and that would last me till the end of my days— something that no one could ever take away.

Two days later we walked into base camp. Almost immediately I felt sick as a dog: nauseated, bloated, my stomach clenching in spasms. It was probably a combination of altitude and something I'd eaten—and was probably the first of many such attacks—but because everything at altitude is so much more intense, I felt like I was dying. I curled up in the tent with a hot water bottle on my stomach, and thought, *This must be what Phil feels like so often.* But even lying nauseated in the tent couldn't quell my excitement. We were here; in a few days we would be going up; the wait was over.

The next morning we woke to the scent of juniper fire. The *puja*! I stuck my head out the tent door. About 20 feet away the Sherpas had built a tall stone altar next to which they had started the ceremonial fire. Black smoke plumed upward in the stiff wind. The *puja* is a Buddhist ritual in which the Sherpas request the gods' permission and blessing for the climb. Last year's ceremony had been one of the highlights of our expedition. I had felt immensely privileged to be both tourist and insider, witness and beneficiary, as the lama chanted and the prayer flags waved his prayers toward heaven. Now I ran outside to watch the preparations. All around the altar the Sherpas were assembling blankets and pads to sit on, and positioning their offerings—beer, soda, fruit, and candy—on the altar's ledge. An elderly lama in layers of worn down vests and jackets was seated on a blanket, chanting. One by one the members of our team gathered: Mark Tucker; Eric Simonson, one of Phil's partners at International Mountain Guides and the expedition leader; several other IMG guides; three "nonguided" climbers who had used the services of IMG to get to Everest but who, like Phil and me, would be climbing on their own; and our team of Sherpas. We took our seats and accepted handfuls of rice to throw into the fire as a Sherpa in a red parka climbed to the top of the altar and raised a wooden pole. An American and a Nepalese flag unfurled and six strings of prayer flags spread out like spokes of a wheel in every direction. For the next several hours we listened drowsily as the lama chanted from a set of ornately lettered prayer cards, the wind and flags a percussive backbeat to his steady drone. We had just placed our crampons and ice axes against the altar so they could be blessed, when the lama's chanting was interrupted by a loud boom. Adrenaline shot through me, and we all turned toward the noise. Several hundred yards away, on the lower flank of the Khumbu Icefall, a plume of ice and snow was billowing upward. An ice cliff had broken away and cascaded down the mountain—a reminder of why we were holding a *puja*.

Toward the end of the ceremony, several Sherpas, led by Ang Passang, moved around the circle and rubbed each person's cheeks with *tsampa*, a roasted barley flour. When they were done, we had each been given a white beard, a symbol of a long and fruitful life. Then, just before the ceremony broke up into a party of beer drinking and laughter, the lama blessed a set of red strings, which several Sherpas tied around our necks, a tangible blessing for our journey. The year before I had not understood the meaning of the string and had taken it off. This year I had no intention of removing it!

On April 13, almost a month after we'd left the States, we left base camp for our first trip through the Icefall. Our plan was to climb to Camps 1 and 2, spend a night or two at each, and then return to base camp to recuperate and acclimatize. The Icefall is a vertical maze of shifting blocks of ice the size of houses. It is the yeti's playground—a sandbox for those "abominable snowmen" who can scale a hundred feet in a single step. But for human beings who must cling to the sheer ice walls with crampons and ropes, and cross the gaping crevasses on swaying ladders, it is the ultimate gamble, a prayer that today's inevitable collapse will not occur precisely where you are standing. We had started at first light at 5:30 so that we could get through the ice before it softened and slid in the heat of the day. By 7:00 a.m. the surreal land-scape was pearly gray. We had now done the "easy" part of the Icefall. We'd woven our way around and over the jumbled blocks on the lower slopes, and what lay ahead was three hours of harder climbing up vertical ice walls. I was about to step onto the first long vertical ladder when an ominous rumble sounded above me. A second later the ice beneath me shuddered.

"Hold on!" Phil called from the top of the ladder.

I stared up at him, frozen.

"It's okay," he said. "Probably just a collapse farther up."

I looked up, expecting to see the giant blocks rearranging themselves above us, the ropes and ladders of our route disappearing into the churn, but everything looked just the same as it had before. My heart was hammering as if it were about to burst.

"You're okay, come on up."

I grabbed the bottom of the ladder and began heaving myself up, my crampons slipping and sliding on the rungs.

"Whoa," Phil called. "No need to rush." He climbed off the ladder onto a small ice ledge, and a few minutes later I climbed up beside him. "We're okay," he said. "Remember 2001? The Icefall moves a bit. But the chance of us dying here today isn't very great."

Was that true? Despite Phil's years of experience, he no more knew nature's plan for the ice that day than I did. But the steadiness of his voice was reassuring, and when we started up again he continued at the same careful, even pace, as if nothing at all had happened. Gradually my heart stopped its furious beating.

By 11:00 a.m. we had almost reached the top of the Icefall. Despite my earlier terror, the rest of the climb had gone smoothly. I could feel myself moving faster and more confidently than I had the year before, and I had lost the crippling anxiety about what lay ahead. We had just crossed a set of four roped-together ladders spanning a 25-foot crevasse (where Phil had told me a Sherpa joke: "Look down, see America! Fall in, free visa to America!") when his radio squawked. Eric's voice came through the static. "You guys okay?"

"Yeah. What's up?"

"Just heard there was a collapse earlier near the top."

Instantly my insides turned to jelly.

"I think we heard it," Phil said. "Can we get through?"

"The doctors are working on it." The Icefall doctors were a team of three Sherpas who were hired jointly by all the expeditions to fix and repair the route. The 5,000 feet of rope and fifty 8-foot sections of ladder needed constant attention as the ground moved beneath them. "Going to keep going up?"

"Yeah. We'll give it a shot."

I breathed in as deeply as I could. Phil wouldn't let us go up if it weren't safe. And he would turn us around if it seemed dangerous . . .

Perhaps twenty minutes later I was standing at the bottom of a 6-foot ladder waiting for Phil to climb off the top when I heard him whistle. "*There's a man-eater*," he said.

Butterflies rose in my stomach. When I got to the top, Phil was standing on a narrow ledge; in front of him, a sheer ice wall rose 20 feet in the air, clean and shiny as polished marble. Between the ledge and the wall was a black chasm into which our climbing rope disappeared.

Phil planted his ice axe next to his feet and rubbed his gloved hands together. "Good thing we weren't here a couple of hours ago, eh?"

This was the collapse we'd heard earlier and that Eric had called about. *What if we had been here when it happened?* I looked up at the wall. Until a few hours before, its surface had been buried deep inside a cliff. The Icefall doctors had put in a rope, but no ladder. We would have to ice climb the entire thing. I didn't mind ladders; as long as I didn't look down, I felt secure. But clinging to the wall with the pick of my axe and my crampons, and hauling myself up with the strength of my arms, was terrifying.

"You okay?" Phil asked in a tone that suggested that he knew I was—or at least would be, once I got going. "Just pay attention to what you're doing. I don't want to spend the next hour pulling you out of a hole." He clipped into the new rope and stepped gingerly across the narrow shelf at the foot of the wall. Staying just to the left of the hole, he set his ice axe into the wall above his head, pulled up, and jammed his two front crampon points into the ice. Steadily, like Spiderman on the side of a skyscraper, he worked his way up the wall. When he got to the top he leaned out over the ledge and hollered, "Piece of cake! You'll be fine."

Yeah, right, I thought. "Why couldn't you have been a golf pro instead of a mountain guide?" I hollered. I clipped into the new rope and traced Phil's steps to the wall. I tried not to look down, but the black hole yawned just to my right— perfectly positioned to catch me if I fell. I slid my jumar up the rope, checked to make sure it wouldn't slide backwards, took a deep breath, and swung my ice axe. It caught for a second in the ice above my head, then slipped.

"Throw that ice axe. Get a good plant," Phil yelled.

"Thanks," I muttered under my breath. But this time I heaved it as if my life depended on it, and it stuck. Now I had to move my feet. I kicked the points of my right crampon into the ice and then, holding the jumar and ice axe with every ounce of strength I had, pulled myself upward and rammed my left crampon into the wall. It held. I was now fully sus-pended from the ice.

"Good girl," Phil called.

I slid the jumar up again, and swung again with the ice axe. Leaning backwards to throw the axe I was afraid I would fall backwards off the wall, but to my relief, the axe stuck. I jammed my right crampon higher on the wall, pulled myself up, and kicked the left one in as well. My arms were burning.

"You're doing great," Phil called. I couldn't look up, but his voice sounded closer. "You're almost here. Just keep coming."

Once again I went through the steps: jumar, ice axe, pull, crampons. My second crampon slipped out of the ice and I looked down as I felt it slide. The hole was right below me. I began to hyperventilate in an effort to catch my breath.

"Come on, baby. You can do it."

I replaced the crampon, and then quickly, before I had time to stall, slid the jumar, threw the axe, and hauled myself up the last stretch of wall. Phil's arm came into my field of vision. I grabbed his hand and lifted one knee onto the top of the wall.

"Stay on your feet—unless you have crampons on your knees."

I leaned over the top of the wall and kicked into a higher spot so that I had enough leverage to put my upper foot flat on the ledge. He was right, of course. If you come over on your knees, they're apt to slide out from underneath you.

"Good job." Phil squeezed my arm and I leaned against him for a few minutes while I rested my arms and caught my breath. As the tension subsided I felt that wonderful sense of pleasure suffuse me, the relief that comes after a bit of really difficult climbing.

"Okay," Phil said after a few minutes. "Let's put the rest of this puppy behind us." He set off on the next section of the Icefall, where a stack of ice blocks the size of tables lay heaped on top of one another like ice cubes in a freezer bin.

I moved behind him and was just about to step out onto the same block he was standing on when it shifted under his weight. The edge I had been about to step on rose about six inches.

"Whoa," he called, "teeter-totter!" He stepped off that block and onto the next one. The one he'd left settled back in place and the new one shifted.

Darn! I thought we'd finished the area that had collapsed

but apparently not. These blocks must have fallen recently from higher up and not yet frozen into place. Cautiously, I stepped out onto the first block, felt it sink slightly beneath me, jammed my ice axe in to maintain my balance, then stepped to the far side of the block. When I passed the mid-point, the block tipped toward the opposite side.

"Kind of fun, huh?" Phil called. He was walking back and forth across a block, riding it up and down.

"Just a blast." But by the time I got past the second block I'd gotten used to the tipping motion. I actually began to have fun anticipating the moment when the block would tilt. I was sorry when, fifteen minutes later, we came to the end of that section and faced another 20-foot wall. This one, though, had a ladder. Phil scrambled up and I moved quickly up behind him. As my head came up over the top of the wall I had to close my eyes against the glare of the sun.

"That's it," Phil said. "That's pretty much the end of the Ice-fall. We'll have some mother crevasses, but this is the end of the big verticals."

I climbed off the ladder, shielded my eyes, and looked around. In front of us was a long, wide snow-filled valley, bordered on three sides by towering peaks and bathed in sun. It was as if we had come up from the underworld, out of the shaded labyrinth into the light. The temperature was suddenly 30 degrees warmer.

"The Western Cwm," Phil said with a note of pride, as if he himself had discovered it. "Just a short hike to Camp 1."

I sat down in the snow, leaned back against my pack, and closed my eyes. Every muscle in my body melted. The Icefall, one of the scariest parts of the climb, and we had done it! Phil dropped his pack and sat down next to me. With our faces in the sun I could almost pretend we were at the beach.

Phil took my hand. "Great job in the Icefall."

"You too," I said. "Good thing you had me there. Aren't you glad I taught you so much about climbing?"

• • •

Most people don't think of Everest as a place that gets hot, but that's because they haven't been in the Western Cwm (pronounced "coom"). The Cwm is a three-sided basin that stretches from just above the Icefall to the foot of the Lhotse Face. It's bordered by the peaks of Nuptse and Lhotse and Everest's west shoulder, and the reflection of the sun off its snow-covered floor and walls makes it an oven on clear days. In the immortal words of Kevin Flynn, one of the "nonguided" climbers on our expedition, we felt like bugs under a magnifying glass as we traipsed across. By the time we reached Camp 1, forty minutes from the Icefall, we had stripped to our shirtsleeves. When we lay down in our tent the thermometer read 108 degrees. When Sue unpacked her rucksack, she found that her toothbrush had melted into an "L." Nonetheless, we lay down to sleep that night wearing our down parkas. Overnight the inside temperature would drop to zero.

The next morning we left for Camp 2. The terrain now was much flatter. The floor of the Cwm is long rather than steep—a 2-mile slog up a gentle grade where the main challenge is endurance. I joked that Camp 2 is a lot like Muir: You see it in the distance forever, but it never seems to get closer. However, we were in no hurry, and despite the presence of other teams that seemed eager to move ahead, we climbed at our own pace, breaking often to enjoy the view. When we pulled into Camp 2 we saw that the Sherpas had built us a beautiful home-away-from-home, above the camps of other teams, just beneath the face of Everest's west shoulder.

Camp 2 is advanced base camp, so the IMG team had a lot of tents there: a cook tent, a storage tent, tents for guides and Sherpas, a tent for me and Sue, and tents for the three nonguided climbers, Kevin Flynn, Stuart Smith, and Ted Wheeler. We were just settling into our own tent when Bill Crouse, a friend and guide with another team, came over. "Hey,

Phil," he said, "I just wanted to pass the word. We got a fore-cast that there may be some pretty good winds coming through." So several of us went around the camp and checked the guylines on all the tents to make sure they were well se-cured.

The next morning, despite the forecast, we woke up to good weather. Kevin, Stuart, Ted, and several of the Sherpas headed up to Camp 3, 2,500 feet above us on the Lhotse Face, where they planned to spend the night. But two hours later they were back. Fierce wind higher up had made it impossible to climb. With this second warning, we took down the tents of climbers who were not currently at Camp 2 and put additional guylines on all the others. I took some comfort from the fact that there were a lot of us in camp to tie things down if the wind turned out to be stronger than we expected.

In early afternoon it began to blow. Sue and I hung out in our sleeping bags and talked and read. By midafternoon it was getting hard to hear each other over the wind. It must have been blowing at around 40 mph. Fierce windstorms are com-mon in the mountains but are usually short-lived, so I was sur-prised to feel the wind increase as the day wore on. In late afternoon I poked my head out the tent door. About twenty feet away our two dome tents—the cook tent and storage tent—were straining against their ties. There was no way they would make it if we didn't further reinforce the guylines.

"Sue!" I yelled. "I'm going out to tie up the domes! You need to sit against this wall!" I pointed to the side of the tent facing the wind. I was afraid that without weight on that side, the tent might blow over.

Sue climbed over my bag and leaned with all her weight against the tent wall. Pushed by the wind, the nylon wrapped itself partially around her. I scrambled out and in a low crouch crept to the domes. I kept my head tucked to protect my eyes from flying ice grains; in my peripheral vision I could see Mark Tucker doing the same thing. Several Sherpas and the three nonguided climbers were also reinforcing tents. Mark and I piled extra rocks on top of the anchor rocks that kept the tents staked to the ground, and then I crept back toward our tent. From this vantage point I could see that our tent was positioned to get the full brunt of the wind. No wonder it had seemed so unstable. If the wind kept up, it wouldn't make it through the night.

I stuck my head in and hollered to Sue to move everything to another tent that was a little better protected, then I collapsed the tent and joined her. For the next few hours we lay in our bags. The light dimmed and the wind continued unabated. Despite its better location, this tent, too, was heaving to the side. I began to wonder if even it would survive. "We need to sleep with our down suits on!" I yelled to Sue. "Put your boots, gloves, and goggles right next to you." If we had to get out in the middle of the night, we would need to be ready.

The wind howled through the night. Over and over we were awakened by the tent wall slapping our faces and pumice and ice battering the walls. When light came, the wind was as fierce as ever. I looked out and was relieved to see that the two dome tents were still standing, but it was a short reprieve. By midmorning the cook tent had ripped, and big sheets of yellow and tan nylon were streaming off the aluminum poles. Several of us went out into the gale, gathered up spare tent flies, and tried to tie them over the holes, but it was a losing battle; they simply wouldn't hold in the wind. So we carried the contents of the tent—stoves, pots, pans, dishes, cups, and boxes of food— to the storage tent, and then did everything we could to secure that one. If the second tent went, our expedition would be in a world of hurt.

Finally, around two in the afternoon the wind began to calm. When it was clear that the worst was over, I went outside to inspect the damage. Remarkably, the cook tent was the only one damaged. One of the Sherpas suggested that we use blue tarps to cover the ripped sections, and we radioed Eric at base camp to send some up. Then we congratulated ourselves on our team-work. It was only because everyone had pitched in that we hadn't suffered potentially expedition-ending damage.

The following morning, Kevin, Stuart, and Ted left again for Camp 3. But as if the mountain itself were conspiring against them, that night the wind returned. They radioed in the morning to say that conditions were very bad—whiteout, wind, and drifting snow—and they were unsure if they should stay or come down. I counseled them to stay. The route to Camp 3 scales the steep icy side of the Lhotse Face and is difficult in the best conditions. Descending in a near blizzard is a bad idea. Technically I couldn't tell them what to do because they weren't my clients, but I sure didn't want them to get in trouble. They debated for some time and finally decided to come down. I told them to keep me informed of their progress and then went to tell Mark Tucker what was going on.

"They'll probably be okay on the fixed rope," he said, "but they'll have trouble when they get to the bottom." The fixed rope ended at the foot of the Lhotse Face, and there were few wands to mark the route from there to ABC.

"Let's go for a walk," I said, and we each grabbed a bundle of wands.

Unfortunately the wind was blowing as hard at ABC as it was up higher, and fog and blowing snow made visibility nil. We made it less than halfway to the Lhotse Face when we could no longer see where we were going.

"What do you think?" I yelled to Tuck.

"I can think of better ways to kill myself."

"Let's come back later." It would be a few hours before Kevin, Stuart, and Ted started down: They still had to dress, eat, pack up, and get their crampons on. If we were at all lucky, the weather might mellow a bit before they got to the bottom. Meanwhile, if it cleared up down here, Mark and I could go back out.

An hour later I was resting in the tent when my radio bleeped. It was Kevin.

"Phil, we can't find the rope. It's buried."

"Have you tried to pull it out?"

"Yeah, we can't."

"Can you see anything up ahead?"

"No. Visibility's zip."

Apparently the fixed rope had been covered by drifting snow. With no visibility there was no way to know if it was covered for 5 feet or 500.

"What about unclipping and climbing down till we find it again?"

"Don't chance it. Go back up."

"Okay. It's just me and Ted. Stuart never came down."

"Good. Hopefully, he'll have hot drinks for you when you get back."

I lay down next to Sue but I couldn't relax. Part of me was relieved to know they were going back up: They wouldn't have to get back to ABC without wands. But the temperature was around zero, they were at 23,000 feet, and the wind was picking up. That section of the climb was steep and icy and in a few hours it would be dark. They were in deep trouble and there was nothing I could do but wait.

An hour later the radio crackled again and I grabbed it. "Where are you?"

"We're still on our way up."

"How're you feeling?"

"Freezing. Ted thinks his nose is frostbitten and I can't feel my feet. But we're moving."

"Good job. Keep going. Not too much farther."

"We'll make it."

The fact that Kevin was still positive was a good sign, but it was hard to feel much relief. As time wore on, they were getting higher, colder, and more tired, and it was getting closer to dark. I went over and told Tuck they were okay and then, for the next hour and a half, I lay in the tent and visualized them up there. The climb to Camp 3 requires putting one foot in front of the other, over and over again, kicking your crampons into steep, hard ice, and pulling yourself up on your jumar. In the steepest sections, you're on just your front points. It's strenuous, the air is thin, and each step requires four or five deep breaths just to keep going. In good conditions the climb takes three to four hours. But where on the Lhotse Face were they? How many more hours did they have ahead?

It was dark when Kevin called again.

"Where are you?"

"We made it."

I let out a huge exhale, probably the first one in three hours. "You okay?"

"Yeah. A little nip on Ted's nose, but otherwise okay."

"Good. Get something hot to drink. And Kevin—we've got plenty of oxygen at Camp 3. Use it." I knew they had to be borderline hypothermic; oxygen would go a long way toward warming them up.

I got off the radio, told Sue and Tuck the news, and then crawled into my bag and slept as deeply as if I had made the climb myself.

The next morning when I stepped out of the tent, the broad sweep of the Western Cwm lay before me, clear as a crystal bowl. The flanks of the three upper mountains dazzled in the sun. All signs of wind and whiteout were gone. Kevin radioed down to say that the weather was equally clear up at Camp 3 and that two climbers, one British and one Hungarian, had just started down. He, Ted, and Stuart would leave shortly. Sue, Tuck, and I had breakfast in the cook tent, then Sue went back to our tent while Tuck and I stayed to chat with Dave Hahn, Ben Marshall, Jake Norton, and Lisa Rust, other IMG guides who had joined us on the mountain to lead another team. We were standing outside the cook tent when a climber we didn't recognize came walking into camp. The urgency in his manner suggested that something out of the ordinary had happened. He strode up to us and blurted, "There's been an accident. My partner has fallen." He explained that he had been leading the way down the Lhotse Face not far below Camp 3 when he turned around to check on his partner, Peter Legate. Apparently these were the British and Hungarian climbers Kevin had mentioned. Seconds later, for no apparent reason, Peter had begun careening, head over heels, down the slope. As this man, Laszlo Mecs, watched, Peter had hurtled past him at tremendous speed and had slammed headfirst into the bergschrund at the foot of the Lhotse Face.

Lisa volunteered to stay behind to watch camp, and the rest of us geared up to walk with Laszlo out to the 'schrund. Fifteen minutes out, we met Kevin, Ted, and Stuart on their way down. Without exchanging a word they knew what we were doing. They had followed Peter's bloody trail down the mountain. When we reached the bergschrund a single glance confirmed what we already knew. Peter had slammed into the ice wall of the glacier where it was separating from the mountain and dropped 20 feet into the crevasse that had formed where the glacier pulled away. He was lying head down in the snow so that only one of his boots was visible. We lowered Laszlo into the crevasse so that he could confirm that Peter was dead, and after strenuous digging, he was able to free Peter's pack, which he brought up to give to the man's family. There was no practical way to retrieve the body or to arrange to send it home, so standing on the edge of the crevasse we held a short memorial, honoring a man whom most of us had never met. Then we walked with Laszlo back to Camp 2.

. . .

We knew the minute Phil and the others came back to camp what had happened. Phil's face was ashen and his eyes were glassy. It reminded me of how he had looked after Chris Hooyman died. As soon as he made sure that Laszlo was cared for, we went back to our tent and lay down. I put my arm around him, over his sleeping bag, and we were silent for a long while.

"It's such a waste!" he said finally. "Such a stupid waste. Marty, Kerrebrock, Hooyman, Peter . . ."

I imagined Peter's family back in England hearing of his death. I imagined his friends and all the people who knew him, grieving.

"You never get comfortable with it," Phil said. "I never *want* to get comfortable with it. I don't ever want to be someone who handles death well."

I thought back to 2001 when Babu had died. I had not handled that death well. On our way into Camp 2 we had passed a young, grinning Sherpa goofing around, standing on his head at the side of the trail. Phil had said, "That's Babu," and I had felt a quiver of excitement. Babu Chiri Sherpa was a legend. He had summited Everest ten times, had achieved his dream of spending twenty hours on the summit without oxygen, and had set the record for the fastest ascent from base camp, making it in seventeen hours. He was using his renown to raise money to build a school in his village. Now he was leading an international team of climbers and staying at Camp 2 at the same time we were. Our first morning in camp we woke up to a commotion on the radio. Our first thought was that there had been an accident, and we dressed quickly, thinking we would help with the rescue. But as the voices continued it became clear that it was not a rescue, but a body evacuation: Someone was being carried off the mountain. The someone turned out to be Babu. He had been out the evening before, apparently taking pictures of the summit, and fallen through a snow bridge over a hidden crevasse. Several guides and Sherpas had retrieved his body earlier in the morning.

Babu's death had paralyzed me. He was one of the best in the world and he had died; what in the world was I doing up here? Phil and I talked about it at length. We took a day off from climbing. I couldn't shake the fear that death had seen us.

"Susan," Phil said, "Babu's death was an accident, a fluke. We all feel terrible about it, but it doesn't change anything for us. This mountain is no more dangerous today than it was yesterday. If we're going to take anything from his death, let's just focus more closely on what we need to do."

The following morning we continued up, but it took several days of climbing for me to lose the heightened fear that Babu's death had brought. After that I checked my jumar and harness a hundred times a day.

And now a second death: Peter's. This was different from Babu's. This time I didn't feel afraid, but I felt terrible for Phil because he had seen it and it had shaken him so badly.

We were quiet for a little longer, each lost in our own thoughts. I kept imagining what it must have been like to fall. "I hope he didn't suffer."

"Sue, it's not like he just slid to the bottom. You don't just slide down really steep ice. It's violent. You hit the ice once and then you're airborne. You somersault and then you hit again . . ." Phil let out a deep sigh. "All we can hope is that the first bounce knocked him out. He was probably dead long before he hit the bottom."

I tried to push away the images that came to mind. "Why did he unclip? Do you think he didn't realize?"

"I don't know."

"Do you think he unclipped because the rope was buried?"

"Sue, I don't have a clue. We'll never know why. But why is not important. The important thing is to stay clipped in up there. To check and double-check."

Phil had adopted his guide voice. For the moment anyway, his grief was giving way to his professional reason, to the need to look ahead at how to move on from this situation. I knew we *would* check and double-check. I knew that in all likelihood we would be fine. What had happened to Babu and Marty and Hooyman and Peter would not happen to us because we would not unclip, we would check our safety harnesses, we would remind each other to the point of being redundant. If something were to happen to us up here, or on any other mountain, chances were it would be an avalanche or a collapse in the Icefall, something beyond our control. Oddly, I took a kind of reassurance from that because it meant that if anything happened to Phil, it would happen to me too.

. . .

After Peter's death Sue and I moved to Camp 3, where we stayed for a night of acclimatization. Then we went back down to base camp where our main job was to wait and be patient. The next time we left it would be for the summit. Unfortunately the decision to leave was not entirely ours. In order to summit we needed good weather up top, which meant we needed a good forecast—minimal snow, no jet stream winds— six to seven days in the future. We also needed to have the fixed ropes in place. Sherpas had put ropes in as far as high camp and were now pushing them up toward the Balcony, but the final stretch to the summit had not yet been completed. Whichever team got there first would finish the job. On May 9, our eighth day at base camp, the Internet weather forecasts all agreed: Winds would be at their ebb on May 16. All around base camp, teams were hearing the same news. It was time to go.

The climb through the Icefall to Camp 1 and then on to Camps 2 and 3 took us four days. The weather was consistently clear; we were well acclimatized, and lest I jinx us by feeling too optimistic, I tried to bite back my sense that this time Chomolungma, Mother Goddess of the World—as the Sherpas call Everest—was smiling on us. On May 14, when we reached Camp 3, Sue and I put on our down suits. Neither of us said it but I'm sure we were thinking the same thing: The next time we take them off, the climb will be over, one way or the other.

The following morning we got an early start. Unlike the previous year, we wanted to get to Camp 4 early in the afternoon so we would have time to rest and hydrate before leaving at 10:00 p.m. for the summit. It was pleasant going up. There was no wind and filtered sunshine and, occasionally, snow flurries that gave the craggy summits around us a snow globe air. We climbed up through the Yellow Band and over the Geneva Spur—Everest landmarks I had read about as a child and become familiar with as an adult. I had time to appreciate the fact that now I was climbing them with my wife. When we got into high camp it was 2:30 in the afternoon, just as we had planned.

The difference between high camp this year and last year couldn't have been greater. The site where last year we had been barely able to stand, and where blowing snow had made visibility next to nothing, was as calm and clear as our Seattle backyard. Colder by 75 degrees, but perfect summit weather. In fact, maybe too perfect. Half of base camp seemed to be up here waiting to summit. I looked around at the clusters of tents scattered across the South Col and thought about 1996, the year twelve climbers died between this point and the summit. Yes, a severe storm had contributed to their deaths, but bottlenecks along the route had been another factor. Climbers who might have survived the storm had died because they had been unable to descend in a timely fashion. *Didn't we learn anything from 1996?* I thought. Facing potentially the same situation, how could I let us go up? For several minutes I agonized over the decision. We had plenty of oxygen; we could easily wait a day while the other climbers went, then try ourselves the following day. But how could we come this far and not try to summit when the weather was absolutely perfect? I went back and forth, mounting equally persuasive arguments on both sides. Finally I came to an argument I couldn't counter: Weather was the one variable we couldn't control; what if we waited and the weather turned bad and we lost our chance? *We'll figure it out,* I decided. *It'll be crowded but we'll be careful.*

That afternoon we paid minute attention to details: what we would wear, what we would carry, the condition of our equipment. To travel light we stripped our provisions to the barest essentials: candy bars and water bottles in our pockets; new batteries in our headlamps; extra gloves, hats, and batteries in our packs. I stuck our little point-and-shoot camera in an inside pocket so it wouldn't freeze. Then at 5:00 we went to bed. I lay in my bag listening to the groan of the ice and the occasional sounds from other camps and thought about the eight ball. For thirty years now on Rainier we'd kept a fortune-telling eight ball at Camp Muir, and every night before a summit climb we'd jokingly consult it. Somebody would intone in mock seriousness, "Will we summit tomorrow?" Then he'd shake the ball and watch the answers swirl around until one swam up into the viewing window. Several answers were possible: *yes, no, can't tell you at this time . . .* If we got one we didn't like, we just shook the ball again until we got the answer we wanted. Now I imagined holding the eight ball in my hand. "Will Sue and I summit tomorrow?" I asked it and watched as the answers swirled around. I wasn't at all surprised at the one that surfaced: *Signs say yes.*

. . .

When we got up at 9:00 p.m. the Sherpas were already melting snow for water. Phil, of course, was out of the tent in a flash. Dorjee Lama and Danuru Sherpa had come to join us at high camp; they would be accompanying us for this last part of the climb. Phil had especially asked for Dorjee be-cause he felt he had denied him the summit last year, and Eric, who as expedition leader assigned the Sherpas, had graciously offered us Danuru, who was one of the strongest climbers. Now the four of us would be a team. When Phil came back a few moments later, I was out of my sleeping bag and fumbling with the laces of my boots.

"I've been talking to Dorjee," he said. "The ropes aren't completely fixed yet."

I looked up.

"A couple of Sherpas are working on it just above the Balcony."

"How long do you think it'll take them to get to the top?"

"Four, five hours; hard to know."

I looked down at my boot. We hadn't come this far just to get turned back by the ropes.

"I'm not saying they won't make it," Phil said. "They're ahead of us, and right now that's all we need. I'm just saying this might not work out."

With new vigor I pulled the laces tight. The weather was perfect, we were strong, and everything had been going well. I was not going to believe that a few thousand feet of rope were going to stop us from getting to the summit. I remem-bered what Phil had told me about imagining the eight ball. "Signs say yes," I said to him.

Phil just nodded.

Almost from the beginning, I was in a groove. Everything was so much better than last year! There was just a light wind, no blowing snow, no troublesome crampons. We were wear-ing goggles (no eye problems!) and after all that training, I was noticeably stronger. The steps that had felt like benches the year before were now their actual size. I was still anticipating the moment when the climb would start to feel impossible when I realized we had reached the Balcony.

We found a spot on the ledge and sat down on our packs. Phil changed both of our oxygen tanks—"It's amazing what you can do when you can see," he joked—and was just about to have a snack when he noticed that the train of lights ahead of us had stopped. "Looks like there's a bottleneck up above." He reached into his breast pocket and pulled out the radio. "Eric?"

Eric's voice crackled up out of the darkness. "Yo, Phil."

"Looks like there might be a bottleneck above the Balcony."

"Yeah, I hear the guys are still working on the ropes. That's probably what's hanging everybody up."

Phil clicked off the radio and put it back in his pocket. "It's a crapshoot," he said.

I felt a stab of angry determination.

After a snack we inserted ourselves back into what was now a slowly moving line. By this time the sun was rising and I could see the climbers in front of me. In their down suits and oxygen masks they looked like colorful alien snowmen trundling uphill one slow step at a time. All around us the sharp ridges of neighboring peaks were differentiating themselves from the darkness. We were on a narrow ridge, just a few feet down from the crest, and were moving single file, everyone stepping orderly into the steps of the previous climber. After fifteen or twenty minutes, the climber in front of me stopped. I looked up. There must have been twenty-five climbers in the line, all standing perfectly still. I looked back at Phil, who shook his head.

"It's not looking good."

I will stand here all day if I have to, I thought. We would not be stopped by those ropes! I knew we couldn't really do that. We had to either summit or turn around by early afternoon, before we got too cold and tired, before we ran out of oxygen, before afternoon storms made the mountain unsafe. I couldn't bear the idea that we had come this close only to be turned away again.

As if he could read my mind, Phil said, "The weather's

good. We can stand here for a while. You okay staying here for a little while?"

We stood for another half hour. To rest my legs I shifted my weight back and forth, relaxing first one leg then the other.

Phil shook his head again. "It's too slow. I don't think we can wait it out."

I didn't even acknowledge that he had spoken. I just stared upward as if the intensity of my gaze could laser through the holdup and get the ropes in place.

Finally, after another half hour, word came down the line: Willie Benegas, an Argentine guide with another expedition, and Apa Sherpa were fixing the ropes to the top. I looked up and, sure enough, I could see them: two small shapes, barely moving, making their way toward the south summit. They crept upward, then stopped, crept and stopped, in a painstaking crawl up the 45-degree face. I felt a chill of vertigo knowing that they were hanging on the side of the mountain without a fixed rope.

At the same time I felt a flood of elation. They were there! They were doing it! We would be able to go up! For the first time that day I felt patient, as if my eagerness had been willing them upward and now that I could see them making it, I could relax. I turned my back to the mountain and looked out. Close below us, snow-cragged peaks fanned out like a sea of sharks' teeth, their pointed tops just catching the pinking light. Behind them, another sea of peaks, softer, bluer, merged with the sky. And superimposed on all, like a sign from another world, lay a perfect, dark, sharp-edged triangle: the shadow of Everest cast by the rising sun. *Remember this, Sue!* I thought. *Take it in, lock it in your brain, keep it forever!* For the next forty minutes, as the light grew and the pinks and blues faded and the peaks crystallized into sharp black-and-white relief, I stared out at the Himalayas and tried to fix that image in my mind. For those forty minutes, there was no place else in the world I wanted to be.

After a while there was a stirring up ahead. I looked up to where Willie and Apa had been fixing the ropes and saw that they had disappeared over the top of the slope. A few minutes later the line began to move. Now we progressed steadily. At the south summit (which, despite its name, is still two hours from the actual summit) we stopped to make our last oxygen bottle change. Then, after a short, steep pitch, we began the long narrow ridge that leads to the Hillary Step. "Look down!" Phil hollered. "You've got Nepal on one side, Tibet on the other!" but there was no way I was looking down, except to check my jumar and harness. Ever since we'd left the Balcony, Danuru, who was climbing with me, had been speeding up. He was in a hurry to get to the top. Now, just before the Hillary Step, he grabbed my arm and pulled me around several slower climbers. When I looked back, Phil and Dorjee had stayed behind. "What about Phil and Dorjee?"

Danuru waved his hand. "They catch up," he said, and hurried on. I had no choice but to follow.

The Hillary Step made me very nervous. It is a 60-degree slope, half rock, half snow, that demands as much courage and rock-climbing skill as it does strength and stamina. I am not a proficient rock climber in the best of conditions, and now I was at 29,000 feet, in a down suit, holding an ice axe and jumar, wearing an oxygen mask and goggles that obscured my vision. The fact that Phil was not behind me made me even shakier. I followed Danuru, hoping to put my feet and hands where he put his, but he was so quick that I was soon left to find hand- and footholds on my own. The rope was so tight against the rock I could barely slide my jumar, and in places there were four or five ropes and I didn't know which to use. I could barely see my feet, much less know where to put them, and with every third or fourth step, my crampons slid backwards down the rock, leaving me hanging by my arms. Each time I looked up, I saw Danuru getting farther and farther ahead, turning occasionally to motion to me with his arm.

After half an hour of climbing there was only a single rock outcrop between me and the top. The rock was taller than I was, and to get over it I had to hoist my whole body up and over. I didn't dare thrust myself upward. I was clinging to this precipice like an ant on the side of a table with nothing but empty air behind me. What if I fell? I tried to inch up slowly, but I got nowhere. There were no cracks into which I could put a hand or foot. I could feel the pressure of the people on the rope behind me. Again I wished it were Phil behind me, but I was also glad it wasn't; I didn't want him to see how poorly I was climbing. *Just go, Sue! Just do it!* I reached up with the jumar and planted my ice axe into a snowy spot above my head, then jumped and pulled at the same time. My chest came to rest draped over the rock, my head facing downhill on the other side. Below me a serrated ridge of knife-edged rocks sloped away. I couldn't move. I knew I had to hoist one leg over the rock and push, but I was paralyzed with fear. If I fell the rocks would cut me to shreds. Suddenly I felt myself being hoisted through the air. A second later I was flat on my stomach on the uphill side. Danuru had grabbed my pack and pulled me over. *Thank God!* I wanted to kiss him. Inching forward on my belly I unclipped the jumar and clipped it to the next rope, then I crawled away from the edge. Danuru was already moving forward up the gentler slope that led toward the summit.

"Danuru! Wait!" I didn't want to go farther without Phil. I knew there was nothing difficult between here and the summit, and I didn't want to get there without him. But Danuru was marching briskly along, eager to reach the top, and didn't hear me. I hiked as fast as I could behind him, stopping every now and then to holler. Finally he turned around. "Wait for Phil!" I shouted.

"He catch up," Danuru hollered back.

I shook my head. "I'm stopping!"

Dutifully, Danuru came back and we sat down in the snow and waited. Other climbers moved past us. I listened to the crunch of their crampons in the snow and the rhythm of their heavy breathing, and as I sat there a feeling of intense joy came over me. We were going to do it!

A few minutes later Phil and Dorjee came up over the top of the Step. I leaped to my feet. I felt like shouting, "We're going to make it! We're going to make it!" but that little voice that says, "Don't tempt fate!" stopped me. Instead, I just grinned at Phil from inside my oxygen mask. Behind his mask I knew that he was grinning too.

We let Danuru and Dorjee go ahead, and Phil walked right behind me. It was much less exposed here: The ridge was wide and covered with snow, and instead of peaks below us there was a sea of clouds. What would the summit look like? I had built it up so in my mind. Fifteen minutes later Phil inched up beside me. Ahead of us the sky met the ground in a smooth arc.

"We're going to make it! We're going to stand on top of the world together!" I screamed inside like a child.

They say that at the moment of death your whole life flashes before your eyes. Well, now I know that sometimes that happens when you're at the height of your life too. In that moment I saw *both* my lives—my life with Phil and the one I would have lived without him. The other life was as clear to me as the real one: a life of friends and pleasures, challenges and rewards, a good life by any measure—but a life without a heart. And then I saw the whole progression of my life with Phil—from the lusty days at Sun Valley, to my first climb of Mt. Rainier, to the mind-opening trip to Kilimanjaro. I saw us building our house, getting engaged in Sikkim; saw Phil's surgeries and the Everest attempt last year—and I felt such a swell of wholeness and love and gratitude that my eyes welled up behind my goggles, and the crystalline line between the snow and sky became a blur. Then I heard a familiar sound: prayer flags whipping in the wind. I looked up and the splotches of red and yellow, green and blue, were only a long stone's throw away. Next to me, Phil pulled aside his oxygen mask and leaned his face close to mine. "You made it, baby!" he said, and I started to cry.

"Phil! We need a summit picture!"

Phil was busy talking to three climbers who had come up the north side. A few moments later he came over to where Dorjee, Danuru, and I were standing. "Time to get off this thing."

"After we get a picture."

"Sue, I really want to get us down." His guide side had taken over. We'd had our fifteen minutes of victory; now he was focused on getting us off the summit safely.

"Phil, we're not going without a . . ." But he had already turned and was heading toward the trail.

In a flash Dorjee grabbed the camera from me. "Phil! Wait!"

Phil turned, and in that second I sprinted to where he was standing just below the crest of the summit. I stood there in my big saffron suit, grinning from ear to ear, holding the American flag I'd brought for the occasion. Phil stood behind me, caught between his competing desires to record the moment and to get us off the mountain safely. Dorjee snapped the picture, and Phil turned back down.

"Wait, Phil! One more! Someone else in picture!"

Dutifully, Phil turned around and Dorjee snapped another. It was almost exactly as I had seen it in my mind's eye a year before, the day Phil told me to buy the Suunto.

September 2002

Phil,
My life's-work direction is changing. I cannot find the words to
express my appreciation of your support. If alone, I do not believe I
would have taken this risk. And alone, I would never have
experienced such happiness in all aspects of my life. Love you, my
partner.

                                                    Sue

February 2003

Susan,
I love the mountaintops and the valleys with you. That's the key . . .
with you. Other guys are very jealous of me, they just want a Susan
of their own. But I've got the original. Have a good day, gorgeous.

                                                    Love,
                                                    Phil

8

THE FALL

May 18, 2002

It took us two months to get up and two days to get back down, and every step down was a paradox. On the one hand, I wanted to get off that mountain as fast as possible; on the other, I wanted to burn every sight, every sensation into my brain because I knew I would never be here again. I wanted to prolong and savor the pure, unadulterated thrill. *We had done it.*

At our last big crevasse near the bottom of the Icefall, Phil decided to use up the rest of the tape in the camera by filming his feet stepping across the ladder. "I can't wait to see this!" I laughed. I settled myself in the snow on the other side as he began moving across slowly, the camera glued to his eye. After a minute, he stopped. "You get a little vertigo looking through that thing."

"Oh, come on, Phil, you've only got another ten feet to go."

He gave me a wry look and continued on, narrating as he went. "Yup, this is a pretty big one, one hundred feet deep, maybe twenty across . . . almost there . . . Don't be nervous, Mom . . . *Shoot!*"

"What!"

He was standing at the edge of the ladder where it met my side, staring at the camera. "I forgot to take the darn lens cap off."

"Well, jeez, Phil, just go back and do it again."

He stepped off the ladder and rewound the tape. There was the black screen with Phil's narration in the background, followed by "*Shoot!* I forgot to take the darn lens cap off," and my voice saying, "Well, jeez, Phil, just go back and do it again." Phil turned off the camera and tucked it in his pocket. "Come on, let's get off this sucker." We looked at each other and started to laugh.

Back at base camp Eric, Tuck, Kevin, Ted, and Stuart ran out to greet us. One of the Sherpas brought us hot tea, and then we all descended on the mess tent. Ever since we'd left high camp the previous morning I'd been visualizing the real food we'd get at base camp—mashed potatoes, fresh vegetables, rice, meat—instead of the cookies, candy bars, and hot cereal we ate up high, and sure enough, within minutes Pemba had put out a big pot of potatoes. I dolloped heaping spoonfuls onto my plate, but after a few mouthfuls I had to put down my fork. My mouth was willing, but my stomach still thought it was up at 26,000 feet. I sat back, closed my eyes, and waited for the queasiness to pass. All around me, the other climbers were sharing war stories from the climb.

Phil was telling the lens cap story when Igor Tsarouk came over, bearing Russian chocolates and a bottle of Georgian brandy. Igor was a tall, thin antelope of a man; he and Phil had guided together on Mt. Elbrus for years. Now he and a team of Russian climbers were here at base camp. They were warm and boisterous, and they had turned base camp into an ongoing party. They also had provided me with a visual memory I will never forget. They had built themselves a sauna out of rocks and tarps, and every morning as I stumbled out to the cook tent in my down coat to get my morning coffee, I'd see a big, burly Russian standing on a rock, bright red and stark naked except for a tiny Speedo and a pair of hiking boots. It was a better wake-up than the caffeine! Now Igor came in, bearing his treats. His team had left the day before, but he had waited behind to extend his congratulations. I leaned back in my chair, my head against Phil's shoulder, and as I listened to the stories, a feeling of ease and exhaustion came over me. It hadn't been a hard day—I had felt really energized coming down the mountain—but now, as if the effort of the whole two-month ordeal had just caught up with me, I couldn't wait to get into my sleeping bag and go to sleep.

Unfortunately, that turned out not to be on the agenda. Back in Seattle our friend Dan McConnell, who was managing director of DDB Public Relations, had heard from Eric via satellite phone that we had summited, and had notified the Associated Press that the first couple in history had scaled the Seven Summits together. Shortly after we got back we called Dan ourselves, and he informed us that most of the Seattle media wanted interviews, as did Fredericka Whitfield of CNN. The idea of being on national TV was exciting; the only trouble was, because of the time difference between Atlanta and Nepal, we had to do it at midnight—at least six hours past what I had hoped would be my bedtime. After dinner we went back to our tent and lay down. We tried to read, to write in our journals, to play a couple of games of hearts, but with each activity it got harder and harder to keep our eyes open. It was just so warm and comfy in those down sleeping bags, on level ground . . . Finally we gave up and set the alarm for 11:30. I fell asleep thinking, *This is a mistake; with only two hours' sleep I'm going to wake up completely blotto.*

At 11:45 we put on our down parkas and headlamps and dragged ourselves out of the tent. I knew it was an excellent thing that Fredericka Whitfield was about to interview us, but I sure wished I could do it lying in my bag. We walked to the communications tent, where Anya, the IMG communications guru, would field the call, and at 11:59, from halfway around the world, we heard Fredericka's upbeat voice. Fortunately, Phil spoke first. He sounded so polished—so untired!—you'd have thought he was a media professional. I thought, *Oh, boy, I'm going to sound like an idiot compared to him!* After a few questions Fredericka turned her attention to me.

"Congratulations, Sue," she said, "how's the view so far?"

The view? I thought. *What view? We're sitting in a tent in the middle of the night.* Then I realized she meant the view from the summit. "Oh, the view from up there? Oh, it was absolutely beautiful. You could see forever." She asked which of us had kept the momentum going to do all Seven Summits. I blabbered for a minute about how the climbs had gradually evolved, but admitted that I was the one who had pushed for doing Everest. Then she hit me with the whammy. "So, how in the world do you top this? What do you plan to do next?"

Do next? I haven't even made it down from here! Who knows what I'm going to do next! "Well, Fredericka, I think I'm, uh . . ." I said the first thing that popped into my head. "I think I'll work on lowering my golf handicap." Fredericka laughed, then I laughed, then we both laughed at the same time, then she congratulated us once more. And then, mercifully, it was over. Within five minutes I was back in my sleeping bag, dead to the world.

Two days later, in one of our last acts at base camp, we took down the American and Nepalese flags from the *puja* altar. Phil grabbed them almost before they were off the pole, and we both saw Ang Passang register a fleeting look of disappointment. "Here, you take it," Phil said, holding the Nepalese flag out to him, but Ang Passang shook his head. So Phil folded the two flags and stuffed them into his duffel.

"Don't you think we should try to get Ang Passang to take his flag?" I asked Phil later as we were walking out of camp.

He gave me one of those slightly annoyed looks, as if I were underestimating him. "That's why I wanted it. I was planning to give it to him. I just wanted to present it to him at the party."

I should have known. "What a nice guy you are, Phil." I gave him a little poke in the arm. "And what's your plan for the American flag?"

He got a little glimmer in his eye, as if this time he was pleased to be caught. "If my dad were alive I would have taken it for him. Instead, this is going to your father."

For what felt like the umpteenth time in twenty-four hours, my eyes filled with tears.

The walk out to Namche Bazaar was like regaining our sight after being blind. It was sensory overload. For three months we had seen nothing but gray, white, and blue and heard nothing but wind, breath, ice, and crampons. Now we were hiking past 8-foot rhododendrons covered with hand-size pink blossoms. Birds warbled in the branches and with each step our boots kicked up the smell of warm earth. A river, swollen with runoff, raced and gurgled, and the air was so thick and warm we could feel it against our skin. Just outside of Namche we met three ten-year-old girls, each more beautiful than the next, walking home from school. We stopped and took their picture, and traded candy and flowers. It was a simple interaction, no different from the dozens we'd had with villagers during our trek in—yet it was so different because this time my eyes were open! I wasn't focused on the climb, I wasn't worried about what lay ahead; I was free to see and appreciate everything and everyone around me. For one of the few times in my life, I felt truly at peace in the world.

Our last night in the Khumbu valley we had our traditional farewell party with the Sherpas. We gathered in a little teahouse in a village called Syangboche, where batteries kept the boom box going all night and we danced until dawn. At one point people made little speeches and Phil said truthfully, "If we hadn't made the summit it would have been because of us. But we did make it, and in large part it's because of the Sherpas." Then we all draped our arms around each other, and while the Sherpas chanted we mimicked their steps in a traditional circle dance. It was rowdy and sentimental and serious all at the same time. For the last few months our well-being had been in these men's hands and now we would be moving on with our very different lives. Phil and I might return to trek in the Himalayas but we would never again climb Everest together. We might see some of these men again, but our paths would never cross in quite the same way. Celebrating together was a way of acknowledging how much we owed them.

Just before the party ended, Phil clanged his pocketknife against a glass, and when the hubbub died down, he said, "Passang, come here." Ang Passang looked a little embarrassed, but Phil called again and Passang joined him at the end of the room. Phil pulled the Nepalese flag out of his rucksack and cleared his throat. "Remember this flag?" he said. "This flag's for you and all the Sherpas. Its rightful place is here in Nepal."

The next morning an old Russian military helicopter came and flew us out of the Khumbu valley and back to the bustling metropolis of Kathmandu.

And where did we go to dinner? That night Phil and I, with Eric, Tuck, and Dorjee, went to the Rum Doodle. I was so excited that, even though this was the first "real" dinner we'd had in three months, I could hardly eat. After dinner Phil and I went behind the bar and the bartender pointed to the spot where we should sign. The restaurant was full of climbers, most of whom had also just come down from Everest, and they all watched and applauded as we signed. Friends of ours took pictures. Then Phil called Dorjee to come up and sign. Dorjee shook his head as if he didn't deserve the recognition, and the bartender frowned as if he didn't approve of a Sherpa signing (I think they discourage Sherpas simply because so many summit), but Phil made it clear that Dorjee was going to sign the board. Awkwardly, but grinning from ear to

ear, Dorjee went up and wrote his name. Afterwards someone ordered us a round of duck farts, a sweet concoction you
can drink a million of before you realize you're under the
table, and it was hard to tell which of us—me or Dorjee—was
more euphoric.

The next day we flew home. As we sat on the tarmac waiting to take off, I unfolded the English-language newspaper I
had bought, and an article on Buddhist philosophy caught my
eye. It discussed the limited ability of material things to provide deep, long-lasting happiness, and as I read it I thought
how apt it was. Back in my pre-Phil days, I did collect posses-
sions. The boat, the condo, the nice dinners and the fine
wines, all made me feel that I had achieved. But over the past
decade I had come to see the fallacy of that way of thinking.
The things that gave my life meaning now were far less tangible: the interactions with other people, the sense of personal
achievement, the experiences that had stretched and
changed me, and, above all, the sharing of my life with Phil.
The article posed a question: If you could take one thing with
you when you die, what would it be? and I knew the answer
immediately: my wedding ring, because it would be a way of
taking Phil and Everest and all the experiences we had
shared, and keeping them with me forever.

I looked down after takeoff hoping to see Everest one last
time, but before I was able to pinpoint any landmarks, the
snowcapped peaks disappeared beneath the clouds.
Nonetheless, a tremendous feeling of contentment flowed
through me. We had done it. Everest. The Seven Summits.
The whole dang dream. I looked over at Phil. "You know, if I
died now, I'd be okay."

Phil looked at me skeptically. "You weren't so ready to go a
few days ago when we were in the Icefall."

I punched him in the arm. "I didn't want to die on Everest.
But now that we've done it, I just feel so . . . complete."

"That's good," he said, kissing me, "because we're not going back."

I grinned. He was teasing both of us about our battle the year before.

"You know, I don't think I realized how important this was to you. I mean, I knew it was important, but I didn't realize *how* important. Even last year, when I agreed to go back."

"I don't think I knew, either. Until this very minute, I really don't think I knew." But sitting there on that plane, Phil beside me, I felt such a feeling of wholeness and *relief*: I had finally accomplished the one spectacular thing I had wanted—and I had done it with Phil.

• • •

We came out of customs into the arms of my mom and Sue's parents. John Waechter was there, and Dan McConnell, and many of our other friends along with a passel of reporters. One of the reporters asked me how this was different from 1984, and I said the same true thing I'd said to Sue on the summit, "This time was better." I saw the pride in Sue's parents' eyes and remembered my own father pumping his fist in 1984. I took enormous pleasure in seeing their joy.

From the airport we went to my mother's house for a little party. As the guests began leaving I got out the flag and drew Sue's dad off to a corner. "Roy," I said, "if my father were still alive, I would have brought this flag back for him. But now I want you to have it." He got a big smile on his face and I could see that the gesture had moved him. "Thank you, Phil," he said. "Mary and I both thank you for this—and for bringing Susan home."

Then Sue and I had four weeks to get reacquainted with our home, our routines, our First World life, and then I had to leave again to lead a climb on Mt. McKinley.

. . .

The contentment I'd felt on the airplane was like a perfume that continued to delight me after we got home. It clung to me as we conducted the last of our media interviews (including our "grand finale" with Diane Sawyer on *Good Morning America*), as we unpacked and saw friends, as we readjusted to life at Internet speed. If anything, it grew bolder as we talked about how, if I wanted, instead of getting a job I could now pursue the speaking. It clung until Phil left for McKinley—and then *bam*, it disappeared. The climb was done, our fifteen minutes were over, Phil was gone, and I was alone. For the first time in more than twenty years, I had no job, no office, no team. There was no one waiting for me to turn in sales figures, no one asking me to remove an obstacle, no problem needing my attention. With Phil's encouragement I had decided to postpone looking for a job in order to give the speaking a shot, but the days rolled out, long and open, and I didn't know what to do. *Who was I?* Corporate sales was practically all I'd ever done. It had shown me I could succeed; it had given me my sense of self. The corporation had been my identity, my security, my sense of future. What would happen if I left it behind? I had a flimsy notion of who I *wanted* to be, but that was a dream, not a business, and I wasn't sure how to turn it into one. How much easier it would be just to go back to the corporate world! But each time I thought that, a part of me rose up in disappointment. For four years now I had fantasized about creating my own business. How could I live with myself if I gave up without even trying?

Phil came home and once again, as I had before Everest, I babbled endlessly about what to do. He assured me that we had enough money to weather my "incubation" and urged me to pursue my dream. But that only increased the pressure. I hated the idea of relying on him for money. Giving up my income for even a short time made me feel uncomfortably dependent. Phil left for Rainier and I rattled around the house, wondering whom to call, what to do first, and then one day I got a call from a former boss. He was now with a data networking company in San Francisco and wondered if I would be interested in becoming their Vice President for Western Sales. *Vice President for Western Sales?* It was everything the anxious part of me wanted! The whole time he talked, two voices warred in my head. *Grab it, Sue, it's perfect! Don't do it, Sue, stay true to your dream.*

A week later I flew down for interviews. Afterwards I called Phil. "It's a good company, Phil, and they're making me an incredible offer. Great salary and benefits, great stock options. How can I turn that down?"

"You can if you want to."

I walked down Market Street and looked out across the bay, feeling the yearning for the security the job represented. Ever since my former boss called I'd felt grounded, like my old self again. With the prospect of a corporate job, my confidence had returned. But I couldn't put aside the feeling that if I took the job I would have to live with a sense of regret. I walked along the Embarcadero to Fisherman's Wharf and browsed among the stalls. I liked San Francisco; it would be fun to come here a lot, get to know the city. I replayed the interviews in my mind. They had gone well; the people I'd met with had urged me to take the job, and seeing their confidence in me had bolstered my own. Suddenly it occurred to me that this wasn't my last chance to get a leadership position. If this company wanted me, another one would too. I would not be lost if my business failed. I grabbed a cab to the airport feeling a hundred pounds lighter. The next day I called to say I would not be taking the job.

Back in Seattle, it seemed that things should now be clear, but the challenge was no easier than it had been before. How did one turn oneself into a professional speaker? I forced myself to think through my goals the same way I had thought through sales. What did I want to achieve? Whom did I need to contact? What did I need to learn? I drew up a schedule and a list of concrete goals so that every day I would know what to do. *Make ten networking calls to others in the industry. Make ten calls to corporate contacts. Work two hours a day on marketing and two on the presentation.* Unfortunately, when I sat down to write my presentation, I realized I had no concrete idea of what I wanted to say. I knew I wanted to draw on my experience in sales and in mountain climbing to show that even the most outrageous dreams are possible. The fact that we'd now climbed Everest gave me great material to work with: If a nonclimber like me could summit the world's highest mountain, *anyone* could achieve their dream. But I wanted to send people out of the room with their *own* dreams shining and the firm belief they could achieve them. How did I draw a path from my story to theirs?

I wrote and rewrote, turning out draft after draft that was too long, too disjointed, too *uninspirational.* I read them to Phil and he listened politely, but I could see his eyes wander. Finally, after several weeks, I began to get closer. I narrowed in on the three most basic things I had done in sales and on Everest that had enabled me to succeed. I had *visualized* us on top of Everest just as I had visualized my team blowing away our annual quota. We had *planned* our assault on the summit by "eating the elephant one bite at a time," just as in sales I'd broken our quota into smaller monthly and weekly goals. And we had *persevered,* going back to Everest in 2002, just as my teams went back over and over again to sales that seemed unlikely. Three strategies for turning a dream into an achievement. Three points—three stories—that gave the speech its shape.

As if progress were its own reward, I got an unexpected phone call from George Martin and Todd Greene from the Everest Speakers Bureau. George had reported on our expedition for his Everest News Web site, and they wanted to know whether I would be interested in being one of their speakers. *Would I be interested?* I barely had time to celebrate before Todd called again to say he had a company that might want me in October. Could I send my promotional video pronto?

My promotional video? I raced into action. Through an associate I found a videographer who said he could do it ASAP. "Just send me footage of your past speeches."

"I have no past speeches."

"Oh . . . Well, then, send me anything you've got."

I pulled together tapes of our media interviews and the Everest footage Phil had shot and sent them along. Over the Labor Day weekend the videographer spliced and edited and spun dross into gold. A week later Todd called to say that I was hired. My first presentation! A few weeks later Todd booked me with another company, and then a former boss asked me to speak to his new department. Three speeches! Three companies that actually wanted me to come and present! For the first time since I had hatched the dream of becoming a speaker, I began to believe it would really happen.

Then Sue Larsen asked me to consider working for her at Kinko's.

Sue was a former boss from U S West, who had since become Kinko's Vice President of Western Sales. She told me the company was opening a new division and wanted me to consider being head of the Northwest region. The job offered excellent compensation and, making the deal even sweeter, our former boss Sue Parks would be our boss again at Kinko's, where she now held the number two position.

Good company, good package, great bosses . . . *How could she do that to me now?*

I stewed for days. Yes, I'd begun to believe I could make it. Yes, I was proud I was pursuing my dream (wasn't that what my speech was about?), but the truth was, I also missed going to work. I missed being needed, I missed leading a team, I missed going after goals together instead of working all alone. I wanted to speak, yes, but many people wanted to *knit* and that didn't make knitting a career. How could I reject the security of a corporate job for a "career" that existed only in my mind?

Once again, Phil said, "Don't do it for the money." That should have been enough, but it wasn't—because when I was honest with myself, it wasn't about the money. It was the old insecurity talking: How could *I* succeed in business for myself? What if I failed? I called John Whetzell, who had started Northland Communications and built it into a powerhouse. He knew about risk and he knew me; I could trust his opinion. Methodically, I laid out the pros and cons, and when I finished he chuckled. "Sue, I can hear in your voice where your heart lies. I think you need to follow your heart."

"You do? You think I should stick with the speaking?" I felt like a kid who'd been given $100 in a candy store.

"Sue, you live with a man who has followed his passion his entire life. You *know* how well it can work. You just have to have faith. You have to know you're doing the very best you can, and then you have to trust the work will come."

I wanted to reach through the phone and hug him.

The next day I called Sue Larsen, thanked her for considering me, and with genuine regret, declined the job. I felt sorry—but also ecstatic.

And then Phil told me he had prostate cancer.

• • •

I got back from McKinley in early July and immediately took a group to Russia to climb Mt. Elbrus. When I got back I had a little free time. So I did something I had been meaning to do since I'd turned fifty the year before: I got a PSA test. The normal PSA range is 2 to 4. Mine came back at 24.

"Come back and we'll repeat the test," Marty said, "but in the meantime, I want you to make an appointment with Phil Chapman. He's a good urologist in town."

I made the appointment, but Marty's retest came back at 2. *Whew!* I told him I'd cancel the appointment with Chapman but to my surprise, he said, "Keep it. Let's make sure we know which number is correct."

Thinking (obviously) that the first result was the wild one, I went to see Chapman, who repeated the test. They did the lab work right in the office, and the number came back: 24. Chapman did a digital rectal exam, which revealed hardness in my prostate. It didn't take a medical degree to know I was in trouble. "I'm scheduling you for a biopsy," he said. "Then we'll see where things stand." Two days after the procedure, Chapman's office called asking me to come in to discuss the results. I didn't need an appointment to know what they would tell me.

• • •

September 17, 2002

Dr. Chapman struck me as a bright guy. He managed to be both patient and efficient, and my immediate instinct was to trust him. It probably was unimportant, but I took some comfort from the fact that he was just a few years younger than I: young enough to know the latest advances, but not so young that I would doubt his experience. I sat across the desk from him thinking, *Different doctor, different office, but all too familiar.* I had no idea that the hell I was about to embark on would be worse than what I had experienced in 1999.

As Dr. Chapman explained to me, prostate cancer is a particularly insidious disease because there are no perfect solutions and no clear-cut answers. While I would have several treatments to choose from, none of them guaranteed a cure and all of them risked significant side effects, most notably incontinence and impotence. Compared to '99 when I didn't even learn I had cancer until it was already removed, I would be spending the next several weeks weighing the pros and cons of those treatments and evaluating the risks of each against the parts of my life that I held most dear.

My cancer, he told me, had a "Gleason score" of 7, meaning it was moderately aggressive, and my biopsy had shown cancer in several of the samples, meaning there was a lot of it. These, plus my high PSA number, put me in a fairly high-risk group. The good news, Chapman said, was that prostate cancer is rarely fatal in the short term. The bad news was that long-term survival depends on whether the cancer has spread beyond the prostate capsule, and that was something he didn't know. Only surgery could tell us that for sure. He ordered an MRI and a bone scan, two procedures that can detect the spread of cancer if it has metastasized far beyond the prostate, but warned me that those tests were generally inconclusive. He then looked up my various test scores on something called the Partin tables and calculated that the odds that my cancer had spread were about 50/50.

"Now here's where it gets tough," he said. "If we know for sure that the cancer is contained, I almost always recommend surgery because it's the best way to be sure we've gotten it all out. When there's a chance it *isn't* contained . . ."—he nodded to include me in that group—". . . you can choose either surgery or radiation."

"What do you recommend for me?"

He smiled. "You're asking a surgeon. I'd still recommend surgery. It's the gold standard in treatment and it's the only way we'll know for sure what we're dealing with. The downside is it's major surgery, we go in very close to nerves and muscles, and there is a not-insignificant risk of incontinence and impotence."

Instantly, I thought, *Not me! It hasn't spread! I won't have side effects!* The ideas were simply inadmissible. But almost as soon as I had dismissed them, they mushroomed into full-blown worry. "And radiation?"

"There are two new types of treatment you should look into. They've both been pioneered here in Seattle and they've both shown good results, possibly with less risk of complications."

I felt confused. "If there are fewer complications, why——?"

"Phil, I've been doing this surgery for many years. I've had good results with relatively few long-term complications. You're young, you're fit; I think you have an excellent chance of coming through it fine. And once it's out we'll know, hopefully, that we got it all."

The idea of getting cut again was horrifying. "Tell me about the surgery."

"In your case we'd go in through the abdomen and take out the prostate gland and the adjacent lymph nodes. There are new nerve-sparing techniques that decrease the risk of impotence. Best-case scenario, you're in the hospital three days and healed in six weeks."

I had heard that before.

"Phil, I don't want to talk you into surgery—*or* radiation. The more you get into this, the more you're going to find that there are no absolute answers. The best thing I can tell you is to talk to as many people as you can and then make the decision that feels right to you."

He wrote down the names of the two radiation specialists, then we stood up and shook hands. "Come back after you talk to them," he said. "We can talk more then."

I left his office, got into my car, and drove around Seattle going nowhere. Who in the world was making decisions Up There? Hadn't I had enough already? Hadn't I paid my dues? I'd worked all my life to maintain my chosen lifestyle despite the Crohn's; I'd come back from two surgeries as well as cancer—and now *this?* And prostate cancer! Where in the world did that come from? Colon surgery and colon cancer I understood. They came with the Crohn's; they were practically expected. But prostate cancer? Not even on the radar! It was like I turned my back for a minute and they got me from the other side. And just when we were on such a high!

I couldn't tell Sue. I couldn't even think about telling Sue. What was I supposed to say: *Hey, Sue, I know we just did the Seven Summits. I know you're starting your dream business—but remember that little medical problem I had three years ago? Well, guess what? Here we go again!* There was no way I could tell her until I was farther along myself. I needed more information, a handle on what it all meant, a decision about how to treat it. I couldn't tell Sue until I could also tell her it would be okay.

I spent the afternoon driving around. When I got home it was already dark. Sue brought our dinners into the family room and while I pretended to pick at my food, she talked about Kinko's. She was torturing herself about whether or not to take the job, and I tried hard to listen, but her words ran up against the prostate cancer in my mind and fell away. After dinner, I told her I had work to do and went into my office. Behind the closed door I looked up prostate cancer on the Internet and spent the next two hours scrolling site after site until my vision blurred and I was numb. "Radical prostatectomy," "brachyther-apy," "watchful waiting" . . . Part of my mind lasered in as if simply reading the information would increase my chance of survival. The other part had no idea of what I was reading, or why.

At 11:00 Sue called from upstairs. "Come on up. Let's go to bed."

I knew she was leaning over the half wall of the landing, look-ing in through the glass door of my office, but from where I was sitting I couldn't see her. "You go ahead. I've got more work to do."

"Oh, come on up. It's late."

"I'll be up in a bit."

After a moment her footsteps moved away down the hall.

I turned back to the computer screen, but I had already read as much as I could. I turned off the computer and for the next two hours sat in my office in the dark.

Over the next few weeks I went to see the two radiologists Dr. Chapman had recommended. One specialized in high-dose-rate brachytherapy, or HDRT, in which a high dose of radiation is delivered to the prostate via needles inserted through the skin. The other implanted radioactive "seeds" permanently into the prostate right around the tumor. Both doctors made persuasive cases for their treatments: minimally invasive, rapid recovery, high success rate, lower risk of side effects. After each meeting I felt myself sway toward that type of treatment. Then I would think about Chapman saying surgery is the gold standard, the only way to know for sure . . .

At night I continued to do research online. There were hundreds of Web sites, thousands of pages of information, and I felt I had to read them all. I went from link to link, from the National Cancer Institute to the Prostate Cancer Foundation, to the personal journals of patients who described in excruciating detail their journeys through the disease. Long after Sue was in bed I would click and scroll, unable to extricate myself from the screen, or from the hope that eventually someone would tell me what to do.

During the day I tried to plan my trips. I had three expeditions going out that fall: Kilimanjaro in late September, Mexico in early November, and Antarctica just before Thanksgiving. Somehow I needed to fit them all in—around whatever treatment I chose. I tried to plan and pack, to arrange for flights and in-country logistics. But I couldn't concentrate. Every activity was hijacked by the weight of the disease and the decision. A week or so into my research, I realized I would have to hand off Kilimanjaro. It killed me to do that. It wasn't that we didn't have an excellent guide to replace me. What hurt was that I had made a commitment—I had represented to the customers that I would be leading the program—and I hated to let people down. I told the customers that I had a family medical emergency; I didn't say it was my own.

On October 4, two weeks after I got the diagnosis, Sue and I drove to Tacoma to have dinner with Jerry Lynch. For days now I had been stewing over how to tell her. I wanted so much not to hurt her, but I couldn't keep up the charade. And she had a right to know. We drove home in a light rain. I turned the windshield wipers on and off as I tried to work up my courage. Out of the corner of my eye I could see Sue's profile appearing and fading in the passing lights—her hair pushed back behind her ear, her mouth relaxed in a small smile. After all her work stress in the past few months it made me happy to see her looking so peaceful. The decision to decline the job and commit to speaking had come as a relief; in the last week she'd laughed more than I'd seen her do all fall.

"I, uh . . ." I cleared my throat and she turned to face me. "I have another little problem."

Her focus tightened.

"I really hate to lay this on you, but . . . you have to know." I kept my eyes on the road. "After I got back from McKinley I decided to have a PSA test . . . You know, you're supposed to get it done at fifty . . . Well, the number was pretty high, so I had a retest, and then . . . well . . . the upshot is . . . I have prostate cancer." I glanced at her quickly—just long enough to see that her eyes had filled with tears.

There was a moment of silence, then she said slowly, "How long have you known?"

"A couple of weeks."

"Oh, Phil!"

"I've been talking to doctors, getting educated. I wanted to do due diligence before I told you."

"Phil, why do you go through this alone?" She stopped herself almost before she finished the question. It was a conversation we'd had before; we both knew I wouldn't change. "What does it mean?"

I told her what Dr. Chapman had told me and explained the three treatment options. "So we have some choices to make. Not in the next forty-eight hours, but soon."

She was listening hard and I could feel her questions coming, but I'd said as much as I could handle for the moment. "You know," I said, "they say if you have to get prostate cancer, Seattle's the best place to get it. Andy Grove from Intel came up here to get treated. And Jim and Lou Whittaker had it. I'm in pretty good company."

She smiled slightly and put her hand on my leg. I could feel her swallowing her questions. I gave her hand a squeeze as if to say thanks for not pressing.

We rode in silence for a few minutes, and then she said, "Phil, we're going to beat this. We're going to work together and get in there and just start beating it."

I nodded, but my own eyes were starting to fill.

• • •

Night after night I would wake at 2:00 or 3:00 a.m. with the sense that Phil had not come to bed. I would follow the trail of light downstairs to his office and I would find him sitting at the computer in the muted light of his desk lamp, scrolling, scrolling, as if the answer were there but always on the next page. When I stood behind him to see what he was reading, half the time it was something I had seen him read before. Each day he would attempt to organize the trips to Mexico and Antarctica or do some other IMG business, but when I passed his door he would be sitting at his desk, his eyes far away. Our house, which is normally pretty neat, had become a map of his activity: an ice cream bar on the kitchen counter, melting in its wrapper; a file folder in the bathroom containing the names of hotels in Punta Arenas. He would start something, then set it down and go on to something else, leaving behind him a trail of projects started and then abandoned. He had lost all ability to focus.

I kept thinking he would come out of it: that he would make a decision, get some sleep, and then be better. Instead, weeks went by with no decision, and he only grew worse. He had begun to take sleeping pills, but even they had little effect. We'd go to bed together and I'd wrap my arm around him as if I could tranfuse him with my own sleep, but at 3:00 or 4:00 I'd wake up, feeling he had gone. I began to get scared. Even in the worst of 1999 he'd not been this despondent. Now I was afraid of his despair, afraid that he would crack.

I'm not a big believer in drugs but I suggested cautiously that he might try an antidepressant. I'd been afraid to say it for fear he'd overreact, but he didn't react at all. It was as if he hadn't even heard me. I called my parents, seeking solace and advice. Unlike '99, I'd told them immediately about the cancer—with Phil's approval. Now they empathized—that was all they could do—but it helped to know that somehow they were protecting Phil too. I yearned for the day when he would finally start treatment. Then the deciding would be over and, at least for the brief time he was under anesthesia, he would get some respite and some sleep.

In the meantime my only recourse was to focus him on living, to supply the point of view that he was unable to see. I must have said a hundred times, "You *will* be guiding." I wrote it on a piece of paper and taped it to his computer. I whispered it to him at night as we waited to fall asleep. I couldn't have the cancer for him, I couldn't make the decision for him, I couldn't undergo the treatment. But there was one thing I *had* to do: I had to make him believe it.

One night we got in bed and I brought a paper and pencil with me. "Let's make a list," I said. "Let's just write down all the pros and cons of each procedure and see if that helps you make a decision." I thought if we brought some methodology to it, perhaps one treatment would clearly outweigh the others.

We sat back against the pillows and I drew a line down the center of the page. I labeled one side "Pros" and the other

"Cons," and underneath wrote "Surgery" and "Radiation." For the next few minutes Phil talked and I wrote until we had a complete comparison.

Pros	Cons
Surgery:	Surgery:
cuts it all out (if contained)	getting cut
we'll know if it's gone or spread	surgical complications
gold standard, best cure rate	risk of incontinence & impotence
Radiation:	Radiation:
cure rate as high as surgery?	cure rate as high as surgery?
no getting cut, no complications	not gold standard
short recovery time	we won't know if it's all out
less risk of incontinence & impotence	

When he had finished talking I held the paper out in front of us. He sagged as if making the list had used up all his energy. I searched for someplace to start the discussion. "Which one do you think has a better chance of giving you a cure?"

"Surgery." He said it faster than I'd expected. "That's what's so darn hard. I want to live—but I can't live at any price. I've worked all my life to maintain a lifestyle . . ." He looked at me with such intense pain. "If something screws up and I come out of it incontinent . . ."

He didn't have to finish. He didn't want to live if he couldn't climb.

"So is the answer radiation?"

He made a feeble gesture, half nod, half shrug.

"Phil, whatever you choose, I know you will be out there guiding. And I will be right here with you."

He gave me a forced smile. It wasn't a decision, but at least we had made a little progress.

The next day I was working in my office when Phil appeared in the doorway. I looked up surprised; he rarely ventured into my office. He stood there, looking broken, saying nothing, shaking his head.

"Phil?" I got up and walked over to the door, and the minute I took him in my arms he deflated. Together we sank to the floor. "Phil, Phil, it's going to be okay." I could feel his tears against my cheek. "We'll get through this."

"How many times?" he said. "How many times have I been told to get my affairs in order?"

I held him as tight as I could. "Phil, you're not going to die. You're going to be guiding. We're going to win." I crooned to him like a baby, but I knew he couldn't hear me. He had been through too much. It wasn't just the prostate cancer, it was all of it: the Crohn's, the stomach surgery, the colon surgery, the colon cancer, the fistula. It was thirty-six years of medical problems—finally eroding his belief that he would survive. In 1999 he had been frightened; he had feared he would die. But this time he was hopeless. He saw the decision not as a choice between cures, but as choosing the best way to die.

That night I wrote him a letter.

Phil,

Throughout the years, you have taught me a great deal about winning. Never giving up has been paramount. Regardless of what we are served, we will fight this one and we will win. You are my hero!

A few days later he came up to my office again. He had just scheduled the surgery.

• • •

Once I made up my mind to do surgery I felt as if I had been leaning that way all along. From the first day in Chapman's office I'd had the notion that to cut is to cure—but the talk of side effects had scared me. Now, there was a kind of relief in coming back to where I had started, but the relief was over almost as soon as it arrived. Within days I found myself questioning my decision. Chapman said the risk of incontinence was small, but I was a textbook example of surgical complications—how could I think it wouldn't happen to me? And what if it did happen and a few years later the colon cancer returned, or Crohn's sent me down the slippery slope? I would have sacrificed my lifestyle for nothing. And what was the chance that surgery would actually cure me? What if they opened me up and the cancer wasn't contained? Or what if they cut it all out and it came back? Then I would have risked incontinence and impotence for nothing. These thoughts went round and round in my head until I couldn't put them aside, and I knew I needed to cancel the surgery.

I called Chapman's office and canceled, but there was no relief. Within minutes I began worrying about the risks of radiation. How could I do radiation with my fragile stomach and chopped-up colon? Three doctors—Marty and the two radiologists—believed I could handle it, but another doctor had advised against it. There was a chance that radiation would damage cells in those other organs, and I had too little left to lose. Plus, radiation had a short track record: It produced good results in the short term, but how did patients fare down the road? The refrain I'd heard repeated everywhere—that surgery is the gold standard—haunted me.

Within hours of making the phone call I realized I had made a terrible mistake. Surgery was the solution and I had canceled it! I had canceled my best chance of getting cured! "I screwed up! I canceled it! I shouldn't have canceled it!"

Sue came running down from upstairs and held me tight. "Shh, it's okay. It's okay. You can reschedule it."

"No!" I shook myself free. "Not for another month. I gave up my slot." I was panicked—as if now that I'd canceled, the cancer would grow at an accelerated rate.

"Phil, it's okay. You can reschedule it. They'll fit you in." Her voice was so steady I felt I could lean into it. "Everything will be fine. You haven't been sleeping; you aren't thinking clearly. But really, you can have the surgery very soon if that's what you want."

A few days later I got a phone call from a Dr. Kevin Tomera in Anchorage. It took me a moment to remember who he was; I'd spoken to so many doctors that I couldn't keep them straight. But as he talked I remembered: He was the surgeon of a friend who had recently weathered his own bout of prostate cancer. "I hear you're trying to find your way through the treatment minefield."

"Minefield, that's about right."

"I don't know if I can tell you anything you haven't already heard, but I'd be happy to answer some questions."

Maybe it was the fact that he had taken time out of his schedule to call me when he didn't know me from Adam— maybe it was just that I was finally ready to make a decision— but for whatever reason I found myself open to his words in a way that I hadn't been to the trillions of bits of information I had already taken in. Calmly, logically, he laid out the alternatives, and his words made sense to me. It was as if for the first time, I could draw a straight line from what I was hearing to what I needed to do. And what I needed to do, unequivocally, was have the surgery. I needed to know if the cancer had spread. If it *had* spread, I felt I could "live" with that, but I didn't want to be out on a mountain somewhere wondering if it was growing, if I was slowly dying. The decision to do radiation, I saw, had been a way of hedging my bet. But hedging wasn't going to get me the win I needed. I needed to hit a home run.

I hung up the phone, went upstairs, and talked to Sue. The

next day I called Chapman's office. That night I had my first full night's sleep.

. . .

The night Phil first told me about the prostate cancer, I realized I needed to take the Kinko's job. The decision to forgo my income for a while had been predicated on him being healthy and working, but now that had changed. I didn't say anything at the time, but a few days later I told him that I planned to call Sue Larsen and accept the job. He looked at me intently, as if he were trying to bring me into focus, and said, "I don't want you to take a job because of me. We'll work it out." I wanted to believe that that was possible, although I didn't see how I could. But I didn't call Sue Larsen.

Within the week, though, Phil had begun his slide and I realized that even in that earlier conversation he had been somewhere else, answering me with some other, former, wishful part of his brain. I saw that I'd have to make the decision myself, regardless of what he said. I told him over dinner that I had decided to take the job and, resignedly, he nodded. "Maybe it's for the best."

The next day, embarrassed, I called Sue. To my relief she was delighted. Before we hung up I said, "You know how much I want to pursue speaking. I won't pursue speeches myself and I won't do them if they conflict with my job, but I plan to accept them when they come to me. I need to know I'm not closing the door on my dream." I almost hoped she would say no, as if that would relieve me of the need to take the job, but she didn't.

Over the next few days I continued to pursue speaking contacts and let the decision settle. Downstairs I could hear Phil on the phone making arrangements for climbs and leaving messages for doctors. Then there were long quiet spells when I knew he was staring at the computer screen or into space. It began to seem fitting to me that while he was grappling with cancer I was having to go back to work. There was no comparison between his situation and mine—his was life and death, mine was only work—but it seemed only fair that I should have to give up something that I wanted. There was almost a pleasure in it. It didn't come close to evening the playing field, but it made me feel a tiny bit closer to sharing his pain.

. . .

November 7, 2002

Before the surgery I asked Chapman what he would do if he cut me open and found that the cancer had spread. "Probably just close you back up," he said. Once it was in the lymph nodes there wouldn't be much they could do. So on the way to the operating room I made myself a promise: *No matter how addled your brain is, Ershler, you have to feel for a catheter the minute you wake up.* If a catheter was there, it would mean they'd gone through with the surgery. If it wasn't there, it would mean the cancer had spread.

I must have carried that thought with me through the whole operation because the minute I opened my eyes I remembered what to do. For a split second I hesitated, afraid to know. Then I took a breath and reached down to my groin. The catheter was there.

When they wheeled me up, Sue was in the room and she was beaming. She leaned over cautiously, avoiding my incision, hugged my head, and crowed, "Dr. Chapman thinks he got it all!"

I wanted to answer but I couldn't. Hearing her say it out loud had brought me close to tears.

Remarkably, I had very little pain. They'd gone right back in through the same old incision and I thought, *Maybe those nerves are so beat up by now they don't have any feeling left!* I could talk and laugh without having to clamp a pillow over my stomach, and by evening I was ready to get up and walk around a little. John Waechter came and I felt so good that, despite my reluctance to have people see me in the hospital, I didn't even mind that he was there. At one point, Chapman came in and joked to Sue that he should do a white paper on me because the surgery had gone so smoothly. "It all looked good in there," he said. "The lymph nodes we examined were negative. We'll get the final pathology report in a few days." I felt a chill when I heard those words, remembering the pathology report in '99, but I just couldn't discount how good I was feeling. My intuition told me I was okay.

So I was stunned when three days later Chapman called and asked, "Are you sitting down?"

I was home, recuperating in bed, and I felt my stomach drop away. "No, I'm *lying* down."

"Okay." He paused. "Margins: negative. Lymph nodes: negative. Seminal vesicle: negative.

It took a moment for the meaning to register. *All the tests were negative.* In an instant, the huge weight I had been carrying for the last two months disappeared. "Sue!" I hollered. "Come here!"

"What?"

"Just come here."

Sue's office chair scraped, and a moment later she appeared in the door of the bedroom. "That was Chapman. Margins negative. Lymph nodes negative. Seminal vesicle negative." I grinned at her, waiting for it to sink in.

A moment later she let out a shriek and practically jumped on top of me. "You did it! You did it!" she yelled.

"*We* did it," I said. "I think we may have just hit a home run."

• • •

On January 6, 2003, I flew to Dallas for a weeklong leadership orientation at Kinko's. Unlike 1996, when I was reluctant to leave Phil even for a day, I had no qualms about going—because this time everything had gone right. The surgical wound had healed, the serious side effects he had anguished about had not materialized, he had gone back to working out at the gym, and while I was in Dallas he would be leaving to lead a climb in Ecuador. The irony did not escape me that while I was starting the job I had taken to pay his medical bills, he was back on his feet and guiding, but I didn't care; I was just so happy he was fine. Despite his "home run" we had no assurance about the future; he would be having PSA tests every few months for the next year and yearly thereafter; the cancer could recur at any time. I just wanted him healthy and active and doing what made him happy. And anyway, now that the job was starting, I was excited. I would have preferred speaking full-time, but I looked forward to meeting new people, learning a new industry, helping set up the new division. I had a plush situation: home office, complete flexibility, a leadership team I enjoyed. And I was scheduling speeches on the side. It was not too hard to convince myself that I was getting it all. In a year or two, I figured, the division would be humming, I'd turn it over to someone else, and then I'd move seamlessly into speaking.

Almost immediately, I realized that was a pipe dream. The Kinko's job demanded 150 percent of my time—which would have been fine if the speaking didn't demand 150 percent also. I'd always given that much to my jobs; that was the way I worked. But in my previous jobs I hadn't also been trying to launch a second career. Now I found myself in a bind. I wanted to be the best I could be at both, and it was impossible. I was only speaking once a month, but preparing adequately took a lot of time, and I simply didn't have it. I carved extra hours out of the day by cutting back on sleep, but that wasn't a solution; I needed more energy, not just more hours.

It felt like 2001 all over again, juggling the demands of Everest training and work. Now speaking was my new Everest.

Ironically, despite the fact that I had put the speaking on a side burner, offers were coming in—approximately one a month. If that happened when I *wasn't* marketing myself, what would happen when I *was*? Suddenly I saw that I could really make the speaking business happen! Phil was guiding, we could afford my incubation period, I could quit Kinko's and grow my own business! Ethically, though, I couldn't do that. I had made a commitment to Kinko's and I was not about to break it. I needed to stay until the new division was running smoothly.

Then, in late summer, I was offered an out. Kinko's decided to restructure and I was told that I would be given a vice president or regional vice president position. It was everything I had been afraid of losing when I quit my job before Everest, everything I'd wanted for most of my career, but there was no way I could take it. It would be unfair to the company and my team since I knew I would be leaving in a year or so, and it would be untrue to myself. So I handed in my resignation. It was time to become a full-time speaker.

October 2002

Phil,
You are the answer to all my wishes. Years ago I would wonder about the future, would I be married, would I be in love, would I be happy? You made it all come true. There is *nothing* more I want in my life. How wonderful to be 100% satisfied. I love you endlessly.

Sue

December 2005

Sue,
You and I have become a pair, a match, and I like it that way. We're better as a team than we could ever be apart. You make a great rope mate in life.

Love you,
Philip

9

THE BREVITY OF TIME

In January 2005 I led my annual climb of Ecuadoran volcanoes and my partner, as always, was Romulo Cardenas. Romulo and I had been guiding together since the late 1980s, when we were introduced by our mutual friend Jorge Anhalzer, and although we usually saw each other only two weeks a year, we had become good friends. As Romulo liked to say, my Spanish never got worse, but it never got any better either. His English improved enormously, however, which enabled us to have increasingly close communication. Over the years he had joined me in other parts of the world, and in 1998 he had been with me when Chris Hooyman died on McKinley. Our relationship was as close as I could have come to having a brother.

Shortly after I met Romulo he began living with a woman named Patricia. I liked Patricia as much as I liked Romulo, and I especially liked being with the two of them together because they cared about each other so deeply. In 1995, when their son, Camilo, was born, they wrote to me and said, "Felipe, in Ecuador parents choose *padrinos* for their children because of friendship, partnership, good example, and admiration. We would like you to be *padrino de Camilo.* We hope that someday you will *aconsejar* and talk with him and that he will see you as *un buen ejemplo.*" And so I became Camilo's godfather. It was a tremendous honor, to which I wasn't at all sure I was equal. But Sue's arrival must have increased their confidence because a year later when their daughter, Victoria, was born, they asked both of us to be her *padrinos.*

Now, Romulo told me, the kids were pushing their parents to get married. They wanted to be baptized, which was, of course, the norm in Catholic Ecuador, and in order for them to be baptized their parents had to be married in the church. So after all these years, Romulo and Patricia were taking the plunge, and in order to kill two birds with one stone, they planned to do both events at once, capped off by a big party. "But Felipe," they said, "we can't have a baptism without the godparents." So in May 2005 Sue and I flew to Quito and then drove south along the Pan-American Highway to the little farming town of Uyumbicho.

It was a gorgeous day with a brilliant sky and high white clouds. In the distance, beyond fields that seemed to encompass every shade of green, sat the old volcano Pasochoa. In Romulo and Patricia's small yard, tables had been adorned with white cloths and white umbrellas, and we sat in rows of white-draped chairs among the two large extended families. In a country where religious ceremonies are highly ritualized, Romulo had managed to find a young priest who was completely in tune with the rather irregular nature of this dual event, and he led the ceremony with a spirited and joyous air. Throughout the wedding, Romulo stared at the ground, looking slightly embarrassed but also very proud, and I thought about how long I had known him and how much we had both changed in that time. Back in 1987 I could no more have imagined him married, or a father, than I could have imagined those things for myself. Yet here we were, living at opposite ends of the hemisphere, having followed roughly similar trajectories, and both now living lives in which those unimagined pleasures were central. Next to me Sue was smiling broadly. The fact that her Spanish was limited to *hola, bueno, loco,* and *margarita* had not stopped her from blending right in with the two families. Not for the first time I wondered: If I had met Sue back in the '80s would we have gotten together? And I had to acknowledge that the answer was probably no. In those days I was married to the mountains. Everything took a backseat to my personal ambitions, and my ambitions were limited to reaching summits. Much as I spouted platitudes about the success of the team, inwardly I knew the truth: The success I really cared about was mine. *Thank goodness,* I thought, *that age, or human nature, or some other uninvited magic helps us wise up over time!*

I wondered what it was like for Romulo and Patricia to get married after all these years, after they'd experienced so much together. When Sue and I got married I knew that I loved her, that I could trust her, that she was kind and generous and loving; that she was positive and resourceful and determined to make things happen. I knew that somehow we had a multiplier effect that made us exponentially happier together than we could ever be alone. And I knew that, five years in, my blood still raced at the idea of going home to her, knowing I would walk in the door and we'd pull a bottle of wine from the fridge, climb into bed, and after "getting reacquainted," *talk.* I knew those things in my gut, but what I hadn't yet experienced on the day we married was how deep our partnership would become. We hadn't yet climbed the Seven Summits, with all the intensity and learning that involved. We hadn't weathered the misunderstanding that threatened my self-esteem and temporarily wrenched our marriage. We hadn't faced major illness together. Now that we *had* done those things, our relationship had grown far beyond the "maturity" I assumed it had when we married. I talk all the time about the importance of partners in the mountains: how they look out for you with the same commitment and intensity with which you look out for them. That was exactly what we had found, or created, in our marriage. Susan pushed me when I needed pushing, lifted me when I needed lifting, cared for me when I was unable to care for myself. She made it safe for me to fall because I knew I could only fall so far. She had become my perfect partner.

After the wedding ceremony, the priest walked over to a small fountain that had been filled with holy water. He beckoned Camilo and Victoria to join him, and with the palm of his hand, he cupped water gently onto their foreheads. They looked more serious than I had ever seen them. Then he motioned to Romulo, Patricia, Sue, and me to approach the fountain. One at a time, Romulo and Patricia dipped their thumbs into the water and pressed them to the children's foreheads, then Sue and I did the same. And while we were standing there, the eyes of the extended family on us, I thought how extraordinary it was—and yet how completely comfortable as well—that we were in another country, another culture, taking part in this intimate family moment. All because thirty years ago, when I was still too young to have any idea of what it meant to design a life, some hand had drawn a path for me that brought me face-to-face with people in a remarkably intense and honest way. I didn't know when I started climbing that it was the *guiding* I would come to love, or that, once my youthful "me-orientation" faded, my customers' successes would hold more meaning than my own. Or that after being diagnosed with cancer and thinking I might never climb again, it wasn't the climbing I knew I'd miss, but the sharing of the pleasures and discomforts, the challenges and setbacks, with other people.

On the way to the airport, Sue and I had heard a country-western song on the radio that made me reflective. The singer was listing the things he wanted to do in the limited time he had left to live, and I thought to myself, *I don't have that kind of list. I love my wife, I love my work, I cherish my friends. I've tried to do things that are meaningful and that make me proud. I've made deliberate choices along the way and they've worked out reasonably well. Yeah, I'm fifty-four and I've had cancer and I don't know how much longer I'll be able to guide. But I feel good about the way my life has gone so far. I don't have unfinished business.*

If anything, rather than regret the things I hadn't done, I felt especially thankful for the things I *had* done, especially the second Everest climb. Sue was so darn eager for that climb; even after going there in 2001 she didn't seem to understand what it took to make it happen. But the minute I got the prostate diagnosis I realized that she'd understood even better than I how important it was to grab opportunities when we had them. She intuitively knew what I'd *thought* the cancer, the Crohn's, and the deaths of friends had taught me: that tomorrow may be one day too late.

Throughout the flight to Ecuador those thoughts had come and gone. Perhaps I was anticipating the kind of life reflection that an old friend's wedding can engender. I thought about how my life would have been different if I hadn't had the Crohn's. On the most obvious level, I might not have stuck with climbing: If I hadn't felt so much healthier in the mountains, I might have pursued my original plan and become a doctor! Sue suggested once that Crohn's gave me empathy for helping others and led me to become a guide. That might be right, I wasn't sure; but I did know that it colored my attitude toward my life and the way I wanted to live it. From the time I was sixteen and mending from that first surgery, I knew I was not going to bend my life to the disease: I was going to live as if it weren't there. And when I died I knew exactly what I wanted on my tombstone: *He did in spite of. He never refrained from doing because of.*

When the baptism was over, Romulo made a short speech and thanked all the guests for coming, and then the relatives descended on the four of them, burying them in hugs and kisses. The band struck up a rousing tune with horns, guitars, drums, and Pan flutes, and aunts and cousins began streaming from the kitchen with platters of empanadas, *humitas,* seviche, and *cuy,* the Ecuadoran delicacy—guinea pig. Before we knew it, Sue and I were pulled into a dance, hands clasped above our heads, as everyone lined up to form the sides of a human tunnel. Laughing and holding hands, the newlyweds and their children ducked through.

I winked at Sue. Twenty years ago I could not have imagined being here with her. What would happen in the next twenty years that I couldn't imagine now? A small part of me shuddered at the thought: the part that hated going for that PSA test and colonoscopy every year, the part that knew that Crohn's and time were not the best of friends. But a larger part of me was more curious than concerned. The Sherpas have an expression, *kay garnay,* which means roughly *So be it.* It contains the acknowledgment that there are things in life we cannot control, and the awareness that our only option is to accept them. It is not about giving up or giving out, but rather about accepting our human limitations. Twenty years ago I would not have understood the meaning of *kay garnay*; if anything, I would have fought it. But life has mellowed me since then, and brought me face-to-face with my limitations. Now I see the beauty in accepting what I cannot change—and the importance of living as fully as I can until then.

. . .

In August 2005 I went back to Kilimanjaro with Phil. At the last minute I almost canceled because several speaking opportunities came up, but some wise voice inside me reminded me of what I often tried to forget: Life can throw you a major curveball at any moment. How many more chances would I have to climb with Phil? I declined the speeches and went.

I was incredibly glad I did. From the very beginning it reminded me how important it is to do this. I'm not Phil Ershler, I'm not a mountaineer. It's the contrast that I love; I would never want a steady diet of climbing. But to get out there in the dirt with a team, to work so hard, to experience the sunrise and have such a sense of accomplishment—it reminds me what life is about.

It was interesting to be back in Africa thirteen years later, with so many more experiences under my belt. This time we flew right into Kilimanjaro Airport and stayed in a town called Moshi instead of the village of Marangu, but the scenes outside were almost exactly as I remembered them: the lush foliage, the red-brown earth, the skinny cows, the windowless houses, the red-caped Masai, the men and women walking, walking, usually with heavy bundles on their heads. The difference was how much *I* had changed: how unsurprised I was by what I was seeing, how easy it was to "converse" with people without a common language, how much more relaxed I felt inside, how much less nervous I was about the climb.

Summit day was easier than it had been the first time, but 4,000 feet is 4,000 feet no matter how many mountains you've been on, and just as I had on every summit day on every mountain, I spent much of the time asking myself, *Why? Why am I here with this headache, this stomachache, these frozen fingers and frozen feet? Why must I work this hard? Why do I put myself through this?* Maybe the difference between this time and thirteen years earlier was that now I knew the answer even while I was suffering. The answer was that pain does not last forever, that soon I would reach the top, and that when I did, the reward would be immeasurable. It would be not just the reward of having done it—although that would be reward enough—but the reward of knowing that I had pushed myself to my very edge; that at that moment I was the best I could possibly be.

The night after we summited, our last on the mountain, we stayed at Mweka camp. We had the big Chagga-cooked dinner and the celebratory toasts, and then all the customers disappeared into their tents, exhausted. That was what I had done thirteen years before, but this time I wasn't that tired. Instead I stayed in the mess tent with Phil, Mark Tucker, and Michael, our Chagga guide. We drank beer and played hearts and talked, and it felt so good to be there, surrounded by Phil; Mark, whom I'd known for years; and Michael who, even though I had just met him, felt like an old friend. I thought about the other members of our team and how bonded we had become in the last two weeks, and I felt a pang of sadness, as I always do, that soon we would all go our separate ways. I knew that most of them would go home and say this climb had been one of the most important experiences of their lives. Phil's clients always say that. Many are highly successful professionals, but success in climbing is so different from success in the business world. It is tangible, internal, permanent—life-changing. When I climb a mountain something changes on a cellular level. New neural pathways are created, and new actions, new attitudes, become possible. The pain fades, and what I am left with is a magnified belief in myself. That feeling never leaves me.

I thought about the feeling of contentment I'd had on the airplane coming home from Everest, and the sense that if I died that day my life would be complete. Those feelings still held, and were so different from anything I'd previously felt. It was as if a hole or insufficiency had been filled. That didn't stop me from striving: I now had a vision for my speaking that was as motivating as my vision of standing on top of Everest with Phil, and now that vision made me eager to get out of bed in the morning. But it didn't diminish the completion that the Everest summit had provided.

Phil, Tuck, Michael, and I played a few last hands of hearts. (It was Michael's first game but Phil showed no mercy!) Then Phil and I went back to our tent and settled into our bags. Within minutes, his breathing took on the deep evenness of sleep. Before 1999 it had never occurred to me to worry about Phil. He seemed invincible; even with the Crohn's I never feared for the future. But 1999 shot a big hole in that way of thinking. I believed at the time he would come through it, but I could no longer pretend that he would live forever. After he recovered, and especially after we summited Everest, it was *almost* possible to revert to that old way of thinking, but after the prostate cancer, that option closed. I could no longer trust that Phil would live as long as I would.

For the longest time I couldn't allow myself to think about

Phil dying. How could I? I didn't think I would survive. I remembered a story my father had told me years ago, when I was still a child. He and my uncle had been riding dirt bikes on an old logging road in South Dakota when they came across a rattlesnake. Concerned that the snake would threaten hikers, my father killed it with a rock and cut off the rattles, which he stuck in his pocket. Back at their cabin, he told my brother, who then clamored to see the snake, so the three of them drove out to the spot where they had left it. When they arrived, the first thing they saw was a rattle sticking up out of the grass. My dad couldn't believe it. How could they be seeing the rattles when he had them right there in his pocket? They carefully parted the grass and stepped in for a closer look. There was the dead snake, minus its rattles. But on top of the snake was a second snake, completely coiled around it.

When my father told me that story I immediately believed that the second snake was the mate, a belief I hold to this day. During the prostate cancer that image came back to me as clearly as if I had seen it myself because I knew that would be my impulse with Phil. If he died, I would want to crawl up next to him, wherever he lay, and stay there with him forever. He was my soul mate, hero, best friend, lover, cheerleader, and husband all wrapped up in one. I could not comprehend life without him. How could I live without my heart? After a while, however, I began to think about it differently. Perhaps it was a coping mechanism—a way of keeping Phil—but I realized that what I would do if something happened to Phil was tell the world about him. He has given so much good to people; my mission would be to honor him in whatever way I could.

The idea that I could live to honor Phil became a source of solace, a way to imagine the future. Without realizing it, I began to do that in my speeches. At one point I hired a consultant to help me polish my presentation, and after watching me speak he said, "You know, Sue, the real hero of your talk is Phil. Are you okay with that?"

In a heartbeat, I said, "Absolutely. Phil gave me the courage to tackle my grandest dreams and believed in me so I could succeed. That is exactly as it should be!" As I spoke I realized that everyone needs a Phil—not a husband or a soul mate, necessarily, but a true mentor, someone who believes in him when his own belief wavers.

It wasn't long after that that I realized something else had shifted. Somehow, when I wasn't looking, I had stopped thinking about "what if" and had begun focusing on *living*: on being together, on doing the things that mattered, on making the most of our time together. In light of that awareness I was even more glad that we had gone back to Everest, and that I'd summoned the courage to pursue the speaking; and even that years ago I'd let Walt Yeager talk me into trying sales, and my parents guide me into attending college. All those things that I had once been almost too afraid to try were among the most pivotal experiences of my life.

I began to think that fear is an intrinsic part of every dream, that *overcoming* fear is part of what makes the achievement so fulfilling.

Before I met Phil I had talked about dreams, but I don't think I really *believed* in them—because I lacked the confidence to achieve them. But now I do believe because my biggest dreams have all come true. I believe that we can achieve anything if we want it with all our heart and are willing to work hard to get it. I believe we are much more capable than we give ourselves credit for, and that rather than any special aptitude, all it really takes to achieve is belief in oneself. I believe in finding happiness where you least expect it. I believe in true love. And I believe in Prince Charmings who sweep women off their feet even after they've given up.

*   *   *

The morning after we summited we woke early to the sounds of birds. How different from the windswept, treeless camps higher up! Outside, the air was cold and the ground was wet with dew, but the sun was just peeking over the top of the mountain. In two hours I'd be hiking in my shirtsleeves. I took one last look behind us as we headed out of camp. The summit rose like a perfect dome above the trees, the morning sun glinting off the ice.

For the first part of the morning I walked toward the back of the group, taking it all in, trying to plant the images in my brain so that they would stay with me when we got back home. After our first break, Phil came and walked right behind me. I love climbing with Phil behind me. It makes me feel that I have the best of both worlds: I have the sense of grand adventure as the mountain opens out before me, but I also have the safety of knowing he is right there. Now I thought about how many times we had walked that way, and I realized that this was the first time in almost a decade that we were climbing without a larger goal. Ever since I had stood on top of Aconcagua in 1996, I had believed that we were working toward the Seven Summits. Now that Everest was behind us, that larger goal was gone.

"Hey, Phil," I said turning around, "Kilimanjaro was the first of our Seven Summits."

"Uh-huh," Phil said, as if this was not exactly new information.

"Well, I was just thinking . . . Now that we've done Kili twice, maybe we should do them *all* again."

Phil didn't miss a beat. "Sue," he said, "just keep walking."

GLOSSARY OF CLIMBING TERMS

Ascender

A handheld device that slides up and grabs the rope as the climber ascends. The ascender is attached to the climber's harness by a rope so that it acts as both a handhold and a point of attachment.

Belay

A safety technique in which a stationary climber holds on to the rope attached to the ascending climber (usually by anchoring it in some way to the mountain). If the ascending climber falls, the belayer (the stationary climber) is able to hold the rope taut and brake the fall.

Bergschrund (or 'schrund)

A gap or crevasse that appears at the head of a glacier where it has pulled away from the mountain.

Bivouac

A camp—usually unplanned—that provides little or no shelter from the elements.

Carabiner

An aluminum clip with a spring-loaded gate through which a climbing rope can be threaded. The rope can then be attached to harnesses, safety anchors, and other things.

Cerebral edema (high-altitude cerebral edema, or HACE)

A life-threatening form of altitude sickness that generally does not occur below 10,000 feet. It is caused by an extreme increase in blood flow to the brain that damages brain tissue and causes brain swelling. Symptoms include headache, loss of coordination, weakness, hallucinations, irrational behavior, and unconsciousness. The best treatment is early recognition and immediate descent to lower altitude. People who have suffered from HACE should refrain from ascending to high altitudes again.

Col
A small, high pass between two peaks or a low saddle on a ridge.

Cornice
An overhang of wind-sculpted snow that projects out beyond the crest of a ridge.

Couloir
A steep gully or gorge, usually containing ice or snow.

Crampon
A spiked metal device that attaches to the bottom of climbing boots to provide purchase on ice and hard-packed snow.

Crevasse
A crack in a glacier; may be anywhere from a few inches to over 20 feet wide and from 5 feet to well over 100 feet deep.

Fixed rope
A rope that has been anchored to the mountain; it serves as both a safety device (climbers clip into the rope) and as a route marker.

Ice axe
A tool with a point at one end and a pick and an adze at the other, used for balance, self-arrest, and gripping ice.

Jumar
   A brand of ascender (see above). "To jumar" means to ascend a rope.

Moraine
   An area of rocks and debris pushed into position by the advancing of a glacier.

Piton
   A metal spike that is hammered into rock to support a belay; rarely used any longer because of the damage it causes to the rock.

Protection
   "Setting protection" involves anchoring the climber's rope to the mountain in such a way that the rope will stop him in case of a fall.

Pulmonary edema (high-altitude pulmonary edema, or HAPE)
   A life-threatening form of altitude sickness in which the vessels carrying blood from the heart to the lungs become damaged, allowing blood into the lungs. Breathing becomes difficult and the oxygen level drops in the body. Symptoms include shortness of breath, cough, blood-tinged saliva, gurgling in the chest, and fatigue. Eventually hallucinations and unconsciousness may occur. Treatment requires rapid evacuation and oxygen.

Rappel
   To descend via a fixed rope.

Scree
   Small loose rocks at the base of a slope.

Sherpas
   An ethnic group originally from Tibet who live in the high mountains of the eastern Himalayas. Due to their prowess at

high altitudes they have become indispensable porters on most Himalayan climbing expeditions. "Sherpa" should be used only to refer to members of the ethnic group; it is not a synonym for "porter."

Sirdar
  The head Sherpa on an expedition.

Spindrift
  Blowing snow.

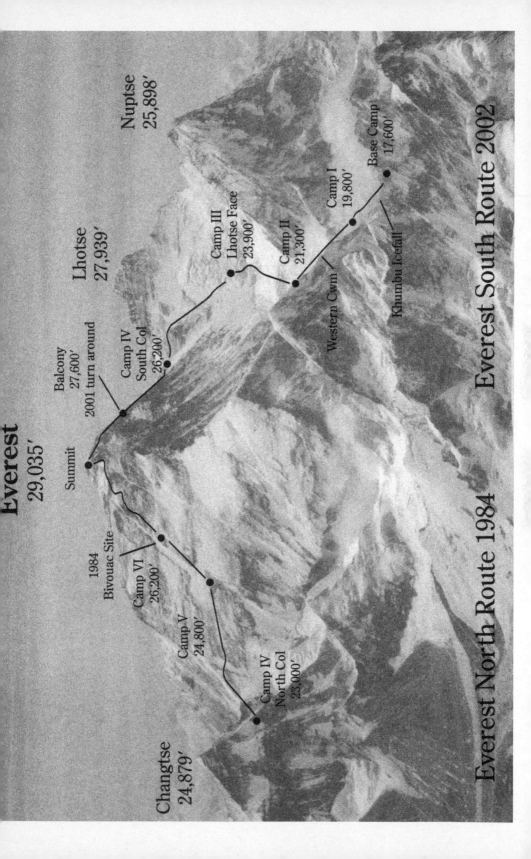

Everest
29,035'

Nuptse
25,898'

Lhotse
27,939'

Changtse
24,879'

Summit

Balcony
27,600'
2001 turn around

Camp IV
South Col
26,200'

1984
Bivouac Site

Camp VI
26,200'

Camp V
24,800'

Camp IV
North Col
23,000'

Camp III
Lhotse Face
23,900'

Camp II
21,300'

Camp I
19,800'

Base Camp
17,600'

Western Cwm

Khumbu Icefall

Everest North Route 1984

Everest South Route 2002

ABOUT THE AUTHORS

Phil Ershler, the first American to summit Mount Everest by the difficult north face (1984), is the world-renowned partner/owner of International Mountain Guides. Phil, his partners, and their guides lead climbs on every continent. For more information, visit www.MountainGuides.com.

Susan Ershler is an international speaker and former executive at Fortune 500 companies. One of the few women ever to complete the Seven Summits and Mount Everest, she speaks professionally about pushing past perceived boundaries, sharing her secrets for success and determination to pursue your greatest dreams. A dynamic and inspiring speaker, she addresses thousands of people each year and provides keynotes for companies such as IBM, Microsoft, and FedEx. For more information about her, visit www.SusanErshler.com.